The Hidden Unity of the Bible

The Use of the Old Testament in the New Testament

Pieter J. Lalleman

T0349776

FAITHBUILDERS

THE HIDDEN UNITY OF THE BIBLE: The Use of the Old Testament in the New Testament by Pieter J. Lalleman. © Copyright Pieter J. Lalleman 2019. First published in Dutch by Buijten en Schipperheijn, Amsterdam.

FAITHBUILDERS
Bethany, 7 Park View,
Freeholdland Road,
Pontnewynydd, Pontypool NP4 8LP
www.faithbuilders.org.uk

British Library Cataloguing-in-Publication Data. A catalogue record for this book is available from the British Library

ISBN: 9781913181161

Cover Design by Patrick Knowles © 2019

Printed and bound in Great Britain.

Contents

Introduction

Many Christians see the Bible as one book, and that is correct. The Bible is the book through which God speaks to us. Yet originally the Bible was a collection of 66 different books from various periods in time, written by diverse authors. These 66 books are divided into two main parts: the Old Testament and the New Testament. Both parts are about the one God of Israel, but in the New Testament we also read about Jesus Christ and about the Christian church which came into being through his ministry.

The authors of the New Testament were well aware of the existence of the Old Testament. (It was not the *Old* Testament as long as there was no New Testament. They often called it 'the Scriptures' or 'The Law and the Prophets,' Matthew 5:17; 21:42; 22:29.) These writers, including Matthew and Paul, used the Old Testament in many ways in their own writings. In this way they created all kinds of connections between the two main parts of the Bible. Old Testament themes come back into the New, and the New Testament quotes the Old, but sometimes the writer only makes an allusion that not everyone notices…

Although Jesus Christ is only mentioned in the New Testament, a knowledge of the Old Testament is essential for us to understand him. You will find him there not only in direct words of prophecy – he and his work are present in many ways in the Old Testament, even in ways which the Old Testament writers themselves did not yet see. However, you only hear this when you listen respectfully to the Bible and accept its authority. When reading in this way, you will notice that you don't always have to take everything in the Bible literally, because many images and themes can only be understood as imagery.

The many cross-references give the Bible much richness and depth. In this book I will deal with some of this richness and depth. To say the same in more theological terms, this book is an argument for the unity of Scripture and for the value of the Old Testament.

This book is in no way 'complete.' It is not intended to describe all cases of the use of the Old Testament in the New. I have limited myself to a personal selection, which is influenced by my teaching in a theological college. Incidentally, I also made many fresh discoveries during the writing process. I begin with several parts of the Old Testament, followed by a number of themes and people that occur all around the Bible, and I conclude with a discussion of most books of the New Testament. The final chapters are on average longer than the earlier ones. You can read the chapters in random order, because there is no thread running through the book. I do, however, sometimes refer from one chapter to another, but the index of texts at the back is your best source of cross-references.

If you are looking for a complete overview, try G. K. Beale and D. A. Carson (eds), *Commentary on the New Testament Use of the Old Testament* (Nottingham: Apollos, 2007), but don't try to read it as a novel!

For a further account of the theoretical background to my work in this book, please see the final chapter.

Some Technical Aspects

1. I have used the 2011 edition of the NIV unless otherwise stated, because it is still the most widely used version of the Bible. An added advantage is that the NIV sometimes makes sentences in Old and New Testament look more similar than they are in actual fact, which helps the reader see connections. However, the NIV is often such a free translation that I had at times to resort to the NRSV or the ESV. I have also translated some texts myself. Uniquely among the modern translations, the 2004 Holman Christian Standard Bible, now published as the Christian Standard Bible, prints quotations from the Old Testament in the New in bold type. This is helpful as far as it goes, but it does not identify allusions and other forms of use of the Old Testament in the New.

2. In addition to the term 'Old Testament,' I sometimes use 'Hebrew Bible.' This is not only for the sake of variation, but it also expresses my conviction that the Old Testament is not obsolete. Indeed, one might readily refer to the 'Old' and 'New' Testament as the 'First' and 'Second' Testaments respectively. However, to keep things easy for the reader, I mainly use 'Old' and 'New' Testament in this book.

3. I have tried to avoid technical language, but some was inevitable, the most important being the word 'Septuagint.' This refers to the Greek translation of the Old Testament, which had already been made by the time the New Testament was written. The writers of the New Testament commonly used this translation when they cited the Scriptures, because most of their readers knew Greek rather than Hebrew.[1] Chapter 32 contains more information about the differences between the Hebrew and Greek texts of the First Testament. The numbering of the Psalms and their verses in the Septuagint differs from that in the Hebrew text and in our translations, but I have ignored this.

    Another term you will encounter is Synoptic Gospels. This refers to the first three Gospels, Matthew, Mark, and Luke, which describe the life of Jesus in much the same way.

4. The chapter on Mark provides the best explanation of the technical terms 'quote,' 'allusion,' and 'echo,' which I have used throughout the book.

---

[1] I have used Albert Pietersma and Benjamin G. Wright (eds.), *A New English Translation of the Septuagint* (Oxford: OUP, 2006).

Chapter 1: Genesis 22

Few parts of the Old Testament are used in so many places in the New as the narrative of the sacrifice of Isaac in Genesis 22:1–19. The story is quoted literally only twice, but you find echoes of it everywhere: in the Gospels and in Acts, as well as in Paul, James, and Hebrews. This beautiful story contains several elements which – in retrospect, after the cross and the resurrection – can be regarded as typological. I will discuss these elements, roughly in the order in which they appear in the narrative, and at the end I will say more about the concept of type. I commence this study with the places in the New Testament that comment on the story as a whole. If you don't know the story, I suggest you read it first.

The Whole Story

The unknown author of Hebrews speaks with approval about the faith which was visible in Abraham's activities (Hebrews 11:17–19). He explains this faith as Abraham's belief that Isaac could be raised from the dead, adding that 'in a manner of speaking' Abraham did indeed receive Isaac back from death. Hebrews also uses the word 'tested' for Abraham's experience, which is not used anywhere else in the New Testament with reference to Abraham, although it occurs in Genesis 22:1.

Once you see that Hebrews mentions raising from the dead, you can understand that Paul is probably also thinking of Genesis 22 when he writes in Romans that Abraham trusted God 'who gives life to the dead' (4:17). Paul thus alludes to Isaac as one who returned from the dead.

James also praises Abraham (2:21–22), but he sees Abraham's works primarily as acts of obedience. Abraham was not only faithful in word, but also in deed. James' take on the narrative fits well with the end of the story, where the angel of the LORD praises Abraham because he has been obedient (verses 16 and 18).

When reading these passages in Hebrews, Romans, and James, you may notice that the authors do not quote from the story or even refer to it with an expression like 'as it is written in Genesis.' They simply make clear allusions and they assume that their readers know the story and will see the link.

Let's consider the various elements of the story.

The Only, Beloved Son

Isaac is referred to as the only son of Abraham three times (Genesis 22:2, 12, and 16), which adds emphasis to the fact. Before the time of Jesus, Jewish readers had interpreted this word 'only' as an indication of special love. Therefore, in the Septuagint the word 'only' had not been translated, so that the emphasis fell entirely on 'beloved' (Greek *agapētos*). And the expression 'beloved Son' is also used with emphasis for Jesus in places such as Matthew 3:17 and 17:5 (NRSV; see also Mark 1:11; Luke 3:22). Thus, the one who uses these words in the Gospels – God the Father – suggests a connection between Jesus and Isaac.

Jesus himself also uses these words in his parable in Mark 12:1–12, when he emphatically calls the son of the owner of the vineyard a 'beloved son' (verse 6 NRSV; see also Luke 20:13). Things do not work out well for the son in the parable. Jesus' words show that he knew of his impending death and that he understood it in the light of Genesis 22; as Isaac was willingly sacrificed, so he will be.

The Son is a Willing Lamb

This brings us to the willingness of Isaac. The counterpart of Abraham's willingness to sacrifice his son is that Isaac is (surprisingly!) willing to cooperate (especially verse 9). He voluntarily becomes the sacrificial lamb. At the end of the story his place is taken by a ram (verse 13).

Here for the first time in the Bible we have a sacrificial lamb, when Abraham speaks to Isaac the prophetic words that 'God himself will provide the lamb for the burnt offering' (verse 8). Later in the story, Abraham actually finds a ram in the bushes and sacrifices it (verse 13), but this does not exhaust the meaning of his prophetic words: in Jesus God provides himself with the lamb that dies for the sins of the people.

The thought of the sacrificial lamb also occurs in the story of the exodus from Egypt (Exodus 12:1–13) and it is developed in Isaiah 53. Whenever Jesus is called the Lamb of God in the New Testament, as in John 1:29, 36 and 1 Peter 1:18–19, you can hear echoes of Isaiah 53, the exodus as well as Genesis 22.

The Father Sacrifices the Son – 'Not Withheld'

Father Abraham is willing to sacrifice his only son; in other words, he does not spare his son. God praises him for this by saying that Abraham has 'not withheld' his only son (verses 12, 16). Paul picks up this thought of 'not withholding' or 'not sparing' one's own son in Romans 8:32. Paul does not explicitly refer to the story here, but he sees clear similarities between Abraham and his son Isaac and, on the one hand, and God and his son Jesus on the other. In both cases the father sacrifices the son, resulting in blessing for the whole world.

The best-known verse in the Bible, John 3:16, was probably also written by the evangelist with the story of Abraham and Isaac in mind: 'God … gave his one and only son…' As Abraham was willing to give his only son, so was God. Perhaps John was also influenced by the words of Paul in Romans 8:32, if he knew this letter.

God Swears an Oath

Genesis 22:16 says that God made a promise to Abraham and it contains the unusual expression 'to swear.' The Bible usually uses the word 'speak' for God, and 'swearing' is rarely used. The author of Hebrews also knew this, for in 6:12–15 he writes:

> We do not want you to become lazy, but to imitate those who through faith and patience inherit what has been promised. When God made his promise to Abraham, since there was no one greater for him to swear by, he swore by himself, saying, 'I will surely bless you and give you many descendants.' And so after waiting patiently, Abraham received what was promised.

Hebrews 6:13 is a free rendering of Genesis 22:16, and in 6:14 the writer quotes the first part of Genesis 22:17. Verse 15 is a commentary on the life of Abraham as a whole, who is presented as an example for the readers, as in verse 12.

Two further references in the New Testament to God's promise are more general. In Luke 1:73, Zachariah mentions an oath of God to Abraham, and the word 'oath' suggests a connection with Genesis 22:16. But the content of this oath is not as specific as what God says in Genesis 22. Therefore, Zachariah apparently does not refer to a particular text, but to God's promises to Abraham in general. Furthermore, in Romans 4:13, Paul writes that 'Abraham and his offspring received the promise of God 'that he would be heir of the world.' There are concrete divine promises in Genesis 22:17–18, but also in other places in Genesis such as 12:2–3, 15:4–5, and 17:4–6. So again, it is not easy to say which text Paul is recalling. But because the words 'be heir' in Romans 4:13 resemble Genesis 22:17 (where the Septuagint uses a form of 'inherit'), it is quite possible that it was precisely the story that was in Paul's thoughts. Indeed, it is probable, because we saw above that Paul also alludes to it in Romans 4:17 and 8:32.

Abraham's Descendant(s)

The content of God's oath to Abraham is that he will have numerous descendants, who will also be a blessing to the world (verses 17–18). This promise is quoted twice in the New Testament with specific reference to Genesis 22. We have already seen how Hebrews 11:17–19 uses the story of the sacrifice of Isaac. Just before that passage, Hebrews makes mention of how much offspring Abraham received, and the author writes, 'descendants as numerous as the stars in the sky and as countless as the sand on the seashore' (11:12). These are almost exactly the same words that the LORD used in Genesis 22:17, and the writer has taken them from there, although he does not refer to Genesis. It is clear that he regards not only the Jews, but also the followers of Jesus as (spiritual) descendants of Abraham.

In Acts 3:25–26 Peter also speaks about the descendants of Abraham, and he quotes Genesis 22:18 literally:

> Through your offspring all peoples on earth will be blessed.

This connection is less visible in the NRSV, where Genesis 22:18 is translated differently:

> And by your offspring shall all the nations of the earth gain blessing for themselves.

However, Peter does not merely quote the text, he also gives it a deeper meaning. For who are this offspring of Abraham? In Genesis, that is Isaac and all people who descend from him. But when you read the context in Acts 3, you see that Peter makes the expression point to Jesus Christ, whom he calls God's servant in verse 26. This highlights that Hebrews regards all believers as descendants of Abraham, while Peter uses the term specifically for the Lord Jesus. Yet these two things complement each other.

Elements Not Used

The striking fact arises that in later times Christians have discovered other things in Genesis 22 than those mentioned in the New Testament. The life and death of Jesus have yet more similarities to the story of Abraham and Isaac. Below I mention the most important:

1. The fact that Abraham and Isaac travel to the mountain called Moriah (verse 2). Later this name Moriah only occurs in 2 Chronicles 3:1, where it says that the temple of God was built on this mountain, which was situated in Jerusalem. Jerusalem is indeed about three days from Beersheba, where Abraham and Isaac lived (Genesis 21:33; 22:4, 19). Later in the narrative this place is called 'the mountain of the Lord' (22:14b; see also for example Isaiah 2:3 and Psalm 24:3). You expect to read in the New Testament that God sacrificed Jesus in Jerusalem, just as Abraham wanted to sacrifice Isaac in the same place, but none of the writers makes this point directly. Incidentally, Moriah is a symbolic name which means 'place of seeing.'

2. Genesis 22 puts some emphasis on the fact that Isaac had to carry the wood for the altar himself (verse 6). John the evangelist emphasizes that Jesus bore his cross himself (19:17) – leaving Simon of Cyrene (Mark 15:21) out of the picture – but he does not openly compare Jesus to Isaac in this respect, as many later readers have done. Perhaps John expects *us* to make the comparison?

3. Abraham says that God himself will provide a sacrificial lamb (verse 8); God will provide (verse 14). This word 'provide' is repeated in the narrative and therefore important, but the New Testament does not explicitly build on it.

4. In Christian readings of the story the parallels run between God and Abraham, and between Jesus and Isaac. Yet some also see a similarity between Abraham and Jesus, namely their inner conflict. The narrative says nothing about this aspect, but it is not hard to imagine that the journey of three full days gave Abraham more than enough time for heart-breaking doubt. He now had to lose either his son or his God. Would he do the will of God or...? The narrator in Genesis 22 repeats the little phrase that father and son 'went on together' (verses 6 and 8) and such repetition is always meaningful. When telling the story to children, you might repeat it even more often. The intense inner conflict of Jesus in Gethsemane is exposed in Mark 14:32–43. Jesus also had to decide whether to do the will of God. Both Abraham and Jesus were obedient.

5. However many parallels there are between the two stories, Abraham's sacrifice of Isaac and God's sacrifice of his son, they end in very different ways. An old children's Bible has:

> And later, much later, when Abraham had been dead for many years, there was again a father who had to sacrifice his only son. But that time there was no-one who cried, 'Hold on, it's enough!' That time the son *really* was the lamb.

Who is the Type?

Looking back over this chapter you will see that there are several types in the story. Some readers may find this confusing and they may try to reduce everything to one type. But it is good to be aware that there are many lines running between the different parts of the Bible. Isaac and the sacrificial lamb both look forward to Jesus; Abraham is both a type of God, the Father who gives his Son, and of the faithful congregation that trusts God without knowing the outcome of events. And at the beginning of the chapter we saw that Hebrews says that both Abraham and Jesus were put to the test, so that is yet another connection.

13

You might wonder how the Jews are interpreting this story in the time after Jesus. Do they not see that it points to him? No, they read this story in a very different way, with great emphasis on the faith and the merit of Isaac. Isaac is the faithful and willing person, and his obedience deserves and earns God's approval. The merit of Isaac is so large that all Jews who live like Isaac can benefit from it and be accepted by God. This is the Jewish way of thinking. This interpretation of the story already existed before the time of Jesus, so it is time-honoured, but that does not make it correct!

Genesis 22 is only quoted twice in the New Testament but is alluded to much more often. You miss the strong influence of the story when you confine yourself to spotting literal quotations and formulas such as 'so that would be fulfilled.' This passage is therefore an excellent example of what I want to show in this book.

Further Reading

Knight, George A.F., *A Christian Theology of the Old Testament* (London: SCM, 1961).

Moberly, R.W.L., 'Christ as the Key to Scripture: Genesis 22 Reconsidered' in R.S. Hess and others (eds), *He Swore an Oath. Biblical Themes from Genesis 12–50* (Cambridge: Tyndale House, 1993) 143–173; see also R.W.L. Moberly, *The Bible, Theology, and Faith: A Study of Abraham and Jesus* (Cambridge: Cambridge University Press, 2000).

Chapter 2: Exodus 33–34

Exodus 33 and 34, and in particular its central part, Exodus 33:12 to 34:10, is a key text that tells us how shortly after bringing the people of Israel out of Egypt, God reveals to them who he is. In this chapter I will show how John picks up the core of the story, while Paul uses the end of the narrative in a surprising way.

John

At the beginning of his Gospel, John makes intensive use of Exodus 33–34. He neither quotes Exodus nor even refers to it openly, but the repeated echoes make the connections obvious. John shows that God's revelation to Israel is surpassed by his revelation in his Son, who first reveals himself to Israel and then to the whole world. To introduce the discussion, I quote from John 1, and you should read the above passage from Exodus alongside it:

> The Word became flesh and made his dwelling among us. We have seen his glory, the glory of the one and only Son, who came from the Father, full of grace and truth. (John testified concerning him. He cried out, saying, 'This is the one I spoke about when I said, "He who comes after me has surpassed me because he was before me."') Out of his fullness we have all received grace in place of grace already given. For the law was given through Moses; grace and truth came through Jesus Christ. No one has ever seen God, but the one and only Son, who is himself God and is in the closest relationship with the Father, has made him known.

God's Tent With Us

John 1:14 says that the word 'made his dwelling among us' or 'lived among us' (NRSV). For dwelling or living John does not use the usual Greek word, but a word that literally means 'pitch a tent.' Just as God had lived with Israel in a tent, the tabernacle, during their time in the wilderness and made himself known (Exodus 25:8; 29:46; 40:34), he has now taken up residence among his people as the Word, Jesus, staying in a tent. And this time, through Jesus, God's glory is much more visible than during the time in the desert. The coming of the Word is a fulfilment of repeated Old Testament promises about God's future living with the people, as you find them for example in Ezekiel 37:25–28; Joel 3:17; and Zechariah 2:10–12. However, in view of the context, John is in particular thinking of the 'tent of meeting' that Moses set up and which is mentioned in Exodus 33:7–11, so just before Exodus 33:12 to 34:10. In the period before Jesus there was already an intense expectation that God would come to dwell with his people. The book *Wisdom of Jesus Sirach*, written in the second century B.C., contains the following application of Exodus 33–34:

> Wisdom praises herself, and tells of her glory in the midst of her people. … 'I dwelt in the highest heavens, and my throne was in a pillar of cloud. … Among all these I sought a resting-place; in whose territory should I abide? Then the Creator of all things gave me a command, and my Creator chose the place for my tent. He said, 'Make your dwelling in Jacob, and in Israel receive your inheritance.' … In the holy tent I ministered before him, and so I was established in Zion. Thus in the beloved city he gave me a resting-place, and in Jerusalem was my domain. I took root in an honoured people, in the portion of the Lord, his heritage.' (Sirach 24:1, 4, 7–8, 10–12)

The 'philosopher' Jesus Sirach says in this passage that wisdom has set up her tent in Israel. It is clear that John is responding to these words, because he sees Jesus Christ as the personification of God's wisdom, the Word of God. John says that it was Jesus who set up his tent in Israel. Hence Jesus Christ also fulfils the expectation of Jesus Sirach. When John writes that the word 'made his dwelling among us,' the 'us' primarily means the Jews in the land of Israel.

The Law

The sections which surround Exodus 33–34 deal with the laws that God gave to Israel. Although modern Westerners often don't have many positive feelings when hearing the word 'law,' for the Jews the law is a source of joy; just think of Psalms 19 and 119! The people of Israel were thankful that God had given them so much good via Moses. John acknowledges this, but he adds that the good gift of the law has now been surpassed because Jesus Christ has brought God's 'grace and truth' (John 1:17). Israel knew God as a 'compassionate and gracious' God (Exodus 34:6), but now in Jesus that compassion and grace has been brought near to us.

God's Goodness

No less than three times in 1:14–18, John writes that we have come to know God's goodness and grace through Jesus. This links with Moses' openly pronounced doubt, about whether God was favourably inclined to him (Exodus 33:12–17; 34:9). The Greek word for favour or grace (*charis*) occurs repeatedly in both passages and it is evident that John's vocabulary was influenced by Exodus.

Seeing God?

When Moses asked to see the glory of God (Hebrew *kabood*; Greek *doxa*; Exodus 33:18), his wish was partially fulfilled: he was allowed to see God from behind (33:21–23). In later times God's glory dwelt in the tabernacle and in the temple (Exodus 40:34–35; Leviticus 9:6, 23; 2 Chronicles 7:1). However, John is in the position to write that in Christ, the only Son, the glory of God has become visible like never before – and to all people. John 1:14 and 18 emphatically use words for *seeing*. The word glory (*doxa*) is a key word in John's Gospel (for example 1:14, 2:11, 11:40, 17:5, 22, 24). His glory is what distinguishes God from human beings: his royal majesty, honour, and splendour, but also his mercy and compassion (Exodus 33:19).

God had told Moses that no-one would survive seeing him in his glory (Exodus 33:20) and Paul follows this thought (1 Timothy 6:16); but John looks at the case from another angle and enthusiastically states that the Son of God has made him known to us (John 1:18). John and his friends have not only seen Jesus, but heard and touched him (see also 1 John 1:1). God's revelation in the Word surpasses the old covenant in every respect.

Miraculous Deeds

The echo of Exodus 34:10 resounds in John 2:11, 3:1, and 4:54, and later in the Gospel when John mentions the 'signs' that Jesus performed.

Jesus brought the definitive fulfilment of God's promise in Exodus 34:10 that the people would see the 'miraculous deeds' (NIV: wonders; NRSV: marvels; NASB miracles) of God.

So far this chapter has shown that the New Testament can use the Old extensively without quoting it. John assumes that his readers know the Scriptures. We will see this one more time below.

Paul

The Run-up

In 2 Corinthians 3:7 to 4:6 Paul responds at length to the story in Exodus 34, the passage which describes Moses seeing God and the wondrous effect it has on him. Paul compares his own work as an apostle with the ministry of Moses. Although there is no doubt that he has Exodus 34 in mind, he does not say so, and like John he does not quote anything from the text. He also refers to other parts of Scripture during his discussion, but I will ignore these. His way of writing shows that Paul assumes that his readers have a good working knowledge of the Scriptures. He may have discussed Exodus 34 with the Corinthians during his long stay in their city (Acts 18:11, 18). In 2 Corinthians 3:3 Paul already announces his subject by mentioning the two stone plates which occur in Exodus 34:29; in this way he alludes to Moses and the making of the covenant at Mount Sinai. In contrast, he states that the new covenant is not engraved on stone but written in the hearts of people. That is an allusion to the fulfilment of prophetic promises such as:

> 'This is the covenant that I will make with the people of Israel after that time,' declares the LORD. 'I will put my law in their minds and write it on their hearts. I will be their God, and they will be my people.' (Jeremiah 31:33)

> I will give you a new heart and put a new spirit in you; I will remove from you your heart of stone and give you a heart of flesh. (Ezekiel 36:26)

The contrast that Ezekiel sees between the outward workings of the old covenant and the innerness of the new covenant determines the way Paul reads Exodus 34:29–35. The old covenant was not bad – but the new is much better. The glory of the new covenant is not momentary but permanent.

Verses 7–13

The actual discussion of Exodus 34 begins in 2 Corinthians 3:7, although Paul begins by mentioning something that is *not* in Exodus. Exodus 34:29–35 centres on the supernatural radiance of Moses' face as a result of his dialogue with the LORD (verse 29). Paul now states that this radiance on Moses' face was not permanent but disappeared again (see also verse 13). Hence Paul himself writes:

> For what was glorious [Moses' face] has no glory now in comparison with the surpassing glory [of the gospel]. (verse 10)

And then follows logically verse 11 (my rendering):

> For if what was set aside [in Christ] came with glory, how much greater is the glory of that which lasts!

In verses 12–13, the NSRV rightly uses 'set aside':

> We act … not like Moses, who put a veil over his face to keep the people of Israel from gazing at the end of the glory that was being set aside.

Verses 14–16

In verses 7–13 Paul keeps close to the narrative in Exodus, but in verses 14–16 he gives his own application. Jews who do not believe in Jesus still have a veil before their eyes, so that they cannot see the truth. Thus, Paul compares Moses' veil to a veil covering the Jews, as an image for hiddenness and spiritual darkness. The veil he has in mind is thus not a piece of sheer fabric, but a kind of burqa or niqab. However, when someone recognises Jesus as Lord, this spiritual veil disappears. And Paul extends the imagery: he puts Moses on a line with the books of the old covenant by writing in verse 15: 'Even to this day when Moses is read, a veil covers their hearts.' As a very positive contrast, in verse 16 Paul likens the experience of Moses to the experience of the believers in Christ: 'But whenever anyone turns to the Lord, the veil is taken away.' Paul's experience is that through the spiritual reading of the Scriptures, people are meeting God! Some interpreters think that verse 16 is a kind of quote from Exodus 34:34, but there are too many differences. Instead, it is an allusion.

Evaluation

In summary, we see that Paul says several things:

- When Moses met with the LORD, he took the veil off his face.

- When Israel finds Jesus, God removes the veil from their understanding.

- When Paul's readers find the Lord, through the Holy Spirit (3:18), they understand the gospel.

- When we understand the gospel, it transforms us (3:18).

- When Paul openly proclaims Christ, people come to faith (4:3–5).

This means that Paul reads Exodus in an eschatological way: the glory of the new covenant had remained hidden from the Israelites and has now been revealed to the church. He does not misread Exodus, but he reads it through the lens of Jesus Christ. And he draws an important conclusion: Moses covered his radiant face, but the followers of Jesus can openly reflect the glory of their Lord. Moses hid his face, but Paul proclaims the Gospel in all openness (with great boldness, verse 12 NRSV; see also 4:2).

Letter and Spirit

When you reflect on Paul's handling of the Scriptures, you may wonder what he means by his remark 'the letter kills, but the Spirit gives life' (2 Corinthians 3:6). Is he not too critical of the written word? No, because he makes a clear distinction between 'the letter' (Greek *gramma*) and 'the Scriptures' (Greek *graphē*). Paul opposes sophistry, legalism, and the 'academic' knowledge of scribes. The old covenant has lost its strength after Christ, but Scripture is God's word for his church, the word that makes us alive by showing us Jesus. Whoever lives through the Spirit will come to know Jesus and find spiritual food precisely in these Scriptures – the Old and New Testaments.

Further Reading

Bauckham, Richard, *Gospel of Glory* (Grand Rapids: Baker Academic, 2015).

Beasley-Murray, George R., *John*. Word Biblical Themes (Dallas: Word, 1989).

Childs, Brevard S., *The Book of Exodus. A Critical, Theological Commentary*, OTL (Philadelphia: Westminster Press, 1974).

Hays, Richard B., *Echoes of Scripture in the Letters of Paul* (New Haven: Yale University Press, 1989).

Tsutserov, Alexander, *Glory, Grace, and Truth: Ratification of the Sinaitic Covenant according to the Gospel of John* (Eugene: Pickwick, 2009).

Chapter 3: Psalm 2

Psalm 2 tells us that the nations of the world are revolting against God's authority and how God responds to this challenge. He gives Israel a new king who extends his dominion over the entire world. God is the heavenly king, but he establishes a kind of representative on earth. The structure of this psalm is as follows:

> Verses 1–3: The problem of opposition to the LORD
>
> Verses 4–6: The LORD sends his Son
>
> Verses 7–9: The Son accepts his assignment
>
> Verses 10–12: Call to the rulers to surrender

Both God and this king speak in this psalm, which is not an ode or a song of praise, but a prophetic message with political overtones. I quote verses 1–2 and 6–9 because they all appear in some way in the New Testament:

> Why do the nations conspire and the peoples plot in vain? The kings of the earth rise up and the rulers band together against the LORD and against his anointed … 'I have installed my king on Zion, my holy mountain.' I will proclaim the LORD's decree: He said to me, 'You are my son; today I have become your father. Ask me, and I will make the nations your inheritance, the ends of the earth your possession. You will break them with a rod of iron; you will dash them to pieces like pottery.'

By mentioning Zion (verse 6), the mountain on which Jerusalem is built, the poet suggests that he is singing about a king from the house of David. However, from the beginning of the exile in 586 BC, Israel did not have such a king anymore. It was expected that God would restore the kingship in the future. So the fulfilment of this psalm would signal the moment when God's future had arrived. This happened with the coming of Jesus Christ, the carpenter from Nazareth who turned out to be God's Son. It is therefore no surprise that this psalm is widely used in the New Testament.

In the order of the New Testament, elements of the psalm appear as follows:

New Testament	Use of Psalm 2	Similarity
Matthew 3:17; Mark 1:11; Luke 3:22	Quote from verse 7	'You are my son'
Matthew 17:5; Mark 9:7; Luke 9:35	Quote from verse 7	'You are my son'
Matthew 4:3; Luke 4:3	Allusion to verse 7	Are you the son?
Matthew 27:54; Mark 15:39	Allusion to verse 7	The Son of God
John 1:41	Allusion to verse 6	Anointed one
John 1:49	Allusion to verse 7	Son and King
Acts 4:25	Quote from verses 1–2	The powers are plotting
Acts 4:28	Allusion to verse 7	Decision made
Acts 13:33	Quote from verse 7	'You are my son'
Hebrews 1:2	Allusion to verse 8	The son is heir
Hebrews 1:5; 5:5	Quotes from verse 7	'You are my son'
2 Peter 1:17	Quote from verse 7	'You are my son'
Revelation 2:26–27; 12:5; 19:15	Allusions to verse 9a	Iron rod
Revelation 11:15	Allusion to verse 7	Beginning of dominion
Revelation 11:18	Allusion to verse 1	World powers conspire
Revelation 14:1	Allusion to verse 6	Sion
Revelation 19:19	Allusion to verse 2	World powers conspire

It is also possible that some echoes of verse 8, in which the Son is encouraged to ask things from God, are audible in the references to Jesus' personal prayer life (e.g. Mark 1:35; 6:46; 14:32–39); but maybe I hear more than there really is. In any case, it is clear that Psalm 2 is very often cited in the New Testament and is only missing from Paul.

When you look up all these texts, you see that everything the psalm says about the king is now being applied to the Lord Jesus. It is assumed that David wrote the psalm, although the text itself does not say so. It is more important that the text is prophetic, and these prophecies are now being fulfilled in Jesus.

Life of Jesus

The most-quoted sentence from the psalm is verse 7, 'You are my son.' It is striking that all New Testament authors add the word 'beloved' to this little sentence, for they write: 'You are my *beloved* Son.' They may derive this addition from Genesis 22:2, where Isaac is referred to as 'your son, your only son, whom you love.' Another possibility is that they had a form of the Hebrew text in which the word 'beloved' appeared also in Psalm 2:7.

Whatever the possibilities, this sentence is used to describe two important events in Jesus' life: his baptism and his transfiguration. Both times he is presented to the people: the first time as the obedient son who is more than an ordinary Israelite, the second time as the incomparable Son of God. Besides the synoptic evangelists, Peter also tells about this from his own experience in 2 Peter 1:17:

> He [Jesus] received honour and glory from God the Father when the voice came to him from the Majestic Glory, saying, 'This is my Son, whom I love; with him I am well pleased.'

The words of God quoted by Peter and the evangelists are, moreover, a combination of two verses from the Old Testament: 'This is my [beloved] son' is a free rendering of Psalm 2:7 and 'in him I find joy' comes from Isaiah 42:1.

Acts 4

The most extensive use of the psalm is in Acts 4. In verses 5–6, Luke emphatically mentions the Jewish leaders who are meeting in Jerusalem, after which he tells us in verses 25–28 how the apostles quote Psalm 2:1–2 with reference to these leaders, saying that the psalm is now fulfilled:

> You spoke by the Holy Spirit through the mouth of your servant, our father David: 'Why do the nations rage and the peoples plot in vain? The kings of the earth rise up and the rulers band together against the Lord and against his anointed one.' Indeed Herod and Pontius Pilate met together with the Gentiles and the people of Israel in this city to conspire against your holy servant Jesus, whom you anointed. They did what your power and will had decided beforehand should happen.

The praying congregation in Acts provides a contemporary interpretation and application of the psalm. Those responsible for the death sentence against Jesus are the same rulers who are now persecuting the church; and they are not only gentiles – Romans – but also the Jewish leaders! The Jews had always read this psalm as a condemnation of others, foreigners, but suddenly their own unbelieving leaders are under attack from their own Scriptures. The use of Psalm 2 explains why more literal translations of Acts 4:27 (NRSV, ESV) have 'the Gentiles and the peoples of Israel.' The words of the congregation reflect the fact that Psalm 2:1 also has two plurals, 'the nations' and 'the peoples.' Luke intends Acts 4:23–31, the longest prayer in the book of Acts, as a model for his readers. It is an example for us because it names the Father, the Son, and the Holy Spirit. The first church brings thanks to God for the liberation of the apostles from the hands of the authorities. Their reading of the psalm leads them to expect that God and his anointed Son will also win the ultimate victory. Our prayers may likewise be based on what God has already done for us.

The congregation in Acts also uses Psalm 2 as basis for their criticism of the Jewish and Roman authorities, and we will see the same in Revelation. But before we look at this, I briefly draw attention to the short scene with the Roman officer in the Gospels (Matthew 27:54;

Mark 15:39). Witnessing the suffering and dying of Jesus, this man is so impressed that he recognises him as the Son of God – and once again the good listener hears an echo of Psalm 2:7! Although many Jews 'conspire against Jesus,' a Roman officer confesses him as the Son of God. The roles have been reversed.

Revelation

Many passages in the book of Revelation tell us how the world is in revolt against God, refusing to submit to him. Readers of Revelation might be surprised at this continuing resistance to God, but those who are familiar with Psalm 2 know that this was to be expected. The expression 'the kings of the earth' (Revelation 6:15; 16:14; 17:2, 18; 18:3, 9; 19:19, and 21:24) refers to the present rulers of the world and is derived from Psalm 2:2 and 10. The promise of Revelation is that Jesus will subjugate them (1:5; 19:16) and this promise of victory is also based on Psalm 2. In many details the writer of Revelation shows that he knows the psalm. The expression 'rule with an iron sceptre' (Revelation 2:27; 12:5; 19:15) is taken from Psalm 2:9. In Revelation 12:5 and 19:15 it is Jesus who wields such a staff as a weapon against his enemies. The use of the psalm in Revelation 2:26–28 is more surprising because these verses form a promise for the believers. The promise that they too will use an iron staff means nothing less than that the victors will share in the role of Jesus Christ as king. To emphasise this great honour, Revelation 2:27 cites also the last line of Psalm 2:9, 'dash them to pieces like pottery.' Our translations of Psalm 2:9 say *'break* with a rod of iron,' while Revelation has *'rule* (or shepherd) with an iron sceptre.' The word 'rule' comes from the Septuagint translation of the psalm. Yet there is little difference in meaning between the two words, for the use of an iron staff symbolises on the one hand the protection (ruling) of Israel – and of God's people in a broader sense – and on the other hand the punishment of Israel's enemies.

The use of Psalm 2 in Acts and Revelation also tells us that it is not surprising when God's children come under pressure from rulers. The rebellion of the powers against God, and hence their enmity against us, was described long ago. Psalm 2:4 says about it:

> The One enthroned in heaven laughs; the Lord scoffs at them.

It comes as a surprise that the end of Psalm 2 is cited nowhere in the New Testament; still, of course, it resonates with the rest of the text. These verses, 10–12, call upon everyone to be wise and to submit to God before it is too late. The psalmist concludes that the people who take refuge with God are happy.

Conclusion

You see that, in the Gospels, Psalm 2 sheds light on the life of Jesus; in Acts on his suffering and resurrection; in Hebrews on his identity as the Son of God; and in Revelation on his coming kingdom.

Finally, have you ever wondered why Jesus of Nazareth has the title 'Christ' everywhere in the New Testament? I think that this psalm played a role in how this came about, for Christ is the Greek translation of the Hebrew title Messiah, which means anointed. In the Old Testament the term anointed is quite common, but it is rarely used for the saviour whom God would send. The Old Testament rather refers to this person as the servant of the LORD (Isaiah), as the prophet like Moses (Deuteronomy), and as the son of David. The fact that this saviour is nonetheless called 'anointed one,' ('Christ'), everywhere in the New Testament must be because God's new king is called 'his anointed' in Psalm 2:2. Moreover, Psalm 2:6 says that God has 'installed' (Amplified Bible) or 'consecrated' his king on Mount Zion, and the Hebrew word used here can also mean 'anointed.' So our psalm is one of the few places where the expectation of God's king and the term anoint are linked. Psalm 2 is a short psalm with great influence!

Further Reading

Gillingham, Susan, *A Journey of Two Psalms. The Reception of Psalms 1 and 2 in Jewish and Christian Tradition* (Oxford: OUP, 2013).

Hays, Richard B., *Echoes of Scripture in the Gospels* (Waco: Baylor University Press, 2016).

Rowe, Robert D., *God's Kingdom and God's Son: The Background to Mark's Christology from Concepts of Kingship in the Psalms* (Leiden: Brill, 2002).

West, Donald S., 'Acts 4:23-31 and a Biblical Theology of Prayer' in Matthew R. Malcolm (ed.), *All That the Prophets Have Declared* (Milton Keynes: Paternoster, 2015) 71–79.

Chapter 4: Psalm 8

This psalm is used in some places in the New Testament, but not as often as you might expect.

Matthew

In Matthew 21:14–17, Jesus' opponents are angry that children in the temple are shouting 'Hosanna for the Son of David' and they challenge him accordingly. (The children are repeating what the adults had shouted during Jesus' entry, see verse 9.) Jesus has no issue with the fact that people are calling him 'Son of David,' for it is a messianic title. He is probably reminded of Psalm 8 at that moment, because the designation comes from the lips of children. Hence in verse 16 Jesus quotes from this psalm, but at first sight he does not do it correctly. A literal translation of Psalm 8:3 is:

> From the mouth of children and infants you are building up a power because of your enemies to stop the enemy and the avenger.

But Jesus says, 'from the lips of children and infants, you, Lord, have called forth your *praise.*' What about that? Has God called forth power or praise? It is a matter of translation. The Hebrew text of the Psalm has 'power,' but the Septuagint has instead 'praise' or 'an ode.' So the words of Jesus are a correct quotation from the Septuagint. In this way he claims that as the Messiah, the son of David, he is also entitled to the praise that is brought to God.

Yet this answer is not fully satisfactory, because it is unlikely that in a discussion with other Jews in Jerusalem Jesus would have used the Greek translation of the Scriptures. Surely they would have normally spoken Hebrew or Aramaic with each other? The Hebrew word in question is *'oz*, a common word in the Old Testament which usually means power or strength. However, it often occurs in a context of honour and praise for God, as in the following two lines from psalms:

> Ascribe to the LORD, you heavenly beings, ascribe to the LORD glory and strength. (Psalm 29:1)

> Ascribe to the LORD, all you families of nations, ascribe to the LORD glory and strength. (Psalm 96:7)

See also Psalm 59:17. These examples show that the two meanings power and praise for *'oz* are not far apart. Hence *'oz* can also mean 'honoured power' or 'praise of his power.' Therefore Psalm 68:34 calls on us to 'proclaim the power of God' or 'ascribe power to God' (NRSV, ESV), although it is more logical that we bring praise to God than power. On this basis the Septuagint could render *'oz* as 'praise,' thus in fact showing the deeper intention of the psalm. For Jesus, his opponents, and Matthew, both meanings of the word were very close together. The little children were praising Jesus' honoured power.

Hebrews

Hebrews 2 contains a quotation and some discussion of Psalm 8. The original psalm gives a timeless description of humanity in their relationship with God, but Hebrews reads it as a short biography of Jesus Christ. A song about all of us is now being read as a description of Jesus. Hebrews interprets every sentence in Psalm 8:5 and 6 as reference to another moment in the life of Jesus. This is not as far-fetched as it may seem, because the psalm is originally in the singular and uses the expressions 'man' and 'son of man' (verse 4, ESV). Hebrews 2:6–9 likewise is originally in the singular, as the ESV brings out, just like older translations such as the KJV, the NASB, and the 1978 NIV.[2] Jesus of course often used the phrase 'son of man' for himself. This made it easy for the author of Hebrews to make the connection between the psalm and Jesus. Here are the key verses on Psalm 8:

Original Hebrew (ESV)	Septuagint
[4] What is man that you are mindful of him, and the son of man that you care for him?	[5] What is man that you are mindful of him, or the son of man that you attend to him?
[5] Yet you have made him a little lower than the heavenly beings	[6] You diminished him a little in comparison with *angels;*

---

[2] The use of inclusive language in recent translations is generally a good thing, but in Psalm 8 and especially in Hebrews 2 it obscures the meaning of the text. Hence for these chapters the non-inclusive ESV is to be preferred.

and crowned him with glory and honour.	with glory and honour you crowned him.
6 You have given him dominion over the works of your hands; you have put all things under his feet,	7 And you set him over the works of your hands; you subjected all under his feet.

Because the author of Hebrews uses the psalm in the Greek translation (Septuagint), he is helped by a difference between the Hebrew (verse 5a) and the Greek text (verse 6a). The text here is not easy to translate. It says something like 'you have made him barely less than *elohim*.' The word *elohim* usually means 'God,' but the Hebrew text has no uppercase letters and in certain places you can take *elohim* as 'divine beings' or 'angels.' And that is exactly what the Septuagint has done here. Hebrews uses this translation and relates the 'him' to Jesus, thus continuing the comparison between Jesus and the angels which has dominated the letter so far.

In Hebrews 2:8b the writer answers a question his readers might have. Psalm 8 says that everything is subject to humanity, 'put under his feet,' as was God's intention according to Genesis 1:26. But we do not experience this in our daily lives, do we? Things in this world are not subject to us at all! Okay, the writer explains, that is correct, but all things are subject to Jesus Christ. The words of the psalm are no longer used with reference to the original creation of humanity in Hebrews 2, but they indicate the experience of Jesus. That is, when he became human, but especially when he died on the cross, Jesus was given a lower place than the angels. Yes, this Jesus did not only die in humiliation, but he was also raised from the dead and received the place of honour in heaven. He is now already 'crowned with glory and honour' (verse 9) and so in him the promise of the psalm has been fulfilled. Psalm 8 helps the author of Hebrews to describe Jesus as the ideal human being. We were meant to be like him, and one day we will be like him.

In Hebrews 2:10 the author uses the word 'sons' (and daughters) to refer to humanity; this again brings out the connection with the one special son, Jesus. In Hebrews Psalm 8 is read with reference both to Jesus' humiliation and to his exaltation. Jesus is seen as the true human, the one who vicariously does everything that is good for humanity and for the world. If Paul had written Hebrews, he would have called Jesus the second Adam.

Just as the New Testament sometimes uses the Old Testament, so also some parts of the Old Testament make use of other Old Testament texts. Psalm 8 refers back to Genesis 1:26–28 by saying that human beings closely resemble God and that they rule over the rest of creation on his behalf. The glory of the creator is thus visible in his people. In turn, Psalm 8 is used by Job, who gives a kind of parody of it:

> What is man, that you make so much of him, and that you set your heart on him, visit him every morning and test him every moment? (Job 7:17–18)

Job uses the psalm as a means of calling God to account for his suffering. He believes that God is either actively afflicting him or allowing affliction to happen. Job selects a well-known song to make his argument stronger, staying close to the text of the psalm. His depressed thought is that all God's attention to humanity has brought him is unhappiness. Job thinks that he will be better off if God would forget him and leave him in peace.

Paul

Paul also connects Psalm 8 directly to Jesus, taking verse 6 as his point of departure. The expression, 'everything you laid under his feet' is biblical language for 'you have made everything subject to him.' According to the apostle, these words are not only true for humans in general, but especially for Jesus. The psalm had a prophetic layer which is now fulfilled in Jesus. Paul's quotation of these words in Ephesians 1:22 speaks for itself, but in 1 Corinthians 15:25–28 the matter is less simple. There it says:

> For he [Christ] must reign until he has put all his enemies under his feet. The last enemy to be destroyed is death. For he 'has put everything under his feet.' Now when it says that 'everything' has been put under him, it is clear that this does not include God himself, who put everything under Christ. When he has done this, then the Son himself will be made

subject to him who put everything under him, so that God may be all in all.

In verse 25, Paul quotes Psalm 110:1 almost verbatim, although most translations do not clearly show this. Paul smuggles in the word 'all' from Psalm 8:7. Psalm 110:1 resembles Psalm 8:6, and that verse is quoted by Paul in verse 27. The context shows that for Paul, Psalm 8 refers to the future: the moment when everything will be subject to Jesus is still in the future. There is thus some tension between Ephesians 1:22 and 1 Corinthians 15:25–28, but this is the same tension that dominates the whole New Testament, and which you also see between Ephesians 1:10 and 1:22. The tension is that many things have already been subjected to Jesus, for in Him God's salvation has come and God's great future has begun – but we are not there quite yet. Death has been defeated, but it is still shaking its tail. Only on the last day *all things* will be fully subjected to God.

Further Reading

France, R.T., *Jesus and the Old Testament: His Application of Old Testament Passages to Himself and his Mission* [1971] (Grand Rapids: Baker, 1982).

France, R.T., 'The Writer of Hebrews as a Biblical Expositor,' *Tyndale Bulletin* 47.2 (1996) 245–276.

Rascher, Angela, *Schriftauslegung und Christologie im Hebräerbrief* (Berlin: De Gruyter, 2007).

Starling, David I., *Hermeneutics as Discipleship* (Grand Rapids: Baker Academic, 2016).

Chapter 5: Psalm 22

This psalm is very different from the previous two. In this personal psalm David complains about his unbearable, lonely suffering. In Psalm 2, the prophetic elements were at the surface, but Psalm 22 lacks words such as anointed and son. Only the word kingship occurs in verse 28 in the ESV ('dominion' NIV), which is in the second part of the psalm, looking ahead to the period after David's liberation. This second part (verses 22–31) is prophetic because it contains the expectation that one day the whole world will know God, but it does not say anything about the Messiah. (It is surprising that verses 27–31 are not cited anywhere in the New Testament!)

When you read Psalm 22 without thinking of other texts, you are likely to take the colourful text as a description of great loneliness, even of being deserted by God, and at the same time as an expression of deep human trust in God. This is how the Jews in Jesus' days read the psalm. No-one connected it with the expected Messiah. But our way of reading changes radically when we lay it side by side with the descriptions of the life of Jesus. Suddenly, we see some striking similarities! We are, of course, helped by the evangelists, and they in turn were put on this track by Jesus himself, who quoted words from this psalm. David, the original speaker, thus unawares reaches out above himself and it becomes evident that he wrote prophetic words. He himself turns out to be a type of Jesus.

The Evangelists

The first quotation from the psalm is taken from verse 18, 'They divide my clothes among them and cast lots for my garment.' It is remarkable that these words are used in all four Gospels (Matthew 27:35; Mark 15:24; Luke 23:34b; John 19:23–24). Although the evangelists give us few details about the crucifixion of Jesus, the clothing is mentioned, as the soldiers think it is important to obtain a part of Jesus' clothing. Jesus is totally humiliated, for he hangs on the cross (almost) naked. This detail of the story probably grabbed the attention of the evangelists because in this incident the Scriptures are clearly and in detail fulfilled. Strictly speaking, the first three evangelists do not quote, they merely use the words of the psalm for their description. It is John who says in so many words, "This happened that the scripture might be fulfilled that said....' In this way he identifies the psalm as a prophecy that has now been fulfilled.

The passion stories in the Gospels also contain other allusions to Psalm 22. The words from verse 7, 'All who see me mock me; they hurl insults, shaking their heads,' are fulfilled in the mockery of the people around the cross (Matthew 27:29, 39; Mark 15:29; Luke 23:35–37). Matthew and Mark add that those present were shaking their heads as a sign of disapproval of Jesus. Jesus is mocked as David was. The parallel between Psalm 22:8 and Matthew 27:43 is even stronger. The words of the psalm are:

> 'He trusts in the LORD,' they say, 'let the LORD rescue him. Let him deliver him, since he delights in him.'

Matthew uses almost the same words to reproduce the way in which the scoffers around the cross taunt Jesus. It also seems that Matthew in this way is consciously preparing for the quotation from Psalm 22:1 that I will discuss below. All in all, Jesus' humiliation is complete.

Another detail in the passion story is that Jesus was thirsty. The way in which John tells this in 19:28 echoes Psalm 22:15a, 'My mouth is dried up like a potsherd, and my tongue sticks to the roof of my mouth…' On the other hand, the evangelists do not mention the fact that at the crucifixion Jesus' hands and feet were pierced, and thus they do not make the obvious connection with Psalm 22:16, '…they pierce my hands and feet.' Yet this is a remarkable detail, because the normal death penalty in Israel was stoning. Crucifixion was a typical Roman punishment and it must be prophetic that David mentions the piercing of the hands and feet. There are further details in verses 14–18 which evoke the proceedings of an execution, even a crucifixion, although David had probably never heard of crucifixion. Although the New Testament does not say so, we can observe that the crucifixion of Jesus was also the fulfilment of Psalm 22:16.

Jesus' Own Words

'My God, my God, why have you forsaken me?' These are the words Jesus shouts from the cross after he has been hanging for hours (Mark 15:34, Matthew 27:46). This cry reflects his misery and agony – and it is a direct quote from Psalm 22:1, which many bystanders would have recognised. Jesus expresses the fact that he is no longer experiencing God's presence while he is suffering. This feeling of abandonment obviously makes his agony all the heavier. Earlier in their Gospels, Matthew and Mark have used Scripture to describe him as the Son of God, but here they show how severely his suffering has hit him.

In the Gospels Jesus himself does not often quote from the Old Testament directly; most of the times it is the evangelists who point out that Jesus was somehow fulfilling the Scriptures. Both Matthew and Mark have recorded these words of Jesus in Aramaic and followed them with the Greek translation. This is striking. Aramaic was probably the language that Jesus normally spoke, like most Jews at that time, but the Old Testament is written in Hebrew. This means that in his death distress Jesus did not use the official Hebrew text of the psalm, but a rendering in his Aramean vernacular. This touching detail once again emphasizes that we should not downplay the severity of Jesus' suffering in any way. Another striking detail is that even in this situation Jesus emphatically says '*my* God,' thus indicating that despite everything he continues to acknowledge the God of Israel as *his* God. His relationship with God is under heavy pressure, but it is not broken. Therefore I don't think that Jesus' cry is a reproach, but rather that it is a lament and a cry for help. This help soon comes in the form of his death – and three days later in the form of his victory over death. This victory guarantees us that although we can be lonely and feeling left by God, just like David and Jesus, he never really abandons us.

I will be emphasising that when someone in the New Testament quotes the Old, the text which surrounds the quoted words in the Old Testament also resonates. This surrounding text is called the context. In the case of Jesus' cry of dereliction and the use of the psalm by the evangelists, the context is the whole of Psalm 22. As stated above, the psalm ends in a positive mood with statements of trust in God and of hope for salvation. This means that in the words of Jesus, too, hope resonates that his death will not be final; he may have thought of the verses 22 and 30–31 of the Psalm:

> I will declare your name to my people; in the assembly I will praise you. … Posterity will serve him; future generations will be told about the LORD. They will proclaim his righteousness, declaring to a people yet unborn: He has done it!

Although the Gospels say little about the meaning of the death of Jesus – for that we must read the Letters – our use of Psalm 22 is a considerable help to understand it.

The Rest of the New Testament

Later in the New Testament, the use of Psalm 22 is less important. The Letter to the Hebrews shows that the whole psalm can now be conceived as Jesus' own words. In Hebrews 2:12, the author quotes Psalm 22:22 as the words of Jesus:

> I will declare your name to my brothers and sisters; in the assembly I will sing your praises.

The replacement of 'people' with 'brothers and sisters' is due to Hebrews using the Septuagint. Likewise, Hebrews 5:7 is an allusion to Psalm 22:24, for both verses state that Jesus' prayers were answered. The allusion is certain because both texts contain a rare Greek word for 'being heard' which is nowhere else used with reference to Jesus. Both verses show how the early Christian church saw the whole psalm as denoting Jesus.

Revelation too uses the second part of the psalm, but here it does not matter who the speaker is in the psalm. Psalm 22:23, a call to all believers to praise God, resonates in Revelation 19:5. And in the important statement that God has become king, a declaration which marks the completion of history (Revelation 11:15 and 19:6), the key words are derived from Psalm 22:28:

> For dominion belongs to the LORD and he rules over the nations.

Thus, Revelation reveals the direct connection between the death of Jesus on the cross and the coming of his kingdom.

In Psalm 22 David describes his enemies as dangerous animals, calling them bulls, wild oxen, lions, and dogs. These images do not appear in the passion narratives, but the metaphor of the lion from verses 13 and 21 is used elsewhere in the New Testament, namely in 1 Peter 5:8 and 2 Timothy 4:17. The writers may have done this under the influence of their study of Psalm 22, the psalm that so aptly expressed the suffering of Jesus. This would suggest that Peter and Paul saw similarities between their own suffering and the suffering of their Lord, as Paul also says in Colossians 1:24.

Further Reading

France, R.T., *The Gospel of Mark. A Commentary on the Greek Text.* NIGTC (Carlisle: Paternoster, 2002).

Hays, Richard B., *Echoes of Scripture in the Gospels* (Waco: Baylor University Press, 2016).

Rowe, Robert D., *God's Kingdom and God's Son: The Background to Mark's Christology from Concepts of Kingship in the Psalms* (Leiden: Brill, 2002).

Chapter 6: Psalm 69

This psalm, attributed to David, is about suffering, and despite the connections not being immediately obvious, this psalm is often used in the New Testament. A possible reason for this 'popularity' is the expression 'your servant' in verse 17. The presence of these words in the psalm probably evoked associations with the servant of the LORD in Isaiah 40–55, whom the first Christians recognised as Jesus. As a result, the psalm may have been combed in search of other elements that shed light on Jesus and his mission. This would explain why Matthew, Mark, John, Acts, and Paul all use the psalm.

Jesus on the Cross (1)

Although Psalm 69 is about innocent suffering, it is only used once in the passion story of Jesus. I will first put the texts together, omitting Luke 23:36 which would not add much to the emerging picture. I am using the Septuagint because the evangelists do so too.

> Psalm 69:22 Septuagint: They gave me *gall* as my food, and for my thirst they gave me *vinegar* to drink.

> Psalm 69:21 NIV: They put *gall* (poison, ESV, NRSV) in my food and gave me *vinegar* for my thirst.

> Mark 15:23 Then they offered him *wine mixed with myrrh*, but he did not take it.

> Matthew 27:34 There they offered Jesus *wine* to drink, *mixed with gall*, but after tasting it, he refused to drink it.

> Mark 15:36a Someone ran, filled a sponge with *wine vinegar*, put it on a staff, and offered it to Jesus to drink.

> Matthew 27:48 Immediately one of them ran and got a sponge. He filled it with *wine vinegar*, put it on a staff, and offered it to Jesus to drink.

The psalm mentions two things that are offered to David, namely gall or poison, and sour wine. Together they represent the bad treatment that David is enduring. The evangelists tell us that Jesus is twice offered something to drink. According to Mark, just before the crucifixion that is 'wine mixed with myrrh.' This drink would have been intended as an anaesthetic and was probably offered by friendly bystanders, not by the cruel soldiers. However, Jesus does not want to be stunned and refuses this drink.

Matthew, however, says that Jesus was offered 'wine mixed with gall,' that is, a kind of poison. Matthew consciously uses these words to make a connection to Psalm 69 and to show that the Scriptures are fulfilled in this detail too. The teacher Matthew knew the Gospel of Mark and it is typical of him that he clarifies its meaning in this way. But, unusually for Matthew, he does not explicitly refer to this event as a fulfilment of Scripture; he apparently expects his readers to know Psalm 69.

Jesus on the Cross (2)

Hours later, when his death is near, Jesus gets offered wine vinegar, a drink that works well against thirst (see Ruth 2:14). The person who wants to give Jesus this drink is one of the bystanders. In this case, the words used by Mark and Matthew are the same; they both allude to Psalm 69, so that it becomes clear that the one who gives Jesus the sponge (Mark 15:36b) or the other people (see Matthew 27:49) intend to taunt Jesus. Recurrence to the psalm clarifies the meaning of the gospel passage. In summary, Matthew shows that the first line of Psalm 69:21 was fulfilled at the beginning of the crucifixion and the second line at the end.

As I said, on this occasion Matthew does not refer to the Old Testament, but John does. This evangelist omits the event at the beginning of the crucifixion to focus on what happened just before the death of Jesus. John writes that Jesus himself spoke, 'I am thirsty,' and that he also drank when he was offered the wine vinegar (John 19:28–30). John sees this as the fulfilment of Scripture. He does not mention which part of Scripture he has in mind, but that is, of course, primarily Psalm 69. In addition, Psalm 22:15 can also be heard resonating. John, too, sees David as a precursor to Jesus and Jesus as the one who obeys the will of his Father.

Salvation for the Nations

Psalm 69 contains impressive promises of salvation for the nations:

> The poor will see and be glad – you who seek God, may your hearts live! The LORD hears the needy and does not despise his captive people. Let heaven and earth praise him, the seas and all that move in them, for God will save Zion and rebuild the cities of Judah. Then people will settle there and possess it; the children of his servants will inherit it, and those who love his name will dwell there. (verses 32–36)

These words at the end of the psalm are meant to indicate that the deliverance of King David also works out positively on his people. We believe that in the same way the resurrection and ascension of Jesus also have colossal positive consequences for his followers. Jesus is the representative of Israel – and so there is salvation for this nation and for all those who are added to it, 'first to the Jew, then to the Gentile,' to quote a phrase from Paul (Romans 1:16).

Judas the Traitor (Acts 1)

We now, however, move to a less positive use of Psalm 69; specifically, to the use of verse 25 in Acts 1:20. Here is the text:

> Psalm 69:25 NIV: May their place be deserted; let there be no one to dwell in their tents.

> Acts 1:20: For … it is written in the Book of Psalms: 'May his place be deserted; let there be no one to dwell in it.'

The quotation in Acts is hardly different from the original psalm; only the plural of the psalm has become singular in Acts, so that it is clear that the words are about one person, Judas.

At the beginning of Acts, Peter and the other followers of Jesus struggle with the betrayal and death of their former colleague Judas, and they seek for an explanation. Peter was likely reading this psalm as a prophecy of the suffering of Jesus, and read verses 21–28 as a criticism of his enemies. Sitting at the heart of this passage, verse 25 is a prophecy of treason and God's punishment of it. Under the inspiration of the Holy Spirit Peter states that this prophecy is basically about one particular person, Judas.

The House of the Father (John 2)

A very different use of Psalm 69 occurs in John 2:13–22, where the followers of Jesus cite Psalm 69:9. Jesus is cleansing the temple and John (2:17) comments: 'His disciples remembered that it is written: "Zeal for your house will consume me."' John does not identify which passage of Scripture they have in mind, but there is no doubt about it. Except that in Psalm 69 it says 'consumes' instead of 'will consume,' there is little difference between Old and New Testament.

The disciples probably did not make this connection between Jesus' action and the Scriptures during the chaotic incident of the temple cleansing, but only later, when they were looking back and reflecting on it. For them, as for Jesus, the temple was the house of God, and they put Jesus on a par with David. He had written these words in the psalm – they had now been fulfilled in Jesus. Through this one reference, the whole of Psalm 69 comes to life. Earlier in his Gospel, John had already dropped hints that Jesus was the new David by using the terms Messiah (1:41) and king of Israel (1:49). It is my conviction that we can read the Old Testament as the disciples did. This is because it contains words which were fully inspired by the Holy Spirit and which come to life in surprising ways in the New Testament description of Jesus and the first churches.

Hatred of the World (John 15)

Psalm 69 also plays a role in John 15:18–27, where Jesus speaks of the hatred of unbelieving Jews against his disciples. The Lord says:

> They have hated both me and my Father. But this is to fulfil what is written in their Law: 'They hated me without reason.' (verses 24b–25)

The words in quotation marks are the translation of only three Greek words, 'they-hated,' 'me' and 'without-reason.' To say almost the same in Hebrew you only need two words, which appear in Psalm 35:19 and Psalm 69:4: 'those who hate me without reason.' What Jesus says in

John 15 is not an exact quotation of either the Hebrew Bible or the Septuagint, but it is very close.

In Psalms 35 and 69 David complains about the unreasonable hatred of people. Of these words Jesus uses those that apply to him and his followers. Like David, Jesus and the first Christians suffer the hatred of the people around them. You see that what was true of David is conveyed to Jesus, but also to his disciples, who are connected with him as the branches with the vine (John 15:1–17).

You may have noted that Jesus here refers to the Scriptures as 'law.' This fits in with the loose use of the word 'law' elsewhere in John, for example in John 12:34, where people say '…we have heard from the Law that the Messiah will remain for ever.' What they really mean is the whole Hebrew Bible, and perhaps especially Ezekiel 37:25b:

> They and their children and their children's children will live there for ever, and David my servant will be their prince for ever.

You see that Jesus and John share the conviction that when you read it in retrospect, much in the Old Testament speaks of Jesus and his followers.

The Unfaithfulness of Israel (Romans 11)

Paul twice draws a verse from Psalm 69, the first time in Romans 11:9–10:

> And David says, 'May their table become a snare and a trap, a stumbling-block and a retribution for them. May their eyes be darkened, so they cannot see, and their backs be bent for ever.'

These words come from Psalm 69:22–23 and any differences are not substantial. Romans 11 deals with the unbelief of the people of Israel, for which Paul is attempting to find an explanation in the Old Testament. Earlier in Romans 11 (verses 3, 4, and 7) he has already quoted from various parts of the Scriptures. The words of Psalm 69 originally express something about David's opponents, of course; but when the psalm is read from a messianic perspective, they refer to the opponents of the gospel. It is not God's fault that these people have sinned and are now hardened, but their own.

But why did Paul quote these words and no others? We cannot be sure, but possibly he does so through association. The expression 'may their eyes be darkened' resembles the words in Isaiah 29:10 from which he quoted in verse 8, which in the Greek are about closed *eyes* and a *darkened* mind. Paul's mind may thus have wandered from Isaiah to the similar words in the psalm.

Bearing Insults (Romans 15)

Later in Romans, in his discussion of strong and weak believers, Paul comes back to Psalm 69. He argues that Jesus did not act out of self-interest and that the strong believers in Rome should not do so either. He then quotes Psalm 69:9b literally:

> As it is written: 'The insults of those who you insult you have fallen on me.' (Romans 15:3)

The speaker in the psalm is David and Paul puts these words in the mouth of Jesus. This does not surprise us in view of what we have seen in this chapter so far. As both David and Christ endured opposition from other people, so believers must endure unkindness from each other. When Paul's readers recall how much Jesus suffered, that will put their own small inconveniences in a new light. The persecuted person in the psalm becomes an example for the believers in Rome. This quotation is typical of Paul, for he often connects the Old Testament to the Christian church, as we will often see in this book.

This chapter has shown how various writers in the New Testament read Psalm 69 as words of the Lord Jesus. It mentions the suffering of an individual and his opponents; it mentions taunting and endurance; but also the importance of the house of God. Undoubtedly, all of Jesus' early followers agreed with reading the psalm in this way. Subsequently, they also applied it to themselves.

This chapter is a good example of how the entire Old Testament played a central role in understanding and processing all the new things that Jesus had brought. The first Christians could not understand him without reference to the Old Testament – and neither can we. We have also seen that the texts were not ripped out of context, but that their use in the New Testament does justice to their context in the Old.

Further Reading

Hays, Richard B., *Echoes of Scripture in the Gospels* (Waco: Baylor University Press, 2016).

Lindars, Barnabas, *New Testament Apologetic. The Doctrinal Significance of the Old Testament Quotations* (London: SCM, 1961).

Chapter 7: Psalm 110

Here's a good question for a Bible quiz: which verse from the Old Testament is most often quoted in the New Testament? It should not surprise you that the correct answer is Leviticus 19:18, the command to love your neighbour as yourself. These words are quoted in Matthew 5:43, 19:19 and 22:39; Mark 12:31 and 33; Luke 10:27; Romans 13:9; Galatians 5:14; and James 2:8. But a good second is, to our surprise, Psalm 110:1. This psalm is about a king of Israel who receives the special honour of being allowed to sit at God's right hand. In Israel and in the rest of the Ancient Near East the place at the right hand of the king symbolised the highest honour, even though in the Old Testament you only see this in 1 Kings 2:19. Psalm 110 has many similarities with Psalm 2, which also contains prophecies about a king – and not just any king, but the one in whom we recognise God's Messiah. Psalm 110 says:

> Of David. A psalm.

> ¹The LORD says to my lord: 'Sit at my right hand until I make your enemies a footstool for your feet.' ²The LORD will extend your mighty sceptre from Zion, saying, 'Rule in the midst of your enemies!' ³Your troops will be willing on your day of battle. Arrayed in holy splendour, your young men will come to you like dew from the morning's womb. ⁴The LORD has sworn and will not change his mind: 'You are a priest for ever, in the order of Melchizedek.' ⁵The Lord is at your right hand; he will crush kings on the day of his wrath. ⁶He will judge nations, heaping up the dead and crushing the rulers of the whole earth. ⁷He will drink from a brook along the way; and so he will lift his head high.

The use of Psalm 110 in the New Testament is limited to verses 1 and 4. The verses 5–7 seem to be about the last judgement and they could have found a place in Revelation, but that book is less bloody than many people think. Perhaps it is significant that these verses are not used in the New Testament!

Verse 1 – Right Hand

It is the Lord Jesus who makes the connection between Psalm 110:1 and himself (Matthew 22:41–46; Mark 12:35–37; Luke 20:41–44). That is striking because the psalm did not play any role in the Jewish expectations of the Messiah. A few days before his death, Jesus refers to this psalm in order to make clear that he is more important than David and that he is truly the expected Messiah. He reads here that in this psalm none other than King David calls him, Jesus, LORD. David also declares that he, Jesus, will sit at God's right hand. Armed with this knowledge, during his trial, when asked whether he is the Messiah, Jesus can answer with a reference to Psalm 110:

> I am, and you will see the Son of Man sitting at the right hand of the Mighty One, and coming on the clouds of heaven. (Mark 14:62)

Jesus does not say that these words come from the Scriptures, but that is the case. His words are a combined quotation from Daniel 7:13 and Psalm 110:1. You see that he uses the Scriptures to understand himself and his calling, and to explain these things to the people. Here he also says in so many words that the enigmatic expression 'Son of Man' refers to himself.

No wonder that after this, Christ's followers also read the psalm in this way. Peter picks it up at the end of his sermon on the day of Pentecost, saying that Jesus is now really seated at God's right hand; a reference to his ascension (Acts 2:34–35). Paul even refers four times to this verse, but in various ways. In Romans 8:34 he describes Jesus as the one who died and rose and now sits 'at the right hand of God.' Paul thus brings the cross, resurrection, and ascension very close together as the important events that show who Jesus is. In the same way, in Ephesians 1:20, he mentions the resurrection and the ascension in one breath; the words 'heavenly realms' and 'at his right hand' clearly show that Psalm 110 is on his mind. This will also be the case in Colossians 3:1. Hebrews also uses Jesus' sitting at God's right hand a number of times in order to emphasise how far he is elevated above all created persons (1:3, 13; 8:1; 10:12–13; 12:2). Someone in this high position is himself also God.

Verse 1 – Enemies

The fourth time Paul uses Psalm 110:1, in 1 Corinthians 15:25, he alludes to another element of it, namely the subjugation of Jesus' enemies. He literally cites the Septuagint translation of the psalm, without saying so. He probably also changes the meaning of the psalm. His words are 'until he has put all his enemies under his feet.' The subject of this sentence is the Lord Jesus, who puts his feet on his enemies to humiliate them.

Verse 4 – Melchizedek

> The LORD has sworn and will not change his mind: 'You are a priest for ever, in the order of Melchizedek.'

Psalm 110:4 is the only place in the Old Testament that interacts with the short reference to Melchizedek in Genesis 14:18–20. The reason for this interaction may be that the psalm's author, David, and the people around him were aware that their new capital city, Jerusalem, was the same city as the Salem of King Melchizedek, as mentioned in Genesis 14. Because David is regarded as the author of the psalm and because he is speaking of himself, a connection originates between the role of David and the role of Melchizedek. And it turns out that these two have far more in common than the kingship: to our surprise the psalm speaks of an eternal priesthood 'in the order of Melchizedek' (NRSV: 'according to the order of Melchizedek'). David sings that the LORD has given him, the king of Israel, the promise that one day he will also be a priest, even a priest 'for ever,' just like Melchizedek. However, this promise was not fulfilled during David's lifetime or in the Old Testament era. Therefore it passed to a descendant of David. This fact is elaborated in the Letter to the Hebrews.

Jews in Jesus' time had been writing much about Melchizedek, but these writings did not make it into the Bible. Some of these apocryphal texts saw Melchizedek as equal to the angel Gabriel and expected his return to earth. The New Testament, however, sees him in a different way: as a type of Jesus.

A central theme of Hebrews is the conviction that Jesus is high priest 'in the order of Melchizedek.' With great rhetorical skill the author first announces this theme several times (2:17; 3:1; 5:6, 10; 6:20) before he actually comes to discuss it in Hebrews 7. He first prepares his audience, making them curious, before he really tackles the subject.[3]

But look first at Hebrews 8:4, where the writer states that Jesus could not be a priest at all. Why was that? For two reasons. First, Jesus' lineage: he belonged to the 'wrong' tribe, for he was from the tribe of Judah while the priests belonged to the tribe of Levi (7:13–14). Secondly, the laws of Israel contain a fundamental separation between the roles of high priest and the political leader of the people. This separation is already visible in Exodus, where Aaron became the high priest and Moses the political leader. After them, Aaron's descendants were the high priests, while the political leadership often changed hands but never was in the hands of a priest.

In practice, this separation between political and religious leadership was not always maintained, for David and Solomon sometimes brought sacrifices (2 Samuel 6:17; 1 Kings 8:62–64). Perhaps they were inspired by the story of Melchizedek, the king who was also a priest, and by the fact that they now also reigned in Jerusalem. God had also said that the whole nation of Israel would be priests (Exodus 19:6), which became the ideal for the future (Isaiah 61:6). In the period before the birth of Jesus there had been leaders who combined the duties and titles of king and priest, in particular the Maccabees in the second century BC (see the apocryphal book 1 Maccabees 14:41), but the New Testament does not include information about these things.

So how could Jesus become a priest and even a high priest? Not on the basis of his origin, like the ordinary priests and the high priest, but through a side door. Jesus is high priest 'in the order of Melchizedek,' for that is what Psalm 110 proclaims! The psalm connects David and Melchizedek, but the promise to David that he will be a priest like Melchizedek is only fulfilled to his descendant Jesus.

---

[3] This approach is typical of the Jewish way of explaining called midrash. But midrash is a complicated and potentially confusing term that I will avoid.

Hebrews 7

Hebrews 7 explains what Psalm 110:4 means for Jesus and for us. As in many Jewish explanations of Scripture, you see the following things:

1. The starting point is a text in the Old Testament, which is later also quoted (in verses 17 and 21).

2. There follows a detailed explanation of the text.

3. Another text is brought on board, in this case of course Genesis 14, but this text is not explicitly mentioned.

4. The conclusion contains a clear application.

In verse 2 the interpretation of the psalm pays attention to the name Melchizedek. At that time the name Melchizedek was generally interpreted as 'righteous king' or 'king of righteousness.' In the name of Salem we, like the Jews in the time of the New Testament, recognise the Hebrew word *shalom*, peace. By combining the names Melchizedek and Salem, Hebrews is able to characterise Jesus as the king of righteousness and peace. Yet the writer does not use this great title; he rather focusses on Jesus as high priest. (The combination of the two words, righteousness and peace, also occurs in Psalm 85:10 and Romans 14:17.) It is remarkable that the author of Hebrews here shows that he knows these Hebrew words, because everywhere else he merely works with the Septuagint.

With help of three arguments, Hebrews now shows that Melchizedek is superior to Abraham and therefore also to all Israelites who descend from Abraham. First, the writer uses the fact that Genesis says nothing about the origins of Melchizedek (verse 3). The reasoning is, it is not mentioned, so it is not there. While someone was only a Levitical priest on the basis of ancestry, the descent of Melchizedek was unimportant. So it is also irrelevant that Jesus did not descend from Aaron. It is even an advantage, because it equates him to Melchizedek. Melchizedek had a timeless feel – Jesus is from now on 'forever' high priest. The verses 22–25 explain this further.

Second, verses 4–6 and 8–10 explore the tithing mentioned in Genesis 14. The tithes were a kind of tax described in Numbers 18:21–32 and other places. According to the writer, Genesis 14 shows that Abraham recognised Melchizedek as one who had a higher status than himself, and therefore gave him tithes. In addition, the unspoken thought is that the deeds of the ancestors affect the children. The conclusion is that Melchizedek is higher in rank than the later priests, because their ancestor Abraham gave tithes to Melchizedek.

Thirdly, verse 7 mentions the blessing which Melchizedek gave to Abraham. The author refers to the principle that the one who blesses is more important (greater) than the one who receives the blessing. This is not a biblical principle, but one that is widely acknowledged. In this case it means that Melchizedek is the superior person, for he blessed Abraham and not the other way around. And as a successor to Melchizedek, Jesus is superior to all who descended from Abraham. You see that Hebrews makes good use of almost every word in Psalm 110:4! And you also begin to understand that the person of Melchizedek in himself has little meaning for the first readers of Hebrews or for us; he merely points to Jesus.

The rest of Hebrews 7 is based on the notion that Jesus was not always a high priest, but that he acquired the role at his ascension. At that moment he replaced the priestly order of Aaron, because they had not attained perfection (verse 11). Henceforth there was no more need for animal sacrifices because the new high priest had given himself as a sacrifice (verse 27). In Scripture it is again in Psalm 110:4 that Hebrews finds evidence that the old priesthood would be abolished. In verses 11–16 the author sets out the rationale for this change – and in response he uses Psalm 110:4 in verse 17 as the trump card.

The later verses of Hebrews 7 (20–22, 28) make still further use of Psalm 110:4, but now of the first half of the verse: 'The LORD has sworn and will not change his mind.' The author notes that this oath is better than the law of Moses by which the priestly order of Aaron was instituted, because it came later (verse 28). Hence the psalm surpasses the law, which allowed people 'who are subject to weakness' (NRSV) to be priests, and so the psalm is the basis on which Jesus is our great high priest.

Further Reading

Hurtado, Larry, 'Two Case Studies in Earliest Christological readings of Biblical texts' in Matthew Malcolm (ed.), *All That the Prophets Have Declared* (Milton Keynes: Paternoster, 2015) 3–23.

Lane, William L., *Hebrews 1–8*, Word Biblical Commentary (Dallas: Word, 1991).

Lee, Gregory W., *Today When You Hear His Voice: Scripture, the Covenants and the People of God* (Grand Rapids: Eerdmans, 2016).

Rowe, Robert D., *God's Kingdom and God's Son: The Background to Mark's Christology from Concepts of Kingship in the Psalms* (Leiden: Brill, 2002).

Chapter 8: Psalm 118

This psalm is meant to be sung in – or on the way to – the temple and is about God's faithfulness to his people. In some verses it appears that a king is singing, and several verses clearly have a prophetic element. In the time of the New Testament the Jews used the psalm as a prayer for the restoration of the kingdom of David, and the Lord Jesus recognised himself in a number of verses. It is therefore no wonder that the psalm is often quoted in the New Testament. Let us walk through this psalm:

Verse 6

> The LORD is with me; I will not be afraid. What can mere mortals do to me?

This verse is quoted literally in Hebrews 13:6. The small difference between the text in the psalm and in Hebrews is caused by the use of the Septuagint in Hebrews. Just as the singers of the psalm have confidence in God in times of difficulty, so the readers of Hebrews may trust God in times of persecution. The basis for this trust is expressed in the preceding verse, Hebrews 13:5, where the writer transmits a promise of God from Deuteronomy 31:6 to his readers.

Verse 10–11

> All the nations surrounded me. … They surrounded me on every side.

The Gospels often tell us that people come to Jesus, but in John 10:24 we have the special situation that the Jews place themselves in a circle around Jesus. John here uses the same word that occurs twice in Psalm 118, which is translated as 'gathered round him.' It is likely that John deliberately borrows the word from the psalm, thus suggesting that the action of the Jews is hostile, just like the action in Psalm 118. And this makes sense, as in context they want to stone Jesus a little later (John 10:31–32)!

Verse 21

I will give you thanks, for you answered me.

These words closely resemble what Jesus says when he asks his Father to bring Lazarus back to life again (John 11:41). Jesus does not really quote; his words are rather an echo of the psalm. But since Jesus cites the psalm on other occasions, it is quite possible that he is thinking of Psalm 118 here as well.

Verses 22–23

The believers are singing about the temple of the LORD in this psalm (verses 19–21), but then the following words appear unexpectedly:

The stone the builders rejected has become the cornerstone; The LORD has done this, and it is marvellous in our eyes.

The image is that of an irregularly shaped stone that did not seem to fit anywhere in the building, but suddenly turns out to be suitable as the important capstone in an arc or a gate; for 'cornerstone' it is thus better to read 'capstone.' The meaning of the verse within the psalm is unclear; maybe it refers to the people of Israel, who were scorned by the gentiles. However, hundreds of years later, Jesus of Nazareth unexpectedly applied these words to himself, at the end of his parable of the vineyard (Mark 12:1–9; Matthew 21:33–46; Luke 20:9–19). This parable ends in a very gloomy mood with verse 9 as the son of the owner of the vineyard is killed and the wicked winegrowers punished for his murder. The subsequent quotation from Psalm 118 in Mark 12:10–11, surprisingly, sheds some positive light on this event: people may reject Jesus, but God will not do so! He is going to make the rejected stone the capstone. How can Jesus give this positive twist to his own sad parable? Only because he is convinced that his death will not be the end, and that he will be resurrected!

There are in fact two connections between Mark 12:1–9 and 12:10–11:

1. In the parable Jesus refers to the story of Joseph in Genesis. The caretakers of the vineyard say: 'Come, let's kill him' (Mark 12:7). The brothers of Joseph use exactly the same words in Genesis 37:20 (Septuagint). Jesus is therefore suggesting that his fate will be

similar to that of Joseph: he will suffer a great deal yet be delivered from that misery. The words from Psalm 118 express this same certainty about the unexpected outcome: just like a rejected stone gets a place of honour in a building, so a crucified person, one who died a most humiliating death, will be honoured as the risen Lord.

2. In Hebrew the words for 'son' and 'stone' resemble each other. The word 'son' (Hebrew *ben*) is central to the parable – the word 'stone' (Hebrew *'eben*) is central to the unexpected addition in verses 10–11. Jesus is making the pun that the *'eben* will be treated just like the *ben*.

Jesus had used Psalm 118:22 before, but not in such a noticeable way. In the announcement of his death in Mark 8:31 (see also Luke 9:22 and 17:25) he said that he would be 'rejected' by the leaders of the people. The word rejection is rare enough to be sure that it comes from (the Greek translation of) Psalm 118. And Jesus alluded to the same word from Psalm 118 again a little later, when he repeated that he would suffer and be rejected (Mark 9:12), although not everyone will have heard that.

So Jesus saw himself as the rejected and rehabilitated capstone, and it is of course under his influence that this image recurs later in the New Testament. Peter tells his Jewish hearers very clearly:

> Jesus is 'the stone you builders rejected, which has become the cornerstone.' (Acts 4:11)

Peter adds the accusatory word 'you' to the word builders, thus directly accusing the Jewish leaders – just as Jesus had done – that *they* are poor builders who had failed to accept Jesus as God's representative. The contradiction is enormous: the Jews despised Jesus, but for God he is the cornerstone or capstone of the plan of salvation. Peter's words also imply that the things which were in the future when Jesus spoke in Luke 20:17 (and throughout 20:9–19) have now become a reality as a result of the resurrection. Jesus *is* now the main stone. Therefore the church around Peter and John, which is under threat from the Jewish leaders, can also confidently sing Psalm 118:5–12.

If you look closely, you see that whenever Psalm 118:22–23 is quoted, the similar prophecy in Isaiah 28:16 also resounds. Both texts speak about God's choice of a stone for an honourable task. Both texts helped the Lord Jesus to process the brutal reality that he, the Messiah and the Son of God, was rejected by the majority of the people of God. This tragic rejection of the most important stone had already been foretold in the Scriptures!

This rejection is again mentioned in 1 Peter 2:7–8, this time in connection with the contrasting human responses to the coming of Jesus. Peter first uses the word 'stone' in 2:4, which forms the basis for his application of the imagery to his readers in verse 5: they are living stones. But then he comes back to the idea of the stone and in 2:6 he quotes Isaiah 28:16 (literally from the Septuagint) as a positive description of God's activity. God has made Jesus the capstone of his new temple, the church. Finally, in 2:7–8, Peter uses Psalm 118:22 in combination with Isaiah 8:14 to describe the potential negative effects of this divine decision – not everyone is accepting Jesus as the central stone and people are rather stumbling upon him.

Verses 25–26a

> LORD, save us! LORD, grant us success! Blessed is he who comes in the name of the LORD.

The words 'save us' are a rendering of Hebrew word *hosanna*, which means such things as 'save,' 'give salvation,' and 'give victory.' In the Greek New Testament (Matthew 21:9b; Mark 11:9b; John 12:13a) it appears in its Hebrew form, untranslated. And because it is translated here in the psalm, it is difficult to see that during Jesus' triumphal entry into Jerusalem the crowd sing the very words of Psalm 118:25.

The following verse in the psalm, verse 26, is one of the few verses from the Scriptures that is cited by all four evangelists; but none of the four tell us that it is a quote! Like verse 25, it was sung by the crowd during Jesus' entry (Matthew 21:9c; Mark 11:9c; Luke 19:38; John 12:13b). According to Luke and John, the crowd adds the belief that Jesus is coming as a king; this shows that they are combining Psalm 118 with Zechariah 9:9. And 'son of David,' the title used by Matthew (21:9), is also a royal title. According to Mark, the people add to the psalm: 'Blessed is the coming kingdom of our father David!' Whichever evangelist you follow, it is evident that the crowd has understood the messianic meaning of the psalm and of Jesus' entry into the nation's capital city. That is why they spread their cloaks and branches on the road, because this was common practice when a king passed by. Jesus accepts what the people say and do; in this way he confirms that he is indeed their king.

It is easy to overlook the fact that the words 'Blessed is he who comes in the name of the LORD' are cited more often in the New Testament. Matthew (23:39) and Luke (13:35) also use them in the passage about the judgement which will come over Jerusalem at the second coming of Jesus. And this time it is not the people who speak the words of the psalm, but Jesus himself. He complains that the city will be left to its own devices until his return. Only then will the people say (again): 'Blessed is he who comes in the name of the LORD.' Jesus' pronouncement may contain an allusion to the warning in Jeremiah 22:5. Note that Luke (13:31) introduces the warning passage with a reference to King Herod, who was certainly not the promised king. This creates a sharp contrast between the bad King Herod and the good King Jesus.

Luke also expects us to hear an echo of Psalm 118:26 in the question that John the Baptist asks in 7:19–20 and that he repeats for emphasis: is Jesus 'the one who is to come?' In the Greek there are only two words, 'the coming-one,' which here form a messianic title. This title is therefore derived from Psalm 118, which also sings about a king. Read against this background, the question of John the Baptist, who is kept prisoner by Herod, is a political question, because Israel was expecting a king who would free them from the Romans. Jesus' answer dodges the political side by pointing to the good things that he is doing for people.

Further Reading

Hays, Richard B., *Echoes of Scripture in the Gospels* (Waco: Baylor University Press, 2016).

Lindars, Barnabas, *New Testament Apologetic. The Doctrinal Significance of the Old Testament Quotations* (London: SCM, 1961).

Rowe, Robert D., *God's Kingdom and God's Son: The Background to Mark's Christology from Concepts of Kingship in the Psalms* (Leiden: Brill, 2002).

Chapter 9: Isaiah 6–12

Within the book of Isaiah, chapters 6 to 12 form a distinct unity. To later readers they appear like a mountain range with various beautiful summits, with smaller mountains and sections that you can easily overlook in between. The summits are clearly messianic passages, and some of the other texts can be read as messianic as well, by virtue of being close to the passages which are more explicitly messianic. In this chapter I follow the order of the text.

Isaiah 6

An allusion to the entire call vision of Isaiah 6 occurs in John 12:41. The connection is clear, not only because Isaiah 6:10 is quoted in John 12:40, but also because the Septuagint in Isaiah 6:1 uses the word 'glory,' which is adopted here by John. In the Gospel of John this word glory refers to the divine majesty, the splendour of Jesus. John's use of the word here therefore shows his view that Jesus was involved in the vision of Isaiah, which he interprets as a vision of God as Three-in-one.

Revelation 4:8 contains the words 'Holy, holy, holy' from Isaiah 6:3, because those on heaven are saying day and night:

> Holy, holy, holy is the Lord God Almighty, who was, and is, and is to come.

Of this three-part sentence the beginning comes from Isaiah 6 and the middle comes literally from Amos 3:13. The final part of the sentence does not have a direct parallel in the Old Testament, but it recalls Exodus 3:13–14. It takes the place of the words 'the whole earth is full of his glory' from Isaiah 6, probably because Revelation gives more attention to history than to creation. Once you are convinced of the relationship between Revelation 4 and Isaiah 6, the six wings of the four living creatures in Revelation 4:8 will remind you of the six wings of the seraphim (angels) in Isaiah 6:2; other angels, the cherubim, have two wings (Exodus 25:20 and 37:9).

At the end of his vision Isaiah receives a difficult assignment: he must speak to his own people, but they will not listen, and God will harden their hearts (6:9–10). The reason for this harsh punishment is indicated in the preceding passage. In Isaiah 5:12–25: the people have turned their back on God and thus have themselves to blame for the judgement. This hardening took place in Isaiah's own time, but God's severe words reappear in various places in the New Testament. According to the Synoptic Gospels, Jesus himself quotes from Isaiah 6 in a conversation about his parables. Jesus' situation corresponds to the time of Isaiah, as can be seen from the fact that the passage on disbelief in Isaiah 5:12–25 has a parallel in Matthew 12:22–32, 38–45 (Mark 3:22–30), where the unbelief of the Jewish leaders is discernible. Just like Jesus' family (Matthew 12:46–50; Mark 3:31–35), the leaders of the people also placed themselves outside the covenant.

In Mark 4:10–12 and Luke 8:9–10, Isaiah is not mentioned by name and the superficial reader easily overlooks the connection of these passages with Isaiah 6. These two evangelists render the words of the prophet freely, but without much change to their meaning. Jesus declares that, just like God at the time ensured that Isaiah's message was not believed, he is now speaking in parables with the result that his words are not believed by everyone. The parables which he tells because of the unbelief of some hearers are therefore more than pleasant stories.

Mark 8:17–18 contains similar criticism of Jesus on his hearers; the words he chooses here are taken verbatim from Jeremiah 5:21. Jeremiah's words, in turn, may form an echo of Isaiah 6:9–10 because of the emphatic use of the terms heart, eyes, and ears. Jeremiah literally says, 'Listen to these things, foolish people *who have no heart*; who have eyes but do not see; who have ears but do not hear.' (My translation, but see also the footnotes in the NASB and the CSB.)

Matthew is the only Synoptic evangelist who mentions the book of Isaiah as the source of Jesus' words. This evangelist first has Jesus summarise Isaiah's words (13:13) before he quotes them literally (13:14–15). In this passage, Matthew uses the Septuagint of Isaiah 6, in which God's judgement is expressed in milder terms than in the Hebrew text. The Hebrew text of Isaiah contains commands ('*Make t*he heart of the people insensitive, *stop* their ears, *close* their eyes'), but in the Greek translation of Isaiah 6:10 and thus in Matthew 13:15, the hardening is the result of the existing unbelief of the hearers.

In his Gospel Luke only refers briefly to Isaiah 6:9–10, probably because he wanted to use the passage later. At the end of Acts (28:25–27) Luke tells us how, after many conversations with them, Paul responded sharply to the persistent unbelief of the Jews in Rome. Paul used Isaiah 6:9–10 to denounce his hearers and then left them to their fate. The blame for the Jewish unbelief in Jesus is laid entirely with the people, which means that they also hold the key to changing the situation. Again, Isaiah's message as passed on by Paul is that whoever refuses to believe the preaching of God's word will suffer the consequences of their decision.

John also cites Isaiah 6:10 (in 12:40), in combination with Isaiah 53:1 (in 12:38). He does this in a sort of evaluation of the public ministry of Jesus before he goes on to describe the teaching of Jesus to his disciples (John 13–17). John's conclusion is as bleak as that of Jesus and Paul: Most Jews do not believe in Jesus as their Messiah – but see the exceptions in 12:42.

Isaiah 6:9–10 is a difficult text, but it is striking that it does not cause any contradiction between Old and New Testament. There is no question of a harsh Old Testament over against a nice, friendly New Testament. In both parts of the Bible unbelief is seen as sin, but God has the freedom to save people or to allow them to perish.

Isaiah 7

With Isaiah 7:14 we reach the first mountain peak of Isaiah 6–12. This verse must be read as part of the story of King Ahaz of Judah in Isaiah 7:1–17. The key question is whether in the coming war the unbelieving Ahaz will trust God or his worldly allies. God offers him a sign of encouragement, but he refuses this offer, and therefore God one-sidedly gives him the sign anyway (7:12–13): a young woman will have a son and call him Immanuel. This birth would only be a real sign for Ahaz if a young woman he knew personally would unexpectedly, perhaps in a miraculous way, become pregnant and give birth to a child. Isaiah does not mention any details about what exactly happened, but it is possible that Ahaz himself unexpectedly had a son, the later King Hezekiah (2 Kings 16:20). He was a descendant of David. The evangelist Matthew tells that this prophetic promise received a second fulfilment in the birth of Jesus, who was also called Immanuel. In Matthew 1:20–23, the angel, Joseph and Mary are discovering a deeper level of significance in this promise than Isaiah had been aware of. The prophet had used the general Hebrew word for 'young woman,' *'almah*, which probably always – but not necessarily – indicates a virgin (see for example Genesis 24:43 and Psalm 68:25). The Septuagint translates *'almah* with the more specific Greek word *parthenos* which means 'virgin.' By using the Septuagint Matthew is able to emphasise that Mary was still a virgin when Jesus was conceived. Isaiah mentions Immanuel again in 8:8 and he plays with the name in 8:10. This suggests that the new-born Immanuel was a special person. It will also have helped his Jewish readers to see 7:14 as messianic prophecy, and as a result these verses reverberate in Matthew 1:23. Although Isaiah had promised Ahaz and his people God's presence, the child who was born at that time was of course only a *sign* of this presence. The Immanuel-promise was fulfilled much more completely in the coming of Jesus, in whom God himself is truly present.

Isaiah 8

Isaiah 8:12–13 is a personal note in which the prophet reports his response to his hearers. God advises him not to be afraid of the things for which they are afraid; instead, he must look up to God. This encouragement is taken over in 1 Peter 3:14, literally from the Septuagint. The basis for doing this is that Peter's readers are living in the same climate of fear as Isaiah and his audience. The words of the prophet may also be heard in Jesus' words in Matthew 10:28 and Luke 12:4–5. The next verse, 1 Peter 3:15, is based directly on words from Isaiah 8, on verse 13 to be exact, as you can see in my translation:

> The LORD Almighty, make him holy. (Isaiah 8:13a)

> Christ the LORD make holy in your hearts. (1 Peter 3:15)

'To make holy' means 'to recognise, to treat as holy'; and the parallel between Isaiah and Peter shows that Jesus is entitled to receive the same honour as the God of Israel.

The next verse in Isaiah, 8:14, calls the LORD 'a holy place' ('sanctuary,' NRSV and ESV) for those who trust him, but also 'a stone that causes people to stumble.' It is therefore a text that emphasizes the division between believers and unbelievers. Because this verse is close to the verses 8 and 10, in which Immanuel is mentioned, it could easily be applied to Jesus, the person over whom the Jewish people were so deeply divided. This is what happens in 1 Peter 2:8, where Peter quotes the words 'a stone that causes people to stumble' and 'a rock that makes them fall' from Isaiah 8:14. Also in Romans 9:32–33, Jesus is called 'a stone that causes people to stumble and a rock that makes them fall,' but Paul's words are closer to Isaiah 28:16 (Septuagint), a verse very similar to 8:14.

In Isaiah 8:17–18 the prophet is still talking about himself, but what he says is cited in Hebrews 2:13 as words of Jesus. Isaiah speaks about his own 'children,' and Hebrews applies this term to the believers. By the way he quotes the writer of Hebrews gives the impression that he is dealing with two separate sections, while these phrases are in successive verses of Isaiah.

The author of Hebrews uses the idea that the believers are children of God also in 2:10 and more at length in 12:4–13. In the preceding verse, 2:12, he likewise quotes a phrase from Psalm 22:22 (see NRSV or CSB) about brothers and sisters as if they are words of Jesus.

Is it acceptable that New Testament authors take words of a prophet and put them in the mouth of Jesus, also spiritualising their meaning in the process? Yes. When you believe that the Hebrew Bible is a prophetic book, you can hear Jesus in and through the words of all the authors. And this is especially true for Isaiah 6–12, where so many other elements are clearly messianic. As we read in this way, Isaiah 8:17 speaks to us about Jesus' trust in God and 8:18 about the fact that we belong to him. Believers are children of God!

Isaiah 9

The second mountain peak in this section is 9:1–7, a messianic passage which you should read for yourself. Although the word 'Messiah' does not appear, yet this very person is clearly the subject of Isaiah's expectations. Isaiah receives the promise that the territory of Zebulon and Naphtali will be honoured as a result of the coming of the Messiah, and Matthew 4:13–16 shows how this promise was fulfilled when Jesus went to live in Capernaum. Isaiah also mentions other areas which will receive blessing through the Messiah, and this promise was fulfilled as well, for Jesus' work was not limited to Galilee, as you see in Matthew 16:13, 24:14, 25:32, and 28:19.

The passage 9:1–7 begins beautifully, using light as a symbol of God's redemption and the coming of his kingdom. This imagery is also reflected in Matthew 4. The evangelist has rendered 'walking in darkness' (Isaiah 9:1a) as 'living in darkness' (Matthew 4:16a). He probably took this word 'living' (literally: sitting down) from Isaiah 42:7 and as a result all of Isaiah 42:1–9 resonates. By means of a small adjustment to the text the evangelist has thus brought together in one quotation two messianic passages from the Old Testament, both of which are about light and darkness. You can be sure that this combination is not a coincidence, because there is a second connection between Isaiah 42 and Matthew 4. Isaiah 9:2 originally mentions a light that shines (NRSV, ESV) or dawns (NIV, CSB) on the people, whereas Isaiah 42:9 says that new things will 'rise' or 'go up' (Greek *anatellō*, also in Isaiah 60:1). This verb 'rise' is typically used for the rising of the sun, and Matthew has included it in his quote from Isaiah 9. The English translations generally use 'dawn,' but more literally Matthew 4:16 says:

> On those sitting in the land and the shadow of death a light has *risen*.

As a result of these minor changes by the evangelist the two passages from Isaiah have become a programme for Jesus' work. For those who believe in him, Isaiah 9:2 now means that Jesus is the light in the darkness of the world. Indeed, he calls himself the light without referring to Isaiah, but undoubtedly with the words of the prophet in mind (John 8:12). No wonder that the same symbolism is used in other places in the New Testament as well (Luke 1:78–79; John 1:9; 2 Corinthians 4:6).

To my surprise, 9:6–7 are not cited in the New Testament. These verses clearly show that the Messiah will be no ordinary person, but the New Testament makes this clear in different ways. These verses do reverberate in the announcement of Jesus' birth to Mary (Luke 1:32–33) and you also hear them in the song of the angels in Luke 2:14, but because of their richness you might have expected that more use would be made of them.

Isaiah 10 and 11

Isaiah 10:3 contains the expression 'the day of reckoning' (NIV) or 'the day of punishment' (NRSV, ESV, CSB). This combination of words occurs in one other place in the Bible, namely in 1 Peter 2:12, where NIV and CSB have 'the day he visits (us)' and NRSV 'when he comes to judge.' (The Greek words are *hēmera episkopēs*.) I would translate them in 1 Peter as 'on the day of punishment' and advise the CSB to print the words in bold, because it is likely that Peter is quoting literally from Isaiah. This is the more likely because both passages are about the oppression of innocent people. Many interpreters of 1 Peter are uncertain as to whether Peter is thinking of something positive (a day of renewal) or something negative, but I would suggest that the parallel with Isaiah is evidence that Peter means the day of judgement on God's enemies.

The passage 11:1–10 is the last peak in this Isaiah ridge. The occurrence of the name Jesse at its beginning and end shows that the promised saviour will be a descendant of David, the son of Jesse (1 Samuel 16:11–13; Psalm 72:20). Verses 1–2, like 9:5–6, you would expect to be popular in the New Testament, but they are only quoted infrequently. Matthew (2:23) uses both Isaiah 11:1 and 11:2, as I will show in chapter 23.

Isaiah 11:1 contains the image of a fallen tree stump, creating the impression that the house of David is at its end. Such was indeed the situation when Jesus came to earth. His father Joseph had no social status, according to Luke 2:24, for he made the sacrifice that was prescribed for poor people.

Many places in the New Testament tell us that the Holy Spirit directed Jesus in his work, for example Luke 3:22 and 4:1, 14, 18. Yet the only place that openly uses Isaiah 11:2 is 1 Peter 4:14. Isaiah had written, 'The Spirit of the LORD will rest on him' and Peter repeats the key words of this promise, yet applies them to his readers. That is a beautiful thought: precisely because the readers must suffer like Jesus, they know that the Holy Spirit dwells in them.

The phrase 'you are blessed' in 1 Peter 4:14 renders the same word that forms the beginning of the Beatitudes: 'Blessed are...' (Matthew 5:3–12). Peter thus combines the prophecy of Isaiah with an expression used by Jesus. In John 7:24 you find the following advice from Jesus, who himself always judged correctly, to the Jews:

> Stop judging by mere appearances, but instead judge correctly.

In this plea you hear both Isaiah 11:3 and 1 Samuel 16:7, where the prophet corrects Jesse's judgement; and these echoes are certainly not coincidental. Isaiah 11:10a gave us the expression 'the Root of Jesse,' a kind of messianic title which is taken up as 'Root of David' in Revelation 5:5 and 22:16, first by an elder and then by the Lord himself. Thus Jesus claims his place as king of Israel and of the whole world.

The clearest use of verse 10 occurs in Romans 15:12, where Paul quotes verbatim from the Septuagint. Paul uses the verse in a chain of texts which he takes from the Books of Moses (Deuteronomy 32:43), the Psalms (117:1), and the Prophets (Isaiah 11:10), all of which contain the word 'nations' or better 'gentiles.' The attention in these quotations is therefore focussed on the community of believers from the nations, not on the Lord Jesus. Paul often uses the Scriptures in this way: they refer to us, the church of the Lord. Part of Isaiah 11:10b, 'the nations will rally to him,' had been translated into Greek as 'in him the nations will hope,' and that is how Paul quotes it in Romans 15:12. Similar words about hope also occur in Isaiah 42:4, a text that is literally quoted from the Septuagint in Matthew 12:21. Isaiah 42 is the passage about the work of the servant of the LORD among the nations that was also described in Isaiah 9:1–7. Matthew uses these words of Isaiah as the response of the people to the outstretched arm of the servant: if he wants to do these things for us, we should hope in him alone!

Finally

In each of the three messianic sections in Isaiah 6–12 (7:14, 9:1–7, and 11:1–10), the prophet speaks of a child that is to be born. As a result, these passages reinforce each other and the interpretation of each of the three is aided by our understanding of the other two. We do not know why this part of the Hebrew Bible places such emphasis on the birth of the Messiah.

Further Reading

France, R.T., *Matthew*, Tyndale New Testament Commentaries (Leicester: IVP, 1985).

Hays, Richard B., *Echoes of Scripture in the Gospels* (Waco: Baylor University Press, 2016).

Schibler, Daniel, 'Messianism and Messianic Prophecy in Isaiah 1–12 and 23–33' in Philip E. Satterthwaite and others (eds), *The Lord's Anointed. Interpretation of Old Testament Messianic Texts* (Carlisle: Paternoster, 1995) 87–104.

Chapter 10: Zechariah 9–14

The prophets of the Old Testament mainly speak about their own time, but Zechariah is an exception among them. The second part of Zechariah is almost entirely about things that are still in the future for the prophet. Zechariah 9–14 resembles Isaiah 6–12 because it is teeming with messianic texts, interspersed with sections that are less likely to grab our attention. For us these passages of the Bible are difficult because they contain prophecies that have already been fulfilled by the Lord Jesus, mixed with prophecies about things that are still in the future. Jesus himself relates some of Zechariah's images to himself, such as the king, the shepherd, and the pierced person. The last two of these make it clear that he knew from Scripture in advance that his work would encounter strong opposition.

The King (9:9–13)

In 9:9–13 Zechariah presents the coming king of Israel. Zechariah 9:9 resembles Zephaniah 3:14–15 and has forerunners in other texts which make a connection between a donkey and the role of Messiah or king, such as Genesis 49:11 (about Judah and his descendants) and 1 Kings 1:32–33, 38, 44 (about Solomon). Jesus himself knows this prophecy and he consciously sets out to fulfil it; to this end he chooses to mount a donkey for his entry into Jerusalem. This choice shows that Jesus wants to be a simple, non-violent Messiah, but the above parallels with Judah and Solomon (and 2 Samuel 18:9) also suggest that a donkey or mule was considered a royal animal in Israel. In any case, it was usual for conquerors to enter a city on horseback. Yet while the martial elements of Genesis 49:11 are appropriated in Revelation 14:20 and 19:13, Zechariah's king is not a fighter. The four evangelists handle this prophecy in different ways. Although Mark and Luke tell us that Jesus entered Jerusalem on a donkey, they do not establish a direct connection with the words of Zechariah. On the other hand, Matthew (21:5) gives one of his formal fulfilment quotations: 'This took place to fulfil what was spoken through the prophet...' Yet he begins the quote with, 'Say to Daughter Zion' and these words come from Isaiah 62:11. Matthew 21:5 is thus a combined quotation from Isaiah and Zechariah.

At the same time Matthew omits the words 'righteous and victorious' from Zechariah 9:9. Matthew makes yet another striking change. Whereas the other evangelists mention only one donkey, Matthew emphasizes that two donkeys were involved in Jesus' entry (21:2–3, 7). The best explanation for this is that he interprets the words of Zechariah, 'on a colt, the foal of a donkey,' as a reference to two different animals.

In the description of Jesus' entry, John 12 first reports (verse 13) that the crowd was shouting Psalm 118:26 and then mentions the donkey (verse 14). John quotes only part of Zechariah 9:9, but of course the entire text reverberates. In verse 16 John adds that Jesus' disciples only perceived the relationship between Jesus and the prophecy of Zechariah after the resurrection. Zechariah 9:10 belongs with the preceding verse and promises that the coming of the Messiah will bring peace to the whole world. Yet the evangelists do not use it in their descriptions of Jesus' entry, probably because this promise has not yet been fulfilled. It is not uncommon that one part of a prophecy has already been fulfilled in Jesus whereas another part is yet to be fulfilled. Any Christian reading the Old Testament needs to have the flexibility to recognise and acknowledge this.

Here are two texts side by side:

> May he rule from sea to sea, and from the River to the ends of the earth. (Psalm 72:8)

> His rule will extend from sea to sea and from the River to the ends of the earth. (Zechariah 9:10)

World peace is an important theme in Psalm 72. The prophet Zechariah takes from this psalm the idea that God's king will be the bringer of this peace and is even inspired to turn this aspiration into a prophecy. In this way Zechariah turns the 'may he' of the psalm into a fact, albeit a fact that is still in the future because the dominion of King Jesus does not yet extend all over the world. Zechariah updates the words of the psalm, in the same way as the writers of the New Testament update the Old Testament. And because they were all writing under the guidance of God's Spirit, their words are normative for us. (The word River has a capital in both passages because it refers to the Great River, the Euphrates; see the paraphrase in the CSB.)

The expression 'the blood of my covenant with you' from Zechariah 9:11 re-appears in Matthew 26:28 and Mark 14:24, and it can be heard more remotely in Luke 22:20 and 1 Corinthians 11:25. Because this expression stands near verse 9, a verse that meant so much for Jesus, it is quite possible that Zechariah influenced Jesus' choice of words. In the Old Testament, sacrificial blood is always the blood of animals, but Jesus applies these words to his own death.

Bad and Good Shepherds (11:4–17)

Zechariah 11:4–17 is a very difficult passage, in which good and bad shepherds play the central roles. The criticism of the wicked shepherds strengthens our hope in the Lord Jesus as our good shepherd.

Zechariah seems to be responding to Ezekiel 34, where God promises the people that he will be a good shepherd to them and that he will set a descendant of David over them. In Zechariah 11 God seems to have second thoughts about this promise, for he announces that he no longer wants to be the shepherd of the people (verses 8–9). And while in Ezekiel 37:15–22 God uses two sticks to illustrate the renewed unity of his people, two sticks are broken in Zechariah 11:10 and 14. The contrast between Ezekiel 34:16 and Zechariah 11:15–16 is especially striking: instead of a good shepherd, a bad shepherd comes. Yet this is not the last word, because Zechariah 11:17 immediately announces the end of the worthless shepherd. This development in prophetic expectation can best be explained from the events in the land of Judah in the period after the people's return from the Babylonian exile, so the period between Ezekiel and Zechariah. The people were not developing as God had hoped. At the same time, Zechariah also describes the coming rejection of Jesus and the inevitable judgement on Israel that would follow.

In verses 8–9, God serves his resignation as the shepherd of the people, adding:

> I told them, 'If you think it best, give me my pay; but if not, keep it.' So they paid me thirty pieces of silver. And the LORD

said to me, 'Throw it to the potter' – the handsome price at
which they valued me! So I took the thirty pieces of silver and
threw them to the potter at the house of the LORD. (Zechariah
11:12–13)

God is asking the leaders of the people to pay him the wages he had
earned as a shepherd. The amount of the payment will show him how
much he is worth in the eyes of his people. They should, of course,
have offered him a huge amount. Thirty pieces of silver, on the other
hand, is ridiculously little, merely the legal price of a slave (Exodus
21:32). This remuneration is thus a heavy insult to God, who
comments ironically: 'the handsome (lordly, NRSV, ESV) price at
which they valued me.' He refuses the money and throws it away.
That the money is thrown to a potter is difficult to explain. The NRSV
here has 'into the treasury,' a translation which requires a small change
in the Hebrew text. In any case, Matthew sees this incident as
prophetic and uses it twice in the story of Jesus' death. In Matthew
26:14–16 he reports that Jesus was betrayed by Judas for the same low
amount of thirty pieces of silver. This passage contains no reference to
Zechariah and it is not a quote, but the good listener will realise that it
is the same amount. Jesus is thus given away for the same low amount
that the people had offered to God for his services. Matthew 27:3–10 is
a more complicated passage. Judas does not want to keep the money
he had first accepted and throws it into the temple in despair. The high
priests then use it for charity. Once again the evangelist sees the
Scriptures being fulfilled:

> Then what was spoken by Jeremiah the prophet was fulfilled:
> 'They took the thirty pieces of silver, the price set on him by
> the people of Israel, and they used them to buy the potter's
> field, as the Lord commanded me.' (Matthew 27:9–10)

Note that this time it is not Jesus who refers to this prophecy, but
Matthew. The parallel is that in both situations the same amount of
money was given to a potter. Yet the words of the evangelist raise a
few questions. In the first place, is this really a quote? No, it is rather a
paraphrase. Matthew also changes the order of the clauses. In
Zechariah God's command comes first but in Matthew it comes at the

end, and Matthew has added the field. Yet he has not distorted the meaning of the text.

In the second place, is it a quote from Jeremiah or Zechariah? Before saying that Matthew is wrong, consider that Matthew's words have similarities with three stories in Jeremiah: Jeremiah 19, in which potters extract their clay from the Valley of Ben Hinnom, and which contains a reference to 'the blood of the innocent' (verse 4); Jeremiah 18, in which Jeremiah visits a potter; and Jeremiah 32:6–15, in which the prophet buys something for pieces of silver. No wonder Matthew thinks of Jeremiah, although the words he quotes largely come from Zechariah. Like Matthew 21:5, this is a combined quotation, not a mistake.

The One They Have Pierced (12:9–13:1)

Zechariah 12:9–13:1 is another messianic prophecy of which some elements have already been fulfilled and others not yet. The core verse is 12:10: 'They will look on me, the one they have pierced' (NIV). It is not known whether Zechariah thought of this pierced person as a contemporary, but in any case, his words acquired a deeper meaning through Jesus. John 19:34 tells us how Jesus' body was pierced on the cross and in 19:36–37 John gives two quotations, stating that this event was a fulfilment of the Scriptures. The legs of a crucified person were normally broken, but this did not happen to Jesus. Instead, a spear was stabbed into his side, which John (19:37) sees as a fulfilment of the words of Zechariah.

As the positive consequence of the death of 'the one they have pierced' Zechariah foresees that there will be forgiveness of sin for the people (13:1). We believe that Jesus' death indeed brings this forgiveness of 'sin and impurity,' yet this beautiful promise from Zechariah 13:1 is not quoted in the New Testament. This might be because the Septuagint did not translate the words fountain, sin, and impurity accurately. The prophecy in Zechariah 12:10, on the other hand, did give rise to many reactions:

- Revelation 1:7 voices the expectation that in the future *all* people will see Jesus as the pierced one.

- In Matthew 24:30, an assertion about the return of the Son of Man, the words 'see' and 'mourn' echo the Septuagint of Zechariah 12:10. These words of Jesus show how he applied the prophecy of Zechariah to himself.

- The first part of the verse, 'A spirit of grace and supplication,' probably also had some influence. Indeed, the Septuagint of Zechariah 12:10 contains the expression 'spirit of grace' (Greek *charis*) which occurs again in Hebrews 10:29.

The Murdered Shepherd (13:7)

In Zechariah 13:7 God speaks to a sword: 'Strike the shepherd, that the sheep may be scattered' (NRSV). It is well-known that Jesus saw himself as the good shepherd. He also applies these words of Zechariah to himself, for in Mark 14:27 (Matthew 26:31) he quotes the text as follows:

> You will all fall away ... for it is written: 'I will strike the shepherd, and the sheep will be scattered.'

What is a command in Zechariah is a plan of action ('I will kill') with Jesus and Mark. In other respects, the quote is also not quite literal. As a result of the changes to the text it is now God himself who will do the inconceivable: he will kill the shepherd, that is, Jesus! Mark does not add anything to explain the prophetic text, but a few verses earlier he gave us some explanation, as Jesus says that his blood will be poured out, meaning he will die, 'for many,' so for humankind (Mark 14:24). Apparently, God only saw one possibility to redeem humans, namely the death of Jesus as it took place on the cross at Calvary. The last part of the text says that, as a result of the death of their leader, the sheep, his followers, will be scattered. According to Mark 14:50, this prediction was fulfilled to the disciples of Jesus, who fled to all sides as soon as he was arrested. Another element of this fulfilment, and also of Zechariah 13:8–9, is the scattering of the Jews over the world after the destruction of Jerusalem in the year AD 70. Jesus himself also spoke about the scattering of his disciples, especially in John 16:32, but he used other words than Zechariah.

Tribulation (13:8–9)

Before Zechariah comes to speak about the final things in chapter 14, in 13:8–9 he still has a frightening passage about the refining of God's people. He uses the words fire, refine, and test, words which also occur in 1 Peter 1:7 and 4:12. Peter probably bases himself on Zechariah, for both texts describe the situation after the death of a shepherd (Zechariah 13:7; 1 Peter 2:24–25) and both do not so much emphasize the suffering in itself as its purifying effect on the believers. If we indeed assume that Peter's choice of words depends on Zechariah, we can also see that 1 Peter 5:1–4 is influenced by the thoughts of this prophet, for both passages are about good and bad shepherds. Taken together, the verses 7–9 (like 11:4–17) state that the coming of Jesus will have both positive and negative consequences. Many people will fail to profit from the blessing of his sacrificial death because of their unbelief.

On That Day... (14:4–21)

Zechariah 14:4–21 contains all kinds of expectations about the end of the world, which is repeatedly referred to as 'that day.' A number of elements of this passage have contributed to the vision of the last battle and of the new world that John describes in Revelation. John does not quote his source literally, but the parallels are clear:

Subject	Zechariah	Revelation
All nations gather	14:2	9:13–19
No distinction between day and night	14:7	21:25; 22:5
Water from Jerusalem	17:8	22:1–2
God king over all the earth	14:9	19:6
The safe, new Jerusalem	14:10–11	21:2, 10–27
Permanent security	14:11	22:3

| Plagues for unbelievers | 14:12–15 | 8, 9, and 16 |
| Annual pilgrimage | 14:16–19 | 21:26 |

Zechariah's vision of the future also resounds in other places in the New Testament. The promise that Jesus will return to the Mount of Olives (Acts 1:11–12) is based on Zechariah 14:4. (Revelation does not mention the location.) When Paul writes about the return of Jesus in 1 Thessalonians 3:13, he uses the expression 'all the holy ones with him' from Zechariah 14:5. These words refer to the angels, as can be seen in Deuteronomy 33:3, Matthew 25:31, Mark 8:38, and 13:27. This in turn means that Paul is also alluding to the words of Zechariah in 2 Thessalonians 1:7. In his letters to the Thessalonians Paul does not quote from the Scriptures, but he 'automatically' makes an allusion, which suggests that his thinking was saturated with them. Zechariah 14:7 contains an expression that is easily overlooked, 'a day known only to the LORD.' This expression says that only the LORD God knows when the end will come. This notion is common to the New Testament, occurring for example in Matthew 24:36 and Acts 1:7.

Zechariah 14:8 states:

> On that day living water will flow out from Jerusalem.

This is one of the verses that resounds in Jesus' promise about living water in John 7:38, along with, among others, Psalm 78:16 and 20. But Jesus also uses the expression 'living water' in his conversation with the Samaritan woman (John 4:10). In both situations he promises blessing to those who believe in him. Revelation 22:1 expresses the expectation that there will be living water on the new earth. Once again, we have here a promise of Zechariah which was only partially fulfilled in Jesus. Zechariah's words about water are never taken literally in the New Testament. The expectation of the water is even disconnected from Jerusalem and the water is perceived as an image of God's blessing, of his abundance, and of the activity of the Holy Spirit. It is therefore unlikely that this verse would contain a promise about the future geographical situation of the Holy Land.

Zechariah 14:9 emphasizes God as the only God, not only of Israel but also of the gentiles. The same emphasis occurs in Paul:

> Or is God the God of Jews only? Is he not the God of Gentiles too? Yes, of Gentiles too, since there is only one God. (Romans 3:29–30a)

It is probable that when writing this Paul had in mind not only Deuteronomy 6:4, the confession that God is one, but also the words of Zechariah, because he emphatically includes the gentiles in his statement.

The book of Zechariah ends abruptly, with a prophecy that there will never again be traders in the temple of the LORD (14:21). Because the rest of Zechariah 14 is about the end times, Zechariah apparently also expects this cleansing of the temple for the distant future. However, we know from Revelation 21:22 that there will be no temple at the end of time. The evangelists do not refer to Zechariah in their description of Jesus' cleansing of the temple, but we can of course hear echoes of the prophet's words in Matthew 21:12–13, Mark 11:17, and especially John 2:14–17.

Closure

Zechariah presents us with a variety of images of Jesus and the future, without explaining how they are related. It is striking that many of these prophecies were only partially fulfilled by Jesus' first coming. This makes it understandable that many Jews find it difficult to recognise Jesus as their Messiah, for will the Messiah not fulfil all prophecies when he comes? Actual quotations from Zechariah only occur in the four Gospels, but his book also had a great influence on Revelation, Peter, and to a lesser extent on Paul. I have not been able to discuss these things comprehensively here. The influence takes a spectrum of forms, right from formal quotations and clear allusions to soft echoes. The influence of Zechariah on the New Testament is so great that he is perhaps the most undervalued prophet.

Further Reading

Duguid, Iain, 'Messianic Themes in Zechariah 9–14' in Philip E. Satterthwaite and others (eds), *The Lord's Anointed. Interpretation of Old Testament Messianic Texts* (Carlisle: Paternoster, 1995) 265–280.

France, R.T., *Jesus and the Old Testament* [1971] (Grand Rapids: Baker, 1982).

Liebengood, Kelly D., *The Eschatology of 1 Peter. Considering the Influence of Zechariah 9–14* (Cambridge: Cambridge University Press, 2014).

Rose, W.H., 'Zacharia' in G.W. Lorein (ed.), *Geschriften uit de Perzische tijd* (De Brug XI; Heerenveen: Groen, 2010) 247–329.

Siebesma, P.A., two chapters in A.G. Knevel and M.J. Paul (eds), *Verkenningen in de oudtestamentische messiasverwachting* (Kampen: Kok, 1995) 184–199.

Chapter 11: Adam

The New Testament tends to speak positively about many people and things from the Old Testament, but that is not so with Adam. He is seen as the source of doom.

Genesis

In Genesis 1–3, the word *adam* is not a proper name, but the designation of the first human being. It is therefore difficult for translators to decide whether to translate *adam* as 'man,' 'human' or as Adam. In Genesis 4:1 the ESV has Adam and the NIV has Adam but with a footnote, whereas the NRSV and the CSB translate 'the man.' In Genesis 1, the word *adam* is even used as a collective term for man and woman together. It is only in Genesis 4:25 and 5:1 that Adam clearly becomes the name of the first male. The same applies to the woman: she is first called 'woman' (Genesis 2:23; 3:2) and only later Eve (from 3:20). This is probably the reason why the names Adam and Eve are rare in the Old Testament and that references are rather to humankind in general.

In the Old Testament

Adam is mentioned again in Hosea 6:7:

> But they, like Adam, have violated the covenant; there they have betrayed me. (CSB, see also ESV)

Here the NIV and the NRSV have 'at Adam,' taking Adam as the name of the small town which is mentioned in Joshua 3:16 and elsewhere. But why would God refer to that trivial city in his accusations against the people of Israel? Adam here should be interpreted as the person, the first human. Hosea says that the people of Israel are still unfaithful to the covenant with God, like Adam was. The entire history of the nation is characterised by sin.

A clear allusion to Adam can be found in Ezekiel 28 where the prophet says to the king of Tyre:

You were the seal of perfection, full of wisdom and perfect in beauty. You were in Eden, the garden of God; every precious stone adorned you: carnelian, chrysolite and emerald, topaz, onyx and jasper, lapis lazuli, turquoise and beryl. Your settings and mountings were made of gold; on the day you were created they were prepared. ...You were blameless in your ways from the day you were created till wickedness was found in you.

You see that Ezekiel twice consciously uses the word 'create.' The king who is described here also has similarities with the high priest of Israel, for the list of the precious stones in verse 13a resembles the description of the breastpiece of high priest Aaron in Exodus 28:15–20 and 39:10–13. Yet these gems themselves were probably inspired by a detail in the creation story (Genesis 2:11–12).

Adam here is the prototype of the proud human being and the king of Tyre is another representative of this type (see also verse 17). Pride is a basic problem of the human race.

Luke

Why did Luke include Jesus' genealogy in such an unexpected place in his Gospel? Matthew presents the overview of the lineage of Jesus at the very beginning of his Gospel, which is a logical place. If Luke preferred another place, he could have linked his list to what he says about Joseph's lineage in 2:4 or to his list of famous contemporaries of Jesus in 3:1–2. Yet he puts the genealogy right before the record of Jesus' temptation in the wilderness (Luke 3:23–38 and 4:1–13). I now understand the reason for this position: the list ends with Adam, the first man who gave in to temptation. The story that follows in Luke, about the temptation of Jesus, is a kind of counterpart to the story in Genesis, for it tells how Jesus did *not* succumb to the temptation. Luke calls Adam 'son of God' (3:38), just as he calls Jesus just before the genealogy (3:22). So these two passages of the Gospel fit together as hand and glove! This connection was missed by the person who divided the Bible into chapters. Seeing it also helps you to understand more of the meaning of Jesus' temptation. He was tempted as representative of humanity, as the first new human. The old human failed when he was tempted – the new human did not.

The Garden

Nowadays you often hear people emphasise the fact that Adam and Eve lived in a garden, a word used repeatedly in Genesis (2:8, 9, 10, 15, 16; 3:1, 3, 8, 10, 23, 24). Adam is styled as a gardener, and it is emphasised that Jesus prayed in the *garden* of Gethsemane, although the Bible does not actually call that place a garden (Matthew 26:36; Mark 14:32). It is also argued that the tomb of Jesus was situated in a garden, but the synoptic Gospels do not say anything like that. John does call the place of the tomb a garden or olive grove (Greek *kēpos*, 19:41), but this is a different word from the one used by the Septuagint in Genesis 2 and 3 (*paradeisos*). The point people are trying to make is that since Mary Magdalene mistakes Jesus for the gardener (John 20:15), Jesus and Adam are both described as gardeners. The New Testament, however, does not support this.

Romans 5:12–21

Although Paul only mentions Adam by name a few times in Romans 5:12–21, he is constantly on the apostle's mind. You can in fact read all Romans 1–5 with the story of Adam at the back of your mind. In one ear you hear words such as law, sin, and condemnation; words reminiscent of Adam. In your other ear, you hear words connected to Jesus such as God's righteousness, love, and faithfulness. In his passage Paul demonstrates how God in Christ tackled the consequences of the fall of humanity. Adam lost 'the glory of the immortal God' (Romans 1:23) which he originally had. Adam was also the channel through which sin penetrated the other people. Every new human in turn gets trapped by sin. Romans 5:12–14 says that death entered the world via Adam. In verse 14, Adam is finally called by name. Paul then contrasts him with Jesus so we can see that Adam's sin has consequences that are the reverse of the grace in Jesus. But, fortunately, this grace is much stronger (verse 15), and Christ overturns the consequences of Adam's sin. Paul does not write very systematically in this passage, but the comparison goes as follows:

Adam	Jesus Christ
Sin and death enter the world (12–14)	Sin and death exit the world (15)
Trespass (15)	Grace (15, 20)
Condemnation (16, 18)	Justification (16, 18)
Reign of death (17)	Reign of grace (17, 21)
Condemnation (17–18)	Acquittal and eternal life (17–18, 21)
Disobedience (19)	Obedience (19)
Sinner (19)	Righteous (19)

Paul calls Adam a 'type' of Jesus (verse 14 NRSV, ESV), but we would rather say that he is the great antitype. After all, Jesus reverses everything! The agreement between them is that their deeds have decisive significance for the people who follow them.

It is quite possible to read the next section of Romans, chapters 6–8, with the difference between Adam and Jesus in mind as well. Just try it out. A person is either 'in Adam' or 'in Christ,' Paul explains. For example, you hear Adam speak in the following words:

> Once I was alive apart from the law; but when the commandment came, sin sprang to life and I died. I found that the very commandment that was intended to bring life actually brought death. For sin, seizing the opportunity afforded by the commandment, deceived me, and through the commandment put me to death. (Romans 7:9–11)

1 Corinthians 15

In 1 Corinthians 15 Paul mentions Adam in a different way. Here he is not mentioned in connection with sin, judgement, and reconciliation, but with the resurrection. Yet once again he is the absolute opposite of Jesus. Adam brought death to humanity, Jesus brings humankind eternal life by resurrection. This is relevant to us because we are either in solidarity with Adam or with Christ. Paul first refers to 'a human being' (NRSV) as the cause of the death of humankind, but then he mentions the name Adam:

> For since death came through a man, the resurrection from the dead comes also through a man. For as in Adam all die, so in Christ all will be made alive. (1 Corinthians 15:21–22)

Later in the chapter Paul mentions Adam once more, again in contrast with Jesus. In this section (15:44–49) Paul explains how our new body after the resurrection will differ from our present earthly body. To explain the present situation, he quotes Genesis 2:7, but he adds two words which I put in italics for the sake of clarity:

> And the man became a living being. (Genesis 2:7b)

> So it is written: 'The *first* man *Adam* became a living being.' (1 Corinthians 15:45a)

Paul thus adds the name Adam to the text of Genesis 2. The meaning of 'living' here is almost equal to mortal. Facing the first Adam, the head of the old human race, stands Jesus, the head of the new humanity, and Paul calls him 'the last Adam.' This Jesus will make the people alive by the power of his resurrection (verse 45b). Verses 47–49 explain the comparison between Adam and Jesus and apply it to humanity:

> And just as we have borne the image of the earthly man, so shall we bear the image of the heavenly man. (1 Corinthians 15:49)

Adam and Christ are the representatives of humankind. Both are situated at the beginning of an era and determine the character of that era. Paul does not comment on any details in Genesis 1–3 but takes the story as such as a description of the fall of humanity.

Philippians 2:5–11

In Philippians 2:5–11, Paul's song about the obedience of Christ Jesus, you hear the echo of several parts of the Old Testament although Paul does not quote them literally. I hear Isaiah 53 and 45:23 as well as

Daniel 7:13–14. Paul also sings about Jesus in contrast to Adam. In verse 6 (NRSV, ESV, CSB) he says that Christ Jesus had 'the form' of God. This word 'form' occurs almost nowhere else in the New Testament, and Paul probably uses it here to characterise Jesus as the image bearer of God. Genesis 1:26–27 tells us that Adam and Eve were made in God's image. The Old Testament does not make use of this thought, but it reappears in the New Testament, where Jesus is the perfect image-bearer of God. Thus, Paul implicitly compares Jesus to Adam. These two persons handled their situation in contrasting ways. Adam tried to become equal to God by eating from the forbidden fruit, after the serpent promised that he would become 'like God' (Genesis 3:5) – but Christ did not cling to his equality with God (Philippians 2:6). While Adam wanted to elevate himself, Jesus voluntarily humbled himself and became 'obedient to death' (verse 8). As divine and human, Jesus is the unique representative of humanity who succeeded where we had failed.

Colossians

Whereas in Philippians Paul merely suggests that Adam and Jesus both bear the image of God, in Colossians 1:15 he says this more openly. Here he also says more about the glory of the Son of God, so that we can better see the difference between Christ and Adam. Christ not only bears the image of God, he '*is* the image of the invisible God'; 'he is [exists] before all things and in him all things hold together' (1:17). In other words, he is God himself and can show us who God is in a way that Adam could not. Paul calls Jesus the firstborn of all creation and in verse 18 he calls him 'the firstborn from among the dead,' thus repeating a key thought of 1 Corinthians 15. Jesus is the prototype of humanity as God intended them to be. Once again Adam is not mentioned by name, but the expression 'image of God' alludes to him.

Later in Colossians Paul also has Adam in mind without mentioning his name. Paul's comparison of the old and the new way of life can easily be read as a comparison between Adam and Christ:

> Do not lie to one another, since you have put off the old man with his deeds, and have put on the new *man* who is renewed

in knowledge according to the image of Him who created him. (Colossians 3:9–10 NKJV, see also Ephesians 4:22–24)

Whoever comes to faith in Christ no longer lives like Adam but like Jesus. Paul describes the transition from the one situation to the other in Romans 6:3–9. That passage makes it clear that we only obtain the new life by being crucified and buried together with Jesus, of which water baptism is an illustration. It is not easy to get rid of Adam.

1 Timothy 2:12–14

In his letter to his co-worker Timothy Paul mentions Adam and Eve in a discussion about the position of women. At that moment Timothy was working in the church in Ephesus (1 Timothy 1:3) and Paul was concerned to hear that there was a lot of wrong doctrine in the church (1:3–4, 4:1–3, 6:3–5). First, he criticised the fact that people occupied themselves with 'myths and endless genealogies' (1:4). Paul also asked Timothy to arrange practical matters and in 1 Timothy 5 he has much to say about what women were doing in the congregation. From 2:12 I gather that some women had a dominant way of teaching, for Paul here uses a negative word for 'assume authority.' You can therefore render this verse as:

> I do not allow a woman to teach a man in an authoritarian way, but she must be modest.

Like other interpreters, I conclude that there was a link between the wrong doctrine and the facts that women were teaching the congregation. It was these women who brought the wrong teaching! With these things in your mind, have a look at the two verses (2:13–14) in which Paul mentions Adam and Eve, and note the tone:

> For Adam was formed first, then Eve. And Adam was not the one deceived; it was the woman who was deceived and became a sinner.

It seems that in both verses Paul is correcting wrong ideas in the congregation, of the kind he had previously called 'myths and endless genealogies.' Apparently, some women in Ephesus said that Eve was created earlier than Adam, and they argued that Adam had been misled in the garden of Eden. Paul contradicts these two ideas and I would paraphrase his words as:

> No sisters, Eve was not created first; that was Adam. And although I know that Adam was guilty of the fall – I myself wrote so in Romans 5:12–14 – it was Eve who was the first to violate God's command by eating the fruit; so she was just as guilty as Adam.

I therefore think that the reference to Adam and Eve does not originate with Paul himself, but with the (female) teachers in the church. Paul is reacting to their erroneous explanation of Genesis 1–3. He puts the record straight and makes it clear that the deceptive teachers cannot appeal to Adam and Eve. In my opinion, he does not forbid all teaching by women, but only the authoritarian way in which it happened at Ephesus and its misleading content. In other places, such as Acts 18:26, 1 Corinthians 11:5, and Titus 2:3, you see that women did teach and prophesy.

My interpretation of 1 Timothy 2:13–14 is unusual. I found it in the commentary of my late friend Howard Marshall, who argues convincingly that Paul does not mention the events concerning Adam and Eve of his own accord. This interpretation sits well with the fact that Paul always writes negatively about Adam, as we saw, and that he never presents him as an example for the believers. Paul does not derive 'creation ordinances' from the Old Testament. On the other hand, he does sometimes reproduce the words of opponents without saying so, for example in 1 Corinthians 6:12, 13 and 7:1, where the quotation marks and the words 'you say' (NIV) are explanatory additions of the translators; compare the NKJV which does not have them.

To Conclude

When you look back on what the New Testament says about Adam, it is clear that the writers are digging below the surface of the Old Testament text. This shows that Jews and Christians had been reflecting on Adam, although the New Testament hardly uses any pre-Christian Jewish traditions. It turns out that biblical faith in Jesus is less individualistic than it has become in our time. What Adam did affects all people, and what Jesus did too. All those who do not (yet) believe are like Adam – and they are like Christ after they have come to faith. Adam and Christ are the representatives of two groups of people. This conclusion implies that in the situation of Genesis 3 every other person would have sinned like Adam did. Sinning is human, as Paul also says (Romans 3:23). So thank God for the second Adam! I am reminded of the following hymn:[4]

> Praise to the Holiest in the height,
> And in the depth be praise:
> In all His words most wonderful;
> Most sure in all His ways.
>
> O loving wisdom of our God,
> When all was sin and shame,
> He, the last Adam, to the fight
> And to the rescue came.
>
> O wisest love! that flesh and blood
> Which did in Adam fail,
> Should strive afresh against the foe,
> Should strive and should prevail.

Further Reading

Blocher, Henri A.G., 'Adam and Eve' in T.D. Alexander and Brian S. Rosner (eds), *New Dictionary of Biblical Theology* (Leicester/Downers Grove: IVP, 2000) 372–376.

Blocher, Henri, *In the Beginning: The Opening Chapters of Genesis* (Leicester: IVP, 1984).

Marshall, I. Howard, *The Pastoral Epistles*. ICC (Edinburgh: T&T Clark, 1999).

Ryken, Leland, James C. Wilhoit and Tremper Longman III (eds), *Dictionary of Biblical Imagery* (Downers Grove, Leicester: IVP, 1998).

---

[4] John Henry Newman (1801–1890).

Chapter 12: The Flood and the Rainbow

Like David, who will be discussed in the next chapter, the person of Noah is not very important in the New Testament. On the other hand, the great flood (deluge) and the rainbow have important roles in it. If you do not know the story about Noah and the flood, you could first read Genesis 6:5 through 9:17.

As a person, Noah mainly receives attention in the list of examples of faith in Hebrews 11:7. The author focuses on Noah's behaviour before the flood and therefore regards him as one of the heroes of faith. Genesis does not mention Noah's faith although it is visible in the story: he believed God's word when he announced the flood; he believed before anything could be seen. In a way that recalls what Paul writes about Abraham in Romans 4, the author of Hebrews says that Noah acquired 'the righteousness that is in keeping with faith.' His obedience saved his family. And because his faith was visible in his actions (Genesis 6:22; 7:5), he also meets the requirement of James (2:14, 18, 24).

Matthew 24:36–39 and Luke 17:24–27

Jesus does not focus on the person of Noah but on the time in which he lived, comparing that era and to the moment when he will return to earth. The behaviour of the people at that time was irresponsible, and so it will be again in the future. People will eat and drink, people will do the 'normal' things, business as usual, unaware that God's intervention is imminent. People will be so busy that they don't see God's judgement coming. The points of comparison are both the wicked behaviour of the people and the suddenness of the event. Jesus voices similar warnings in Matthew 24:42–44, 50 and Matthew 25:13. Noah and his family, on the contrary, were well prepared – so that is also possible. These warnings also affect us. We do not receive information about the date of his return either, yet we can (and must!) be prepared.

2 Peter 2:5 and 3:3–7

The Old Testament does not tell us that Noah spoke to his contemporaries while he was building the ark, but it is probable and even logical that he did. For example, the narrative assumes that Noah knew the distinction between pure and unclean animals, without telling how he acquired that knowledge (Genesis 7:2 and 8:20). No wonder that Peter adds the element of proclamation to the story by calling Noah 'a preacher of righteousness' (2 Peter 2:5).

In 2 Peter 3 Noah is not the subject and he is not mentioned. Peter writes about the possibility that the earth will perish. That is what God did once and he will do it again at the end of time. The people in those days, like most people today, thought that the end of the world is not coming. Noah's contemporaries surely had a good laugh as they watched him build a ship on dry land which no one ever expected to be used. But Peter believes that the unlikely, unexpected thing will happen, just as in Noah's time. A clear difference with the Old Testament is that Peter expects the coming judgement on the world to be by fire, not by water. The difficult verse 5 alludes to the great role of water in the creation narrative of Genesis 1:6–10. According to Peter God is not only the creator but also the judge of the world. If you do not have the Old Testament open, you will not immediately understand what Peter means.

1 Peter

One of the most difficult passages in the New Testament is 1 Peter 3:18–22. Peter here says two unusual things: first, that Jesus 'went and made proclamation to the imprisoned spirits' and second, that there is a connection between Noah's ark and baptism. This is one of those passages which only become clear when you see how Peter uses the Hebrew Bible here and in surrounding passages, although Peter also interacts with Jewish biblical interpretation in his time. Here is a list of the parallels that Peter signals, after which we will unpack the details:

Genesis 6–9	1 Peter 3
Punishment on sin (ancient times)	Punishment on sin (end times)
Seemingly the end of everything	End of time
The ark	Baptism
Many bad people – few believers	Bad people – small congregations
Noah righteous	Jesus righteous
Noah's good lifestyle	The readers' good lifestyle
Noah's testimony and the opportunity for repentance	Testimony of the readers and the opportunity for repentance

To begin with, Peter sees similarities between the flood as God's punishment in the past and God's judgement at the end of history. Earlier in this chapter we already saw that the Lord Jesus had the same perspective, according to Matthew and Luke. Furthermore, Peter knows that the advent of Jesus has inaugurated the end of time – we are now in the last days (see also 1 Peter 1:20 and 4:7). The flood *seemed* to be the end of everything, the coming of Jesus *is* the end of everything. Then you see several negative and positive similarities between the situations of Noah and Peter. On the negative side it is said that the people before the flood were exceptionally bad (Genesis 6:5–6; this had been much emphasised in the Jewish interpretation of these verses). Genesis 6:1–4, an enigmatic passage, is also about the transgression of boundaries through sinful behaviour; and this passage had also attracted colourful interpretations from Jewish interpreters. Some of this is visible in 1 Peter 4:3–4, where Peter likewise gives examples of sinful behaviour. Verse 4 mentions 'reckless, wild living' and the rendering in the ESV, 'the same flood of debauchery,' brings out the intended allusion to a flood of water.

In response to this sinful behaviour Peter tells his readers that they should live in a completely different way, and in 1 Peter 4:7–11 he unfolds this: love, commitment to others, and positive speech. To the flood story of Genesis, Peter adds the suggestion that Noah and his family lived in an environment that scorned and dismissed them, whereas they were expected to have a positive lifestyle. The same expectation is on Peter's readers, so the Noah family should be their example. Peter stresses that only eight people were saved in the ark; the great majority of humanity in Noah's time resisted God (verse 20). His entire letter makes clear that his readers also form small minorities in the great Roman Empire, which is not a safe environment for them (1:1; 2:12–17; 3:13–14; 4:12–19). Many of us live in a similar situation.

On the positive side, the resemblance between Noah and Jesus is first and foremost that both are 'righteous' persons. This is declared about Noah in Genesis 6:8, 9 and 7:1, who is the first person in the Bible to receive this accolade. Genesis also states that he was 'blameless among the people of his time' and 'walked faithfully with God' (6:9). Elsewhere similar praise is limited to Enoch (Genesis 5:22, 24). Later Jewish writings had much to say about what this entailed, and you see this reflected in Hebrews 11:7 and 2 Peter 2:5. This state of affairs explains why Peter emphatically declares the same thing about Jesus (1 Peter 3:18).

Secondly, Noah is an example for Peter's readers because of the good testimony he gave. The text of Genesis does not say much about this, but the later Jewish interpreters do, and so does Peter in 2 Peter 2:5. The seven days in Genesis 7:4 were explained as a final opportunity for Noah to call for repentance, and it was believed that he had done so with utmost urgency. You may have seen an illustration of this proclamation in a children's Bible – Noah addressing his contemporaries with a hammer or saw in his hand. Peter writes that he expects his readers to give just such a good testimony to the people around them (1 Peter 3:15–17). Both in the time of Noah and in Peter's own time, therefore, there is an opportunity for repentance. The ark can be seen as a symbol of the Christian community which is saved from the chaos of the world. Note that in 1 Peter the person of Noah has a role in the argument next to the ark and the flood.

But what about the 'imprisoned spirits' (3:19)? They have no real parallel anywhere in the Old Testament, but the expression is probably based on Genesis 6:1–4, the difficult passage which precedes the flood story. Here the book of Enoch can provide real help. In New Testament times this book was only a few hundred years old and probably quite popular; several passages in 1 and 2 Peter and Judas include allusions to it, and that is also the case here. Enoch tells how the fallen angels of Genesis 6 are awaiting their condemnation in a kind of prison. Peter picks up this idea by saying that Jesus has brought the good news of his victory to these fallen angels as well. Because the message is about his victory, Jesus will have done so after his ascension. The book of Enoch claims that Enoch was instructed to speak to these angels. By saying that Jesus did so, Peter is contradicting the tradition about Enoch. (This shows that he does not regard the book of Enoch as authoritative. Peter and Judas do allude to Enoch in the same way that we refer to a popular book or to something on social media, without recognising it as part of inspired Scripture.) Peter mentions this fact to encourage his readers: so complete is the victory of Jesus over death!

Acts 5:1–11

I think that there is a connection between the story of the flood and the punishment of Ananias and Sapphira in Acts 5. In both cases, God forcefully intervenes against human sin. In Genesis this happens at the beginning of the history of humanity, as a warning that he takes sin very seriously. God has barely finished creating the universe and giving humans a space to flourish, when everything on earth goes wrong. In response God sends the flood as a sharp warning to people who will live in later times, but this punishment is strictly a 'once but never again,' as Genesis 9:8–17 emphasizes.

The death of Ananias and Sapphira also takes place at the beginning of a history, namely the history of the church of Jesus Christ. The church has barely been founded when sin already breaks in, threatening to spoil everything. Again, God sends a warning hard as nails, which intends to say: this may be the era of the new covenant, but that does not mean that I am henceforth going to tolerate sin. Sin is and remains unacceptable, and under no circumstances are you allowed to deceive me and my Holy Spirit (Acts 5:3, 4, 9). Yet like the flood, this warning is a one-off and is not followed by further punitive measures. The abhorrence that emanates from it is hopefully clear enough. I am not sure whether Luke was aware of the parallel with the flood when he wrote about Ananias and Sapphira, but some of his readers have seen it. It helps us to accept the hard story in Acts, which some readers have found unpalatable, if not unfair.

The Rainbow

The bow which God displays in the sky after the flood as a sign of his lasting covenant faithfulness (Genesis 9:12–17) is mentioned in the Old Testament in Ezekiel 1:28 as a symbol of his radiant appearance. In Revelation 4:3 and 10:1, the thoughts of God's faithfulness and his glory come together. The fact that John first sees a rainbow around God's throne and later around the most powerful angel is a reference to God's faithfulness to his covenant with all creation, the covenant he made with Noah (Genesis 9). In this way the book of Revelation shows that God is faithful to his creation. It is precisely for that reason that he destroys 'those who destroy the earth' (Revelation 11:18, clearly alluding to the flood story in Genesis 6:13, 17); people kill the earth, so God kills them. His judgement on those who disfigure and mutilate his creation is righteous and fully deserved. Yet while the flood brought the waters of chaos back into the world (see also Genesis 1:6–7), God's final judgement will rather save the earth, as he discards the water and secures the renewed earth forever. That is what it means that the sea will be absent from the new earth (Revelation 21:1). Thus, the God of the rainbow keeps his promise that he will not destroy the earth again (Genesis 9:11).

Further Reading

Bauckham, Richard, *The Theology of the Book of Revelation* (Cambridge: Cambridge University Press, 1993).

France, R.T., 'Exegesis in Practice: Two Samples' in I. Howard Marshall (ed.), *New Testament Interpretation. Essays on Principles and Methods* (Exeter: Paternoster, 1978) 252–281.

Marcar, Katie, 'In the days of Noah: *Urzeit/Endzeit* Correspondence and the Flood Tradition in 1 Peter 3–4,' *New Testament Studies* 63 (2017) 550–566.

Chapter 13: David

There is no Old Testament character about whom we know more than King David. His adventurous life story fills half of 1 Samuel and all of 2 Samuel, and it is repeated in 1 Chronicles 11–29. If you do not know the story, it is surely worth reading! You will get to know David as a man of flesh and blood, with much blood on his hands, a man with many virtues and perhaps even more vices. Furthermore, David is credited with writing many psalms, and the prophets often refer to him.

The New Testament mentions David more than fifty times, and Jesus is often associated with him. Matthew makes this connection most often: he calls Jesus 'son of David' (Matthew 1:1); a 'king like David' (Matthew 21:9); and once also 'David's Lord' (Matthew 22:41–46).

2 Samuel 7 and 1 Chronicles 17

In theological terms and seen from the perspective of the New Testament, 2 Samuel 7 is the culmination of the stories about David. Here the prophet Nathan brings him great promises of God, which have their climax in verses 12–16:

> When your days are over and you rest with your ancestors, I will raise up your offspring to succeed you, your own flesh and blood, and I will establish his kingdom. He is the one who will build a house for my Name, and I will establish the throne of his kingdom for ever. *I will be his father, and he shall be my son.* When he does wrong, I will punish him with a rod wielded by men, with floggings inflicted by human hands. But my love will never be taken away from him, as I took it away from Saul, whom I removed from before you. Your house and your kingdom shall endure for ever before me; your throne shall be established for ever. (see also 1 Chronicles 17:11–14)

The interpreters rightly refer to this passage as a covenant of the LORD with David, even though that word is not used in the text. The LORD unilaterally makes a formal agreement with David, including a strong promise about the perpetuation of his family as the royal house in

Israel. David refers to this very promise when he transfers power to Solomon at the end of his life:

> The LORD, the God of Israel, chose me from my whole family to be king over Israel for ever. He chose Judah as leader, and from the tribe of Judah he chose my family, and from my father's sons he was pleased to make me king over all Israel. (1 Chronicles 28:4)

The Rest of the Old Testament

In subsequent parts of the Old Testament God's promise to David resounds everywhere: there will always be a king from David's family. That is why you read about the messianic child in Isaiah 9:

> Of the greatness of his government and peace there will be no end. He will reign on David's throne and over his kingdom, establishing and upholding it with justice and righteousness from that time on and for ever. The zeal of the LORD Almighty will accomplish this. (Isaiah 9:7)

Jeremiah confirms this expectation at the very moment when the exile is just beginning, and he even calls the future king by the name David (23:5–6; 30:9 – do read the contexts)! In Ezekiel 37:21–24 the future king is also called David, and his reign is associated with the reunification of the Northern Kingdom (Ephraim) and the Southern Kingdom (Judah). The expectation of such a king from the house of David is always positive. He will be a good monarch who will ensure salvation, peace, righteousness, and justice.

Because David's dynasty is permanent, its capital Jerusalem also becomes an important place (see for example Isaiah 37:35) and many positive expectations in the later books of the Old Testament are therefore linked to blessings for Jerusalem.

2 Samuel 7 in the New Testament

After the people of Israel had gone into exile (586 BC), there was no descendant of David on the throne in Jerusalem. The people may have wondered what would come of God's promise. But in the New Testament we see that God kept his word and did indeed let the saviour descend from the family of David. All four Gospels testify to this, see for example Mark 11:10; Matthew 1:1, 17, 20; Luke 1:27, 32; and John 7:42. In Luke's story about Jesus' birth, you come across the promise of 2 Samuel 7 when the angel Gabriel addresses Mary about the child she will receive:

> He will be great and will be called the Son of the Most High. The Lord God will give him the throne of his father David, and he will reign over Jacob's descendants for ever; his kingdom will never end. (Luke 1:32–33)

Almost this entire promise of the angel consists of parts of Old Testament texts, and 2 Samuel plays the first violin. In addition, you may also hear Isaiah 9:6, Daniel 7:14, and Micah 4:7.

In the long quotation from 2 Samuel 7 above I printed a sentence in italics: *'I will be his father, and he shall be my son.'* Like the angel, the author of Hebrews sees these words as a reference to Jesus (Hebrews 1:5b). He writes this immediately after he has cited Psalm 2:7, which says almost the same thing ('You are my son, today I have become your father'). People who are familiar with the Gospels will find this use of 2 Samuel 7 logical: Jesus is the special son of David, who is also the Son of God at the same time. It is therefore quite striking that when Paul cites the same words in italics from 2 Samuel 7 in 2 Corinthians 6:18, he makes them refer to the church, not to Jesus! Paul quotes God's words, first spoken by Nathan, as follows:

> I will be your father, and you shall be my sons and daughters, says the Lord Almighty. (NRSV)

In this way, Paul extends the scope of the promise in 2 Samuel 7:14. God was not only a Father to David and to Jesus, but he is now also to the believers. Paul makes this move deliberately, for his words 'the Lord Almighty' at the end of the quote come from 2 Samuel 7:8. (There the NRSV and the ESV have 'LORD of hosts,' which translates the same expression.) This shows that Paul had read all of 2 Samuel 7 and was not just grabbing a sentence out of context.

Revelation 21 also applies the words in italics from 2 Samuel 7 to the believers and not (only) to Jesus. Here they find a place in the promise of God, the heavenly king who sits on the throne (verse 5):

> To the thirsty I will give from the spring of the water of life
> without payment. The one who conquers will have this
> heritage, and I will be his God and he will be my son.
> (Revelation 21:6b–7 ESV)

This use of 2 Samuel 7 shows that, thanks to Jesus, believers are also accepted as children of God. But it goes far beyond what Nathan and David could imagine. In and through Jesus, God is doing things that are truly new and great: he adopts you and me as his children!

Christ

The word Christ (Greek *Christos*) means 'anointed one,' so it is not a surname but a title. It is the Greek translation of the Hebrew word *Messiah*. The church confesses that Jesus of Nazareth is God's anointed servant, God's Messiah, and therefore we call him Christ. We also believe that Jesus is the fulfilment of all kinds of promises in the Hebrew Bible. Yet the word 'anointed' is rarely used in what you might call 'messianic prophecies.' Can this be explained? In Israel, priests and kings were anointed to equip them for their important role. The ointment oil was a symbol of the Holy Spirit. To be anointed therefore means to be something like an equipped office-holder. The word occurs in Leviticus with reference to the priests and Isaiah 45:1 calls King Cyrus of Persia the anointed of the LORD. King Saul is emphatically called God's anointed (1 Samuel 12:5; 26:9, 11, 16, 23) and David knows that he is not allowed to kill Saul even though they are enemies.

How could this word Messiah become the main title of Jesus of Nazareth? That is because of David, who is often referred to as God's anointed. We hear in detail how the young David is anointed (1 Samuel 16:1–13) and how this preparatory anointing is repeated at the moment he really becomes king (2 Samuel 2:4 and 5:3). Later on David is also called anointed in 2 Samuel 23:1, 2 Chronicles 6:42 and Psalm 18:50; 89:38, and 132:17. But even more important are the prophetic words in which the term is used, such as 1 Samuel 2:10, 35; Psalm 2:2; 20:6; 28:8; Habakkuk 3:13; and the enigmatic passage Daniel 9:25–26. Together these texts ensured that the Jews sometimes called their expected saviour, the second David, Messiah (see also Luke 3:15).

Jesus' followers see him as the king of Israel from David's house, and therefore Matthew (1:1, 16, 17, 18), Mark (1:1), and John (1:17, 20, 25, 41) use this title with emphasis at the beginning of their books on him.

Root

Two verses in the book of Revelation (5:5 and 22:16) refer to Jesus as the 'Root of David.' This unusual expression is not explained, but because it is about David, you quickly think of the Old Testament. That this is correct is confirmed by Paul, who also uses the word root in Romans 15:12:

> And further, Isaiah says, 'The Root of Jesse will spring up, one who will arise to rule over the nations; in him the Gentiles will hope.'

The term 'root' thus comes from Isaiah. Paul says in Romans 15 that the Jew Jesus has come to bring God's salvation to both Jews and gentiles. To substantiate this claim, in verse 12 he quotes from Isaiah 11:10 in the Septuagint, which is slightly different from the Hebrew text, but has the same positive meaning. As so often, in these few words from the Old Testament the context of these words resounds too; all of Isaiah 11 thus resounds in Romans 15 as well as in Revelation 5 and 22. In this case that is particularly clear because the prophet Isaiah *begins and ends* his wonderful messianic prophecy (11:1–10) with the word root, making it a key word for the whole passage.

We will look a little longer at Isaiah 11, which was also discussed in Chapter 9. The prophet speaks of a shoot 'from the stump of Jesse' – and this Jesse was the father of David, see for example 1 Samuel 16:1–13 and Psalm 72:20. In other words, Isaiah has high expectations of a descendant of King David, who will have superhuman traits. The prophet says at least three things about him in this passage:

1. The Spirit of God will rest on him (verse 2). These words resound in what the four Gospels report about Jesus (Matthew 3:16; Mark 1:10; Luke 3:22; John 1:32). In Acts 10:38 you even read that Jesus was *anointed* with the Holy Spirit. Yet this promise is applied to the believers in Ephesians 1:17 and 1 Peter 4:14. So here the same happens that we saw with regard to 2 Samuel 7, as Paul and others apply an

Old Testament promise, given to David and his descendants, not (only) to Jesus but also to the church.

2. He will act righteously and pronounce judgement (verses 3–5). We see this throughout the life of Jesus, for example in his approach to the woman who committed adultery (John 8:1–11), even though the writers of the New Testament do not refer to these words from Isaiah 11. However, Isaiah 11:3–5 is used in the description of Jesus' judgement on his return (Revelation 19:11, 15, 21; 2 Thessalonians 2:8).

3. His coming will restore peace in creation (verses 6–9). Mark 1:13 says that Jesus lived among the wild animals and seems to make use of Isaiah 11:6–8. Yet the New Testament is also aware that world peace will only be the result of Christ's second coming.

Finally, when you go back to Revelation 5:5 you can see that Jesus' title 'Root of David' has a different meaning than his title 'Lion of Judah.' The latter title mainly refers to his power and divinity, but the former to Jesus' human lineage and to the unexpected elements of his actions.

Symbol

Have you noticed that most of the events in David's life are not mentioned in the New Testament at all? In particular, no-one mentions his bad characteristics. In this respect, the New Testament follows the description in Chronicles rather than that in Samuel, as Chronicles one-sidedly prises the positive traits of David.

There is even a great contrast between David and Jesus. In Acts both Peter and Paul speak about the disparity between the end of Jesus' life and that of David: While David died and did not rise again, God raised Jesus back to life (Acts 2:29–32; 13:37, see also 34–36).

The conclusion, therefore, is that in his behaviour Jesus shows little resemblance to David. Unlike, for example, Abraham, Joseph, and Jeremiah, David as a *character* is not a type of Jesus. The similarities between him and Jesus are in their role as king, in their *status*, and in the promises about this status. David was the first and most important king of Israel; Jesus is his final and definitive successor. In fact, in the New Testament David is more a symbolic persona than a real person. This is in line with the way in which Jeremiah already refers to him

(17:25; 22:2, 4, 30; 33:15–17; 36:30). In this respect, the New Testament makes a very selective use of the Old.

Further Reading

Fitzmyer, Joseph A., *Essays on the Semitic Background of the New Testament* (London: Geoffrey Chapman, 1971).

Knight, George A.F., *A Christian Theology of the Old Testament* (London: SCM, 1961).

Chapter 14: The Temple

The tabernacle and the temple are real buildings which are mentioned everywhere in the Bible. They acquire a new meaning in the New Testament and from then on they are mainly used as symbols. The New Testament writers usually do not quote a particular text from Scripture as they assume that their readers know the temple and the tabernacle. I will therefore begin this chapter with some general historical background information.

Tabernacle and Temple

The temple is the place where the LORD God lives (Psalm 132:13–14). This living or dwelling must be regarded as symbolic because Israel knew well that God was not bound to a particular location (2 Chronicles 6:18; Isaiah 66:1). In Acts 7:48, Stephen reminds his Jewish audience that God, 'does not live in houses made with human hands,' and in verses 49–50 he underlines these words by quoting from Isaiah 66:1–2; he uses the Septuagint which does not differ much from the Hebrew text (and the NIV has the tendency to assimilate the texts, which is helpful for the purpose of this book). Yet God had chosen the temple in Jerusalem as the designated place where he would meet with his people (1 Kings 8:27–30). This temple in the national capital was built by King Solomon (1 Kings 6–8) as the successor of earlier sanctuaries, such as the tabernacle which was used during the period of Israel's sojourn in the wilderness, and the later sanctuary in Shiloh (Joshua 18:1; 1 Samuel 1:3, 24). What I am writing here typically pertains to any of these sacred places.

The temple was the place where the Israelites received all kinds of (spiritual) blessings; see for example 2 Chronicles 6:20–39; Psalm 36:7–9; 65:4; 84; it was also the symbolic residence of justice (Psalm 89:14; 97:2). The temple of Solomon was destroyed by the Babylonians (2 Kings 25) and the second temple, which stood in Jerusalem during the time of Jesus, was built as its successor in the time of the prophets Haggai and Zechariah (Haggai 1:14–15; Zechariah 8:9; Ezra 6). However, this was a much simpler building, and King Herod took it upon himself to enlarge and embellish this temple in order to win the favour of the Jews. The resulting construction work was still underway at the time of Jesus (see also John 2:20) and was bringing about a beautiful building (Mark 13:1; Luke 21:5; Matthew 23:16). In this temple Jesus cured all sorts of people, here he was praised by children, and he gave much instruction (Matthew 21:14–15; 21:23–24:1). But first he had thrown the traders out (Matthew 21:12–13) and called himself 'greater than the temple' (Matthew 12:6). Gentile peoples also had temples, and these too were seen as places where you could meet a god. When Paul and Peter wrote letters to readers with a pagan background, they had no need to explain what a temple is.

No Access!?

There were strict rules about who could come into the inner spaces of the temple. Unlike in modern churches, ordinary people had to stay at a distance, in a court, and only the priests had access to the actual temple. This was because of God's holiness (Leviticus 16:2, 17). Exodus 26:33, Numbers 18:7, and especially Hebrews 9:3–8 tell how in the tabernacle a veil formed the absolute separation between accessible and inaccessible spaces. Likewise in Solomon's temple the rear hall was forbidden terrain (1 Kings 8:6–11). These rules explain why the priest Zechariah was on his own in the temple while the believers were waiting for him outside (Luke 1:8–10, 21; note that Luke does not even tell us where the temple is).

The Synoptic Gospels tell how the curtain (veil) in the temple is torn at the very moment when Jesus dies on the cross (Matthew 27:51; Mark 15:38; Luke 23:45). This must have been a catastrophic event for the priests! It is striking that this heavy curtain tears from top to bottom, not from the bottom up. This shows that it did not happen by human hands and that it was therefore an act of God himself. The implication is that God is giving the people unrestricted access to himself through the death of Jesus. From the moment of Jesus' death, God can be reached by everyone, not only by the priests or the Jews. You can even say that God himself already symbolically begins the demolition of the temple, something the Romans would do in the year AD 70.

The temple had even more rules. Spaces of decreasing proportions were reserved for gentiles, women, men, and priests respectively. To point this prohibition out to gentiles there was a clear boundary mark. In Ephesians 2:14 Paul uses this well-known barrier as a metaphor for the spiritual separation between Jews and gentiles. He is pleased to say that through the work of Jesus this separation has now been removed completely. Although the temple in Jerusalem was still there at the time when Paul wrote his letter, the separation had lost all meaning. In Jesus Jews and gentiles have the same access to God.

Jesus as the New Temple

With the coming of Jesus, the temple has been displaced in God's plan. The new covenant only has a spiritual temple. In the New Testament, both Jesus and his followers receive this honorary title of temple.

Jesus' first visit to the temple (after the visits as a child, Luke 2:22–52) is reported in John 2:13–22. Whoever reads the Old Testament and John 1 carefully will notice that there is something missing from this story in John 2. According to the Old Testament, God's glory (Greek *doxa*) dwelt in the tabernacle and in the temple (Exodus 40:34–35; 1 Kings 8:10–11; 2 Chronicles 7:1), and John 1:14 announces that in Jesus this divine glory has come to earth. So you expect that Jesus' glory will be especially visible when he visits the temple. But John says poignantly that Jesus displays his glory by performing a sign in the village of Cana in the remote province of Galilee (2:11), and he is completely silent about this glory in 2:13–22. This silence does not mean much good for the temple! During this visit Jesus claims that he is the temple in person, and that this temple will be demolished but rebuilt after three days (John 2:19–21). His words have a double meaning because Jesus speaks them in the temple, but he is referring both to the destruction of this literal temple and to the death and resurrection of his body. His words connect well with John 1:14, where John explains that Jesus came to pitch his tent on earth. John thus establishes a connection between the tent of meeting in the desert (see for example Exodus 33:7–11; 40:34–35) and the temple on the one hand, and Jesus as the new meeting place between God and humankind on the other.[5]

---

[5] See also the chapters 2 and 26. What Jesus says about the temple in John 10 I will also discuss in chapter 26.

In Mark 14:58 the witnesses who are accusing Jesus make use of his words recorded in John 2, for they distinguish between a temple made by human hands and one not made in this way:

> We heard him say, 'I will destroy this temple made with human hands and in three days will build another, not made with hands.'

These witnesses probably did not really understand that Jesus was not only talking about the literal temple, yet they are right in claiming that he had indeed announced the destruction of the temple in Jerusalem (see also Mark 13:2). After the destruction at the beginning of the exile in Babel this is thus the second time that the temple will be destroyed, but this time it is definitive, for there is no promise of restoration. (For promises of restoration after the first destruction, see for example Isaiah 56:7 and 60:7.)

In 2 Corinthians 5:1–2 Paul also distinguishes between something made with human hands and something eternal, but here it is about the place of residence of the believers. When we die we will receive 'an eternal house in heaven, not built by human hands.' Yet you can say that these words are also about Jesus, for he is the one who is preparing this dwelling-place for us (John 14:2–3).

The Church as a Temple

In 1 Corinthians 3:16–17, Paul addresses the congregation in Corinth regarding their responsibilities, telling them that they are a temple of God, in which the Holy Spirit dwells. In verse 9 he has already called them 'God's building.' He does the same thing in his second letter (2 Corinthians 6:16), in a statement that you must read in the context of 2 Corinthians 6:14–7:1. To strengthen his words, he adds 'as God has said' and then quotes a series of statements from Scripture about close contact between God and humans. Paul's quotations and their Old Testament sources are as follows:

2 Corinthians 6:16–18	Old Testament
I will live with them and walk among them	Exodus 29:45, Leviticus 26:11–12
I will be their God, and they will be my people	Leviticus 26:12, Ezekiel 37:27
Come out from them [Babylon] and be separate, says the Lord. Touch no unclean thing	Isaiah 52:11
I will receive you	Jeremiah 23:3 (Septuagint)
I will be a Father to you and you will be my sons and daughters	2 Samuel 7:14, with addition of 'and daughters' from Isaiah 43:6
says the LORD Almighty	2 Samuel 7:8

Paul has adapted the text of Scripture somewhat, but the words are well recognisable. This series of quotations shows that God is now fulfilling what he had been promising throughout the Old Testament; he is now present with humans without the mediation of a stone temple, for these people themselves are now the temple. This great blessing leads to the requirement that the believers avoid contact with anything unclean; hence the call to come out from Babylon, taken from Isaiah 52:11, which you also hear later in Revelation 18:4.

Peter uses the image of the temple in 1 Peter 2:5: the church consists of living stones which together form a spiritual temple. To this imagery Peter adds that Jesus is the cornerstone of this temple, and as evidence he cites Isaiah 28:16:

> So this is what the Sovereign LORD says: 'See, I lay a stone in Zion, a tested stone, a precious cornerstone for a sure foundation; the one who relies on it will never be stricken with panic.'

These words promise God's people a better basis for their existence than the leaders in the time of Isaiah offered. Because Jesus has already called himself the cornerstone, Peter can apply these words to him.

Paul and Peter thus call upon the local churches to live a holy life because they are receiving the blessing that the Old Testament connected to the temple.

It is striking that in 1 Corinthians 6:19 Paul does not apply the image of the temple to the church, but to individual believers. Each of us is a temple of the Holy Spirit. Paul puts this thought by the side of his assertion that the body of every believer is a member of (the body of) Christ (verse 15). Both images, temple and body of Christ, mean that God is in command and that we must not defile our bodies by sinning.

Paul uses the temple metaphor in yet a third way when in Ephesians 2:19–22 he does not call the local church but the world-wide church 'a dwelling in which God lives by his Spirit.' He does not use the word temple but the allusion is clear. The church as a whole is a temple, with the Lord Jesus as its cornerstone, built on the foundation of the apostles and the prophets. The peace which results from this state of affairs (verses 15–17) is a partial fulfilment of the promise of peace in Micah 4:1–4 = Isaiah 2:2–4, which promises that in the last days 'the mountain of the LORD's temple will be established.'

Having read this far, you should have no problem understanding that John 4:21–24 also has the church of Christ as its subject. Jesus tells the Samaritan woman that the discussion between Jews and Samaritans about the place where God should be worshipped is no longer relevant. Jews served God in Jerusalem, but the Samaritans had their own sacred mountain of Gerizim. Jesus brings the discussion to a higher level by pointing out that the coming of the Holy Spirit means it is no longer necessary to go to an earthly temple to worship God. True worship comes from people in whom the Spirit of Jesus dwells and who are therefore temples of the Spirit. Someone who wants to meet God in truth will come to a spiritual temple; that is, to us! You can therefore also apply Psalm 48, a song about the temple, to your own church community, asking yourself whether you are living up to this ideal.

The Future

Ezekiel 40–46 contains a detailed design of a temple for the time after the return from exile, but this design was never realised. This temple will not be built in the future either, at least not with God's blessing, for Revelation 21:22 makes it clear that there will be no temple in God's future, in the same way that there will be neither lamplight nor sunlight (Revelation 22:5). The presence of the triune God himself with humanity will make the mediation of a temple utterly unnecessary. This should not surprise you after you saw how Jesus, Paul, and Peter explain the spiritual meaning of the temple. Since the coming of Jesus, the temple of God is no longer a stone building. God's promises are being fulfilled in human beings.[6]

Further Reading

Alexander, T. Desmond, and Simon Gathercole (eds), *Heaven on Earth. The Temple in Biblical Theology* (Carlisle: Paternoster, 2004).

Ellis, E. Earle, *Christ and the Future in New Testament History* (Boston, Leiden: Brill, 2001).

McKelvey, R.J., 'Temple' in T. Desmond Alexander and Brian S. Rosner (eds), *New Dictionary of Biblical Theology* (Leicester/Downers Grove: IVP, 2000) 806–811.

---

[6] More on this controversial topic in my book *Enduring Treasure. The Lasting Value of the Old Testament for Christians* (London: Faithbuilders, 2017), 131–134.

Chapter 15: Shepherd and Sheep

The Bible originated in an agrarian society and consequently it contains many things to do with agriculture and livestock. Some of these subjects also picked up a theological significance, with the shepherd and the sheep among the best-known examples. The fact that the shepherd is such a common image in the Bible is undoubtedly also due to the fact that David, the first good king of Israel, was originally a shepherd. On the one hand David is an example of good leadership, and a good leader is referred to as a good shepherd, on the other hand God promises that the saviour of his people will be a good shepherd who will be a descendant of David.

Sheep

Sheep are mentioned in the Bible more often than any other kind of animal. Shepherds in the West drive their sheep, often with the help of a dog, but shepherds in the Ancient Near East went at the head of the herd and the flock followed them by recognising their voice or their whistle. This leading the way provides a beautiful illustration of the relationship between Jesus as leader and the believers as his followers. When you think of a Western shepherd-with-dog, you are in the wrong show. When the sheep of two or more flocks were together a shepherd could simply call his own sheep to separate them from the others, for his own sheep would recognise his voice whereas the other sheep would not (John 10:3–5). At night the sheep were usually indoors, in a sheepfold (John 10:1); during the day the shepherd led them into fields with grass and drinking water. Psalm 23 gives a picture of the work of a shepherd, but you can easily get an overly romantic impression. Shepherding was a lonely, demanding, and dangerous profession; in a country where predators were roaming free you could not afford to nod off for a moment! (Nonetheless, there were also female shepherds, see Genesis 29:9 and Exodus 2:16–17.)

Although the Bible does not develop the idea, it appears that Abel, the shepherd, is a kind of ideal believer (Genesis 4:2–4). If this is correct, he is a type of Jesus, because he too was an innocent victim of murder.

Good and Bad Shepherds

When a leader is called 'shepherd,' his or her followers are automatically referred to as 'sheep.' Domestic sheep are animals that require a certain level of care and will certainly get lost if they are not properly led. This fact makes it understandable that in the Old Testament lack of good leadership is expressed as the absence of a shepherd (1 Kings 22:17; Ezekiel 34:5; Zechariah 10:2) and that the evangelists use the same image when they describe Jesus' concern for Israel (Matthew 9:36; Mark 6:34); Jesus himself probably used this imagery. Sometimes words such as 'flock' occur without being interpreted as *human* sheep (for example Psalm 95:7; 100:3). The fact that Moses and David were shepherds before they became leader of the people seems to have been a good preparation for their later task. This is also apparent in the following words:

> You led your people like a flock by the hand of Moses and Aaron. (Psalm 77:20)

> He chose David his servant and took him from the sheepfolds; from tending the sheep he brought him to be the shepherd of his people Jacob, of Israel his inheritance. And David shepherded them with integrity of heart; with skilful hands he led them. (Psalm 78:70–72)

God even calls a good foreign leader, namely King Cyrus of Persia, a shepherd of Israel (Isaiah 44:28). Conversely, it is logical that bad leaders of the people come under criticism as bad shepherds, as in Jeremiah 10:21; 12:10; 50:6, and Zechariah 10:3, texts which are very recognisable in our time. Notice that these texts are politically charged!

God as Shepherd

In addition to the image of human leaders as shepherds the Old Testament contains the conviction that God himself is the shepherd of Israel (Psalm 80:1). This imagery usually expresses God's tender care for the people and for individuals (Psalm 23; Isaiah 40:11), as well as his protection (Psalm 78:52); yet sometimes he needs to treat his stubborn sheep like a stern shepherd would do (Ezekiel 20:36–38).

The prophet Jeremiah is the first to receive David's assist from Psalm 23 and to use the shepherd in an extended image. He applies it to the field of leadership in the community of faith and in politics:

> 'Woe to the shepherds who are destroying and scattering the sheep of my pasture!' declares the LORD. Therefore this is what the LORD, the God of Israel, says to the shepherds who tend my people: 'Because you have scattered my flock and driven them away and have not bestowed care on them, I will bestow punishment on you for the evil you have done,' declares the LORD. 'I myself will gather the remnant of my flock out of all the countries where I have driven them and will bring them back to their pasture, where they will be fruitful and increase in number. I will place shepherds over them who will tend them, and they will no longer be afraid or terrified, nor will any be missing,' declares the LORD. (Jeremiah 23:1–4)

Because this section follows directly after passages in which Jeremiah criticises the kings of Judah (Jeremiah 21–22), his biting reproach particularly concerns these kings – who were the direct descendants of David! But Jeremiah's words also relate to the other selfish leaders of his time. The prophet describes God's future salvation of the people as the appointment of *other* shepherds over the people.

The most important passage about the role of shepherds in the Old Testament is Ezekiel 34, which appears to be an extended version of Jeremiah 23. Ezekiel probably knew the words of Jeremiah in written form and delivered a prophetic sermon on them. The verses 2–8 are a test for every government; leadership means care for the people, not benefiting from them! Ezekiel then brings in a new element that he may have derived from Jeremiah 23:5: God himself will become the shepherd of his people. In this way Ezekiel combines Jeremiah 23:1–4 with 23:5–6. Ezekiel 34:11–22 contains the promise that the condition of the people will improve when God dismisses the wicked human shepherds and takes control himself. In particular God promises his people security (verses 25, 27, 28) and enough food. These wonderful promises first and foremost pertain to the return of all Israel from the exile (verse 13). Micah 2:12–13 and 4:6–8 likewise state that God himself will unite the people as a shepherd on their return from the exile. There is, however, a surprising transition in the words of Ezekiel: from 34:23 God suddenly declares that he will appoint another shepherd, his servant David, who is called 'prince' in verse 24; see also Ezekiel 37:24. Here God's promise to David that the latter would be a shepherd over Israel also resounds (2 Samuel 5:2). Of course, the person intended here is not David himself, but a descendant of his, because David lived some four hundred years before Ezekiel. The text here also gets the characteristics of the ideal picture of the future. God promises a restoration of the paradise situation. And the one who will achieve this is the 'David' whom he will appoint.

The last time the theme of the shepherd appears in the Old Testament is in Zechariah 11:4–17, where it again expresses God's judgement on bad leaders. This is an enigmatic passage: God gives his people a good shepherd, but this does not bring a blessing; on the contrary, a conflict arises and the shepherd resigns from his task.

The Synoptic Gospels

Psalm 23 and Ezekiel 34 are never quoted in the New Testament, but these passages are in many different ways present in the background. This once again shows you that a literal quote is not the only indication of the presence of the Old Testament in the New. In the New Testament the terms shepherd and sheep are less frequent than in the Old, but they do occur in Matthew, Mark, and Luke. I start with a few examples of beautiful imagery from Jesus according to Matthew:

> Watch out for false prophets. They come to you in sheep's clothing, but inwardly they are ferocious wolves. (Matthew 7:15)

> I am sending you out like sheep among wolves. Therefore be as shrewd as snakes and as innocent as doves. (Matthew 10:16)

> When the son of Man comes ... he will sit on his glorious throne. All the nations will be gathered before him, and he will separate the people one from another as a shepherd separates the sheep from the goats. He will put the sheep on his right and the goats on his left. (Matthew 25:31–33)

The powerful but sad image of the exhausted sheep without a shepherd in Matthew 9:36 (Mark 6:34), first used by Moses in Numbers 27:17, gains depth when you read it against the backdrop of Ezekiel 34. On the other hand, the image of the shepherd is used positively in Jesus' tale which we call 'the parable of the good shepherd' (Luke 15:1–7). While Jesus criticises the Pharisees and the scribes, he shows God's love at the same time. The image speaks of care for people who have lost their way, and joy when someone returns to God. Jesus does not speak out on the question whether God will act as good shepherd or whether he will take the role upon himself. We might say that God, Jesus, leaders in the church, and also the church as a whole can assume this role. Jesus calls his hearers to take care of each other as shepherds. Even this simple narrative gains much depth for those who read it in the light of the Old Testament background.

John 10

The most important passage about shepherd and sheep in the New Testament is John 10:1–18, a passage both less romantic and much deeper than many think. The Lord Jesus uses two images here, for he calls himself both the door of the sheepfold and the shepherd of the sheep. Yet both images have a similar meaning. Jesus is the good leader, protector, and carer of his followers. Just as Ezekiel strongly criticised the spiritual and political leaders of his time, so Jesus is severely critical of the Jewish leaders in his time, calling them hired hands, mercenaries who abandon the sheep when anything bad happens (verses 12–13), and even thieves and robbers (verses 1, 8, 10). The response of his hearers makes clear that his words hit them hard (verses 19–20, 31–33). It is clear that Jesus applies to himself promises which in the Old Testament applies to the one God. On behalf of the God of Israel he takes care of humankind, for he is God's presence on earth. He brings about the new unity of God's people, in direct fulfilment of Ezekiel 37:21–24:

> I have other sheep that are not of this sheepfold. I must bring them also. They too will listen to my voice, and there shall be one flock and one shepherd. (John 10:16)

This passage suggests that Jesus fulfils all the expectations of the Old Testament. Jesus is both the religious and the 'political' leader of his people. For us these things are often separate, but not in him. What Jesus does for the people according to John 10 even goes beyond the expectations of the Old Testament. Firstly, he gives humanity 'life ... to the full' ('abundantly,' NRSV, John 10:10). Secondly, no one will ever be able to steal the sheep from him (John 10:28). Thirdly, Jesus announces that he will die for the salvation of the sheep: he will give his life for them (John 10:11, 15–18), voluntarily, out of pure love for them. These promises far transcend anything the Old Testament ever says about shepherds. David may have risked his life (1 Samuel 17:34) but he did not die as a result. At the same time, this last promise resolves the tension between the role of God and the role of David's descendant, for Jesus is of course both. The author of Hebrews uses this imagery when he calls the risen Jesus 'the great shepherd of the sheep' (13:20 NRSV).

According to Revelation, Jesus transcends the Old Testament expectations in different ways as well, because Revelation 7:17 contains two new elements. First, that in the future believers will be led to living water like sheep, with the result that no misery whatsoever will be left. Second, that the Lamb – that is Jesus – will herd them like a shepherd (Revelation 14:4). Thus, John mixes the images of Jesus as the Lamb of God and Jesus as the shepherd.

After Jesus

Church leaders in the New Testament are frequently called shepherds, after Jesus; they are also called 'overseers' (Acts 20:28). In Ephesians 4:11 Paul uses the word 'shepherds' (ESV; 'pastors' in the NIV and the NRSV) for particular kind of leaders in the community. The English word 'pastor' renders the Latin word *pastor* which means 'shepherd,' and which is therefore appropriate for use in our churches.

After his resurrection, when Jesus restores the relationship with Peter who had denied him, and gives him a new task, he uses various expressions which of course mean the same thing: 'Feed my lambs,' 'Take care of my sheep,' and 'Feed my sheep' (John 21:15–17). In turn, in his first Letter Peter addresses 'the elders' in the congregation, whom he then calls shepherds of the flock; and he refers to Jesus Christ as 'the Chief Shepherd' (1 Peter 5:1–4). Peter also uses this imagery earlier in the letter, when he addresses the slaves in the congregation and calls Jesus the shepherd of the sheep (1 Peter 2:18, 25). It is worth noticing that to the slaves Peter says things that he could also have said to the rest of the congregation, which indicates that the slaves were fully accepted as members of the church.

That brings us to the church, the sheep. The above has shown that the use of this image in the New Testament is not substantially different from that in the Old. Now as then sheep need guidance – which God provides, often through the good services of other persons. In this way he fulfils the promises of Ezekiel 34:17–22. It is up to us to be willing to be sheep and to follow the shepherd wherever he goes.

Further Reading

Goodfellow, Peter, *Flora and Fauna of the Bible* (Oxford: John Beaufoy, 2015).

Ryken, Leland, James C. Wilhoit and Tremper Longman III (eds), *Dictionary of Biblical Imagery* (Leicester: IVP, 1998).

Chapter 16: Jonah

The main message of the book of Jonah is that God loves not only the Jews but all people. He even loves the cruel Assyrians in Nineveh and gives these people the opportunity to come to faith in him too. The New Testament shows that many Jews had not yet grasped the message of Jonah for they attached too much value to their position as God's chosen people; see for example Luke 15:11–32 and John 8:31–59. A similar attitude may also explain why the first followers of Jesus did not immediately obey his command to go and proclaim the gospel throughout the world (Matthew 28:19–20; Luke 24:47–48; Acts 1:8). The beginning of Acts shows how at first they stayed together in Jerusalem; only from Acts 8 onwards we see them taking reluctant steps to bring the message of Jesus to less familiar territories. At some point in this story someone could have referred to Jonah in order to encourage the apostles to travel into the world. That does not happen, yet the author of Acts does point to some interesting similarities between Jonah and Peter, the first apostle to visit a gentile (Acts 10): both men are sent to the gentiles to proclaim God's word, but both are unwilling to go; both are located in the coastal town of Joppa (Jafo, see also Jonah 1:3; Acts 9:43; 10:5, 8–9, 23); and in both cases God forcefully intervenes to overcome the resistance of his 'servant.'

It is not only Peter who is compared to Jonah in the New Testament, but Jesus himself as well. He himself draws this comparison in Matthew 12:38–41 and Matthew 16:4 (see also Luke 11:29–32). In both situations, the Jewish leaders are asking Jesus for a sign, and both times he refuses the request with reference to Jonah. His sign, his legitimation, will be his resurrection from the dead. Jesus quotes Jonah 2:1 in Matthew 12:40; the only quote from the book of Jonah in the New Testament. The point of comparison is that Jesus, like Jonah, will be dead and buried for three days. Jonah was not literally dead, but inside the big fish he was doomed – and that was how he felt (Jonah 1:17; 2:1–7). According to the modern way of counting, Jesus was not in the tomb for three full days, but people in the East regard part of a day as a whole day, and Jesus was in the tomb for parts of Friday, Saturday, and Sunday. In eastern thinking the parallel is therefore accurate.

At the same time, Jesus also says that he is 'greater' than Jonah (12:41), yet without saying why this is so. In Matthew 12:6, he calls himself 'greater than the temple' and in 12:42 'greater than Solomon.' When you take these three comparisons together, you see that Jesus is more than the priest, the king, and the prophet in Israel.

Jesus' resurrection from the tomb would be a sign for his contemporaries, who were at risk of being even more unbelieving than the inhabitants of Nineveh in Jonah's time. These Ninevites had at least repented in response to Jonah's preaching (Matthew 12:41). The core question in the middle section of the Gospel of Matthew is whether the people of Israel will listen to Jesus during his life or only after his resurrection – or not at all.

When Jesus claims that he 'will be three days and three nights in the heart of the earth' (Matthew 12:40), his words allude to the prayer of Jonah which mentions 'the realm of the dead' and 'the very heart of the seas' (Jonah 2:2–3). These expressions further intensify the connection between Jonah and Jesus.

Back to Peter. A little later in Matthew we read that Jesus addresses his disciple as 'Simon son of Jonah' (16:17–18). It is no coincidence that Jesus alludes to the fact that Peter's father was called Jonah. His words seem like a prophecy of the events in Acts 10. Jesus continues by saying that 'the gates of Hades (hell, ESV) will not overcome' the church (Matthew 16:18). It appears that these words also echo Jonah 2, the part of the book known as 'the psalm of Jonah,' in which the prophet describes his stay in the fish as a journey to the empire of death:

> From deep in the realm of the dead I called for help (Jonah 2:2 NIV)

> I went down to the land whose bars closed upon me for ever; yet you brought up my life from the Pit. (Jonah 2:6 NRSV)

Because Jesus vicariously ended up in the realm of the dead, his church – which is built on the work of Peter son of Jonah – will be safe from the dangers that threatened Jonah.

After we have seen how Jesus and the evangelist Matthew use the book of Jonah, we can perhaps also understand more of Matthew

27:52–53. This brief description of the resurrection of 'many holy people who had died' does not occur in the other Gospels. Matthew probably tells about it because this event shows him and us that although Jesus – like Jonah – descended 'in the realm of the dead' (Jonah 2:2; Matthew 12:40), 'the gates of Hades' did not really 'overcome' him (Matthew 16:18). Even in that unlikely place he displayed his power, so the church will not be overwhelmed by it either!

Two comments in conclusion. The first is that with Jonah you see the same thing as with Noah and David. The New Testament does not set up the person of Jonah as an example for us. There is no suggestion that someone was better than they really were. Instead, certain aspects of God's great deeds to that person are seen as a prefiguration of what God would do again later in Jesus and in his church.

The second is that you might think that Jonah 1:11–15 resounds in John 11:50. Both passages contain the same thought: an innocent person is sacrificed, killed, for the benefit of the larger group, so that this group will be saved. However, this line of thought is not unique to the Bible. It occurred and still occurs in many places. Pagan religions know the idea that humans should kill someone to placate the gods and in modern films heroes also die in order to save their friends. So this is a good idea but it is not specifically Jewish or Christian. Even the fact that the victims may volunteer to be killed has many parallels outside the Scriptures.

Further Reading

Inkelaar, Harm-Jan, Sermon on 31 December 2017 in the Protestant Church of Oud Gastel, NL.

Lalleman, Pieter J., *In the Power of the Resurrection. Studies on the Book of Acts* (London: Faithbuilders, 2019).

McLay, R. Timothy, *The Use of the Septuagint in New Testament Research* (Grand Rapids: Eerdmans, 2003).

Chapter 17: The River

The theme of the river is that of a great promise of blessings. It appears in many places in the Bible, from the first to the last book. It is a striking refrain because it is not a messianic theme, and yet it speaks to us about the blessings of God. In a number of places this theme shows progression from small to large: the river which begins as a small stream soon becomes deep and wide.

Genesis

The river is first mentioned in Genesis 2:10–14:

> A river watering the garden flowed from Eden; from there it was separated into four headwaters. The name of the first is the Pishon; it winds through the entire land of Havilah … The name of the second river is the Gihon; it winds through the entire land of Cush. The name of the third river is the Tigris; it runs along the east side of Ashur. And the fourth river is the Euphrates.

The details in these verses are not easy to comprehend, but you don't have to understand everything to grasp the meaning. We know the Tigris and the Euphrates, but not the Pishon or the Gihon. However, you can keep your atlas closed because you will not find the situation as described in Genesis in there. People who do not take Genesis 1–11 literally would not expect so anyway; and those who do take Genesis 1–11 literally think that the paradise was destroyed and the whole appearance of the earth changed by the flood (Genesis 6–9). This passage says that in the paradise situation the river of God provided water to the whole earth. The ideal world of the beginning, which we call paradise, was a garden with abundant water. The one river had four headwaters because four is the number which symbolises the earth, for example in the expression 'the four corners of the earth' (Isaiah 11:12 NRSV; Revelation 7:1; 20:8).

God gives abundance and his word uses the image of an abundant river to evoke this. That is the more remarkable because the land of Israel does not have any large rivers. The River Jordan is relatively small, and so Israel is largely dependent on rainfall for its fertility. (Remarkably, this insight is already expressed in Deuteronomy 11:10–11.) The Israelites may have looked enviously to the neighbouring countries with their large rivers the Nile, Euphrates, and Tigris. But Genesis looks back to the beginning, suggesting that even the neighbouring countries of Israel are currently in a situation that is only a shadow of the original good creation. The world is waiting for God's restoration.

The Psalms

As I said, Israel does not have large rivers, and the city of Jerusalem lies on a few mountain tops where only a spring provides fresh water. And yet you read expressions like the following:

> There is a river whose streams make glad the city of God, the holy place where the Most High dwells. (Psalm 46:4)

> You care for the land and water it; you enrich it abundantly. The streams of God are filled with water to provide the people with corn. (Psalm 65:9)

Taken literally, these verses are incorrect. They contain poetic and prophetic language. The singers envisage the great river of God which will one day provide the land with abundant water. In the case of Psalm 65 this river might be the Jordan, but Psalm 46 is absolutely prophetic as it does not in any way reflect the reality in the lifetime of the poet. He is looking forward to God's future!

Ezekiel 47

The most elaborate description of the river of God occurs in Ezekiel 47:1–12. Ezekiel sees this vision while he is in exile in Babylon, hence far from the land of Israel. God had said that the land had been contaminated by the sin of the people (see, for example, Ezekiel 36:17–18) and he had therefore allowed the destruction of the temple in Jerusalem. And yet there is a future for Israel. This passage tells us the following things about the river: its origin (verses 1–2), its enormous size (verses 3–5), and its positive effect on the land (verses 6–12). The 'man' is the angel who shows Ezekiel round. Ezekiel sees a small stream of water coming from the temple in Jerusalem, trickling from under the altar and flowing eastward, towards Jericho and the Dead Sea. In the real world this is where the Mount of Olives and a few other mountains are located. Water cannot flow upwards, but in the prophet's vision that does not play a role, for this is God's wondrous river.

Before you think of the estuaries of large rivers like the Thames, the Severn, or the Mississippi, just imagine the insignificant beginnings of an ordinary river. For miles the nascent stream is small, barely visible in the grass, and sometimes it even seems to disappear completely. Only a long way downstream does it take on any significance. Often there are tributaries that provide an increase in the amount of water. Ezekiel's river is very different! The small stream rapidly becomes deeper and wider, and after only a few miles the prophet no longer dares to walk through it. In a miraculous way a powerful, unsurpassable river emerges, which then flows into the Dead Sea. In an instant the poisonous water of that large lake, saturated with salt and minerals, becomes sweet and healthy. What the River Jordan (which also empties into the Dead Sea) never managed to do, will be done by this river. There will be abundant life in the Dead Sea, and as many species of fish as in the Great Sea (verse 10 NRSV; this is the Mediterranean Sea, as the NIV explains, for which the Israelites had great awe). On the banks of the river, fruit trees begin to grow, very special species of trees which bear fruit every month without ever resting in the winter. These trees are very useful because they carry both edible fruits and medicinal leaves. If you hear the echo of the tree of life in Genesis 2 and 3, you have listened well.

Ezekiel 47:11 contains a striking detail. A small part of the water remains salty. Is God unable to make *everything* new? Of course not! The prophet is probably mindful of the useful properties of salt, which is antiseptic, suitable to conserve food, and an important flavouring. So it is by his grace that God leaves some salt on the edges of the new freshwater lake.

This vision is one of the most powerful expressions of hope in the Old Testament. God himself will cleanse and renew the land! It is clear that this prophecy has not yet been fulfilled, and given the supernatural elements it will only be fulfilled on the new earth. This expectation is also reflected in Revelation. The meaning is that God will give blessing from the place where he is present, despite the present miserable situation. For Ezekiel, this place of God's presence is Jerusalem. Despite the fact that they are currently in exile, there is still a future, and even a future of abundance, for God's people – even in a city that is not at the banks of a river at all!

After the Exile

The images that Ezekiel sees are primarily concerned with the wilderness of Judah, where centuries later John the Baptist and Jesus would baptise people, thus making the promise of new life visible. But baptism is not the fulfilment of Ezekiel's words. According to Ezekiel, it is the Dead Sea that is made alive, traditionally the place where the cities of Sodom and Gomorrah were situated, which were once destroyed by God because of their sins. Even for that toxic region there is the possibility of new life.

Ezekiel thus looks forward to the renewal and cleansing of the land after the exile. He brings a promise to those who are in exile at that time, but also to the generation that will return. Yet, in reality, after the exile the situation in Israel was hardly better than before. The prophet expected that the curse which lies upon the earth would be taken away. Paul expressed the same hope in other words in Romans 8:18–25, but these expectations have not yet come true. Only in the future will the earth be transformed. Only then will holiness permeate and renew the ordinary.

Zechariah and Joel

Other prophets also use the theme of God's river, likely in dependence on Ezekiel. Some time after Ezekiel his words resound in Zechariah 13:1, while Zechariah 14:4, 8 expresses a variation in the expectation: the water that rises in Jerusalem will be able to flow eastwards because the Mount of Olives will make way for it, and at the same time a river will flow westwards as well, so to the Mediterranean Sea. The theme also appears in Joel, a prophet whose work is difficult to date:

> Then you will know that I, the LORD your God, dwell in Zion, my holy hill. Jerusalem will be holy; never again will foreigners invade her. In that day the mountains will drip new wine, and the hills will flow with milk; all the ravines of Judah will run with water. A fountain will flow out of the LORD's house and will water the valley of acacias. (Joel 3:17–18)

Here too, the expectation of abundance is connected with Jerusalem. From this city a river will spread blessings in the days of the Messiah. Israel expects its renewal from God.

In countries which often have more water and precipitation than they can handle this theme may not appeal to the senses. But you can imagine that in Israel, a country with many deserts and often extended periods of drought, it was particularly appealing. At last, in the days of the Messiah there will always be plenty of fresh water! And even people in the West know that humans die sooner from thirst than from hunger or any other shortage.

John

When you read literally, you don't notice the theme of the river in the Gospel of John. But you do hear that several times the Lord Jesus relates God's gift of abundant water to himself. At the same time, he also spiritualises the theme. He sits down at a well and offers a Samaritan woman living water (John 4:1–26, especially verse 14); the woman is struggling to understand that Jesus is not talking about physical water. Later he makes the same offer to all his fellow country people during a festival at the temple in Jerusalem (John 7:37–39). And John 10:10 contains the well-known words of Jesus that he came to give humanity life in all its fullness.

In Jesus the Old Testament expectation thus finds its initial fulfilment, but it is clearly not yet the complete fulfilment. However wonderful it is, the availability of living water is still limited to individuals. What is very clear, though, is that it is always about gifts of grace. All Jesus asks of the Samaritan woman and his fellow countrymen is that they come with an empty bucket, empty hands, which *he* wants to fill. The living water is his gift to the people.

The coming of Christ thus brought a personal, partial, and spiritual fulfilment of the promise of the river. Romans 8:18–25 says clearly that the world as a whole does not yet share in the abundant water. That fulfilment is yet to come.

Revelation

In Revelation 21–22 the prophet John offers a description of the new heaven and the new earth that God will give, and this is where the New Jerusalem will be centre stage. In the middle of this kaleidoscope of images it says:

> Then the angel showed me the river of the water of life, as clear as crystal, flowing from the throne of God and of the Lamb down the middle of the great street of the city. On each side of the river stood the tree of life, bearing twelve crops of fruit, yielding its fruit every month. And the leaves of the tree are for the healing of the nations. No longer will there be any curse. The throne of God and of the Lamb will be in the city, and his servants will serve him. They will see his face, and his name will be on their foreheads. (Revelation 22:1–4)

The way in which John handles this wonderful material is almost sloppy. He describes briefly what he sees without bothering to explain it. The reader who does not know that John's vision is based on Ezekiel is likely to miss the connection, because John does not point it out. This is how John almost always deals with the Old Testament. After a few sentences his attention is already drawn by the next marvellous element of his vision: the throne of God and of the lamb. Various elements of Revelation 21–22 are taken from Ezekiel 40–48 as a whole, although John has just contradicted the key element of these chapters. For whereas Ezekiel had provided a detailed description of a new temple, John simply but decidedly writes about the new city of Jerusalem that he did not see a temple in it, 'because the Lord God Almighty and the Lamb are its temple' (21:22).

In Ezekiel's vision the river originates from the throne of God in the temple; John mentions 'the throne of God and of the Lamb' (22:3b), thus indicating that the Lamb of God, the Lord Jesus, is God just as much as God the Father, that he sits with him on one throne, and that together with him he is the source of blessing. This one throne provides the abundant, life-giving water for the new world. Have you noticed that there is no separation any more between literal (ecological) and spiritual renewal? God will lift the curse that lies over the earth!

Finally

The theme of the river thus involves various aspects of blessing:

- It is all by grace, humans add nothing to it.

- It is about the renewal of humanity and of the world.

- God is a God of life and abundance.

- God can turn very little into very much. (We also see this when Jesus feeds thousands of people using a small amount of bread and fish.)

- In Jesus there is already a fulfilment, but there is more to come.

This is a wonderful promise, not just for the future but for our lives here and now! For this reason the theme of the river fits well in the season of Advent. We are looking forward to what God is going to do. Jesus Christ has already come and he has finished his work on the cross and in his resurrection, but we are looking forward to the fullness of what God wants to give us. The new world will have abundance because he will be there!

Further Reading

Bauckham, Richard, *The Testimony of the Beloved Disciple* (Grand Rapids: Baker, 2007) 278–280.

Chapter 18: The Numbers Three, Four, Seven, and Twelve

Not all numbers in the Bible have a deeper meaning and it would be unwise to attach meaning to each number. This chapter does not discuss the symbolic significance of numbers in general, but only some numbers in the New Testament whose symbolic significance can be explained by the influence of the Scriptures of Israel.

Twelve

Jesus had a large number of followers, as you can see, for example, in Luke 6:17; 8:1–3 and 24:18. Yet the four Gospels clearly say that he regarded only twelve of them as his special disciples (for example, Luke 6:13). Jesus will have chosen this number deliberately, because the people of Israel consisted of twelve tribes, the descendants of the twelve sons of Jacob. This number twelve occurs for the first time in Genesis 35:22 and 42:13. Because there were twelve tribes, the number twelve became a symbol of God's people in the Old Testament (for example, 1 Kings 18:31), and the same was true for multiples of it such as 24, 12,000 and 144,000 (for example, 2 Samuel 17:1). On occasions Israel therefore positioned twelve memorials (Exodus 24:4 and Joshua 4:8–9) or built twelve copies of something (1 Kings 7:25; 10:20). This symbolism also suggests that the figure of 24,000 victims in Numbers 25:9 indicates that the entire nation was severely punished. Luke 22:30 establishes the relationship between the twelve tribes of Israel and the disciples of Jesus, and so this verse shows the connection between the use of the number twelve in the Old and the New Testament. The meaning of Jesus' decision to have just twelve disciples would be that God was restoring the people of Israel by means of this group of followers. They did not come from twelve different tribes, but they represented the people as a whole. Because there were twelve disciples, twelve baskets of bread were collected (Luke 9:17).

The followers of Jesus understood this symbolism and therefore they soon set out to choose a successor for Judas, to bring the number of apostles back to twelve (Acts 1:21–26), even though I think it would have been better for them to wait because God had destined Paul for this place.

124

The New Testament letters rarely use the number twelve, but James begins his letter saying that he is sending it 'To the twelve tribes scattered among the nations' (James 1:1). Because James does not only write to Jewish believers, we know that he uses the number twelve as a symbol for the world-wide community of believers.

In the book of Revelation, the number twelve plays a major role again. In Revelation 7, John first hears about a group of 144,000 (= twelve times 12,000) believers, and subsequently he sees 'a multitude that no one could count' (verse 9). In my opinion, this is the same group of people, and it is therefore unhelpful that most modern translations have divided Revelation 7 into two sections with different headers (7:1–8 and 7:9–17).[7] The multitude symbolises the followers of Jesus, the new people of God. Initially it was largely made up of Israelites and could still be counted, but at a time that was still future for John it would become innumerable. (In the time when John wrote Revelation there were still less than 100,000 followers of Jesus. Revelation 7 is therefore a great promise!) This vision of John also shows that in later times the number twelve lost its literal meaning due to the unlimited growth of the church of Christ.

Yet the symbolic value remained, and it helps to understand that the 'crown of twelve stars' on the head of the woman in Revelation 12:1 means that she represents the people of Israel, the people from which the Messiah was born. And in Revelation 21:12–21 the number twelve dominates the dimensions of the New Jerusalem, blurring the boundaries between people and buildings. In this vision of the future, the twelve tribes of Israel (verse 12) and the twelve apostles (verse 14) are once again closely connected; this means that the New Jerusalem will be the abode of all who believe in Jesus, from Jews and gentiles. John does not explain who the 24 (= twice twelve) elders are whom he sees in heaven (from Revelation 4:4 to 19:4), but in the light of the preceding discussion, they must be the representatives of God's people from the eras of the old and new covenants. The number twelve thus always signifies the people of God.

---

[7] See Pieter J. Lalleman, *The Lion and the Lamb. Studies on the Book of Revelation* (London: Faithbuilders, 2016), chapter 6.

Three

Because of our faith in the Holy Trinity, for Christians the number three represents God, while four is a symbol of the earth. Yet in the Old Testament, this meaning of the number three is very rare. The number is related to God in Exodus 23:14, where the LORD ordains three festivals per year, but that is not a big harvest. It happens from time to time that three things are mentioned in connection with God, without the number being given explicitly. For example, the people of Israel are instructed to love God with all their heart, soul, and strength (Deuteronomy 6:5) and the blessing of the high priest has three clauses (Numbers 6:22–27). In Isaiah 6:3, the prophet hears how the angels are calling to each other 'Holy, holy, holy is the LORD Almighty.' This threefold call is probably an allusion to God's Trinity. If so, you can say that God's revelation in the New Testament clarifies the Old. The same 'three times sacred' (*trishagion*) can also be heard in Revelation 4:8, of course based on Isaiah 6.

Some people also explain the number of three visitors to Abraham in Genesis 18 as a reference to the Trinity, but later in the story it becomes clear that we are dealing with the LORD and two angels. Most of the times everyday numbers like three and four occur in the Bible, they have no deeper meaning.

The fact that certain things happen three times would indicate that they are important and undoubted, as in Numbers 22:21–33; 1 Samuel 3:1–9; 1 Kings 18:34 and in the New Testament in Mark 14:32–42 and 14:66–72. But these are not cases of influence of the Old Testament on the New, because this motif is also found in much other literature.

Four

It is typical of the Old Testament that groups of four things or four phrases often indicate generality and universality. Thus there were four rivers on the original earth (Genesis 2:10–14) and the earth has four ends or corners (Isaiah 11:12). In addition, there are four cardinal directions, which are mentioned in Genesis 13:14 and alluded to in Ezekiel 37:9. For this reason the references to four (winds) in Matthew 24:31, Revelation 7:1, and Revelation 20:8 probably depend on the Old Testament. In Ezekiel the entire living creation is represented by four living beings, which occur again in Revelation 4:6–8. The use of the number four in Revelation is based on Ezekiel and on Daniel, but it is the description of the tabernacle in Exodus 25–39 which provides the material for the description of the New Jerusalem in Revelation 21.

Much more often you encounter four things or phrases without the number four being explicitly mentioned, as in Isaiah 58:6–8 and in Revelation 5:9 ('tribe, language, people and nation'), 5:13; 7:9; 10:11 ('peoples, nations, languages and kings'); 11:9; 13:7; 14:6; and 17:15 ('peoples, multitudes, nations and languages'). In all these cases, the worldview of the Old Testament has influenced that of the New.

Seven

The number seven represents completeness, just like twelve, but seven is more about the completeness of what God is doing. To God's people the seven days of creation in Genesis 1:1 to 2:3 are the model for all God's work. As a result, later in Genesis seven again stands for fullness and completeness, both positively (7:2–4; 33:3) and negatively (4:15, 24). This use of the number occurs throughout the Old Testament, positively for example in Joshua 6:4; 2 Kings 5:10, 14; and Psalm 119:164, negatively for example in Leviticus 26:18, 21, 28.

This symbolism influences the New Testament. Moreover, Israel is the only nation of which we know for sure that it had a week of seven days, whereas the number seven was less important to other peoples.

Peter asks Jesus whether he has to forgive someone seven times and in reply he receives the symbolic number of 'seventy times seven' (Matthew 18:21–22), probably with a nod to the revenge of Lamech (Genesis 4:24). The number seven plays a role in the word game between Jesus and the Sadducees (Matthew 22:25–28), but also in Jesus' warning against evil spirits (Luke 11:24–26). After Pentecost, the apostles could have appointed six or eight wise helpers, but they chose the beautiful number of seven (Acts 6:1–6). The author of Hebrews uses exactly seven quotations from Scripture (1:5–14), probably with the aim to make it perfectly clear that Jesus is above the angels.

The book of Revelation is full of groups of seven, sometimes numbered but sometimes unnumbered. A simple example is that John sends the book to seven local churches; there were more churches in that part of the world, but Jesus chose seven to represent the fullness of the world church. In this way Revelation suggests that God will bring his work in the world to completion. Was John aware that the number seven also plays a major role in Genesis 1:1 to 2:3? In Hebrew, Genesis 1:1 has seven words, 1:2 has fourteen and 2:1–3 five times seven (35). The word God occurs 35 times, the words heaven and earth 21 times each. Consciously or unconsciously, Revelation is very close to Genesis 1.

Further Reading

Pop, F.J., *Bijbelse woorden en hun geheim* (Den Haag: Boekencentrum, 1964).

Ryken, Leland, James C. Wilhoit and Tremper Longman III (eds), *Dictionary of Biblical Imagery* (Leicester: IVP, 1998).

Chapter 19: John the Baptist

John the Baptist is a colourful person who evokes recognition in many people: his message is radical and his death dramatic. You understand him even better when you see how the four evangelists describe him against the background of the Old Testament. Incidentally, the name John (Joannes, Hebrew *Yeho-chanan*) means 'The LORD is merciful.'

His Parents

Luke tells us most about the background of John. In the story of his parents, Zechariah and Elizabeth, you already hear many echoes of the Old Testament:

Parents of John in Luke 1	Old Testament element
The man is introduced first, then the woman, verse 5	Like Elkanah before Hannah, 1 Samuel 1:1–2
Obedient to the commandments, verse 6	As instructed in Deuteronomy 4:40; as done by Abraham, Genesis 26:5
At age yet childless, verses 7, 18	Like Abraham and Sara, Genesis 18:11
The woman is barren, verse 7	Like Sara, Genesis 11:30
An angel appears during the sacrifice, verses 10–11	As the angel Gabriel appeared to Daniel at the time of the sacrifice (9:21)
'Your wife will bear you a son, and you must call him…,' verse 13	As with Isaac, Genesis 17:19
The father asks how he can be sure of the promise, verse 18	Like Abraham, Genesis 15:8
The mother declares that she is no longer ashamed, verse 25	Like Rachel, Genesis 30:23

The child is circumcised, verse 59	As instructed to Abraham, Genesis 17:12, and like all his descendants, Leviticus 12:3
The father sings a hymn after the birth, verses 67–79	Like Samuel's mother, 1 Samuel 2:1–10

All this shows that, although God is going to do something new, the coming of John – and also that of Jesus – is not detached from what has preceded. The history of God and the people of Israel is continuing. The story of John's birth as a whole (Luke 1:11–20) has the same form as the stories about the appearance of God in Genesis 15:1–4 and the appearance of the angel in Judges 13. These stories – and hereafter the announcement of Jesus' birth in Luke 1:26–38 – have five elements:

- Appearance

- Human amazement

- Message

- Human objections

- Reassurance and sign

God is doing something new, but it is presented in well-known forms.

Samuel

We just saw that the portrait of Zechariah and Elizabeth largely consists of a compilation of thoughts and texts from the Old Testament. On the other hand, the portrait of their son John is of one piece, because he looks remarkably like the prophet Samuel. Like Elizabeth, Samuel's mother was initially childless, and her pregnancy too was linked to a visit to God's sanctuary (1 Samuel 1). Both new-born prophets get their name from their mother (1 Samuel 1:20 and Luke 1:60). They are dedicated to God from birth and therefore not allowed to drink alcohol or cut their hair (1 Samuel 1:11 Septuagint and Luke 1:15); this shows that they were Nazarites, people about whom you read in Numbers 6. Their respective ministries are the beginning of a great time for Israel. God is going to do something new!

The story contains one striking contrast with the Old Testament, however. There we twice see two mothers who are rivals: Leah and Rachel in Genesis 30, and Peninnah and Hannah in 1 Samuel 1. And twice things do indeed get tricky! The meeting between Elizabeth and Mary in Luke 1:39–56, on the other hand, is a happy occasion for two joyful, pregnant women.

Elijah

The similarities between John and Samuel are obvious, even though Samuel is not mentioned by name. On the contrary, another important prophet, Elijah, is mentioned by name. Indeed, the angel says to Zechariah about John:

> And he will go on before the Lord, in the spirit and power of Elijah, to turn the hearts of the parents to their children and the disobedient to the wisdom of the righteous. (Luke 1:17a)

The angel does not say that he is taking these words almost verbatim from the last verse of the book of Malachi; but note how he has changed the very last words of the prophet. Malachi had quoted God as follows:

> See, I will send the prophet Elijah to you before that great and dreadful day of the LORD comes. He will turn the hearts of the parents to their children, and the hearts of the children to their parents; or else I will come and strike the land with total destruction. (Malachi 4:5–6)

The last words in Malachi contain a serious threat, but the angel instead says to Zechariah that John will:

> Make ready a people prepared for the Lord. (Luke 1:17b)

This positive twist is striking. Malachi expected that the advent of 'Elijah' would bring God's judgement, but the angel now announces the possibility of repentance. This possibility arises because John will act 'in the spirit and power of Elijah.' Like Elijah brought a sea-change in the dark period of Ahab and Jezebel, so John will redirect the people to God. John is therefore the expected Elijah, the messenger who appears before (the Son of) God himself appears.

Luke does not mention any further similarities between the great prophet Elijah and John, but Matthew does. According to him, John's outer appearance resembles that of Elijah, because they are both hairy men with leather belts (2 Kings 1:8; Matthew 3:4). A third agreement is that both Elijah and John are hotly persecuted by a wicked woman: Jezebel in the case of Elijah (especially 1 Kings 19:2), and Herodias in the case of John (Matthew 14:1–11). The reason for their persecution is that both prophets are quite blunt. Elijah mainly focuses on Ahab and Jezebel (1 Kings 18:18; 21:20–26), John addresses Herod and Herodias regarding their adulterous relationship.

Matthew dedicates a long section to the doubts of John (11:2–6) and what the people should think about him (11:7–15). Not many prophets were known for the fact that they had struggled with doubt, but Elijah (1 Kings 19:3–4, 10, 14) and Jeremiah (for example 20:7–18) were. Unfortunately, John is in good company! Jesus concludes the conversation in Matthew 11 by saying that John is the promised Elijah (verse 14), which of course reflects the expectation of Malachi 4:5- 6. In the middle of the passage (verse 10), Jesus quotes the beginning of Malachi 3. This passage reads in full:

> 'I will send my messenger, who will prepare the way before me. Then suddenly the Lord you are seeking will come to his temple; the messenger of the covenant, whom you desire, will come,' says the LORD Almighty. But who can endure the day of his coming? Who can stand when he appears? For he will be like a refiner's fire or a launderer's soap. (Malachi 3:1–2)

Jesus only quotes the beginning, which seems to pertain to John the Baptist. He does not discuss the subsequent words which refer to himself as 'the Lord.' In this way the New Testament pulls apart things which appear together in Malachi. John, the messenger of the Lord, is not himself the Lord.

Following the glorification of Jesus on the mountain, at which Elijah and Moses also appear (Matthew 17:1–8), Matthew renders another conversation between Jesus and his disciples, in which he again calls John the new Elijah (17:9–13). Thus Jesus repeats that the promises of Malachi 3 were being fulfilled in John. A new element in this conversation is that Jesus will also have to suffer, just as Elijah (and

Jeremiah) and John suffered. It is possible that Jesus' contemporaries rejected him as Messiah because they thought that the Old Testament Elijah would precede the Messiah; Jesus tries to help them not to take the words of Malachi too literally: the promised Elijah, that was John the Baptist, so nothing would prevent the coming of the Messiah.

John's Ministry

Matthew and Luke each have a long passage on John's activities, both of which have chapter number 3. Here the words of the prophet John receive more attention than the fact that he baptises people. In Luke 3, verses 11–15 are extra in comparison to Matthew, and these verses deal with a subject which is also discussed in 1 Samuel 8:11–18: the oppressive power of the government in the areas of daily life, taxes, and warfare. John's words remind us of Samuel's concern about possible oppression by the government. Samuel had prepared the way for King David in the same way as John prepared the coming of Jesus.

By calling the people to repentance (Luke 3:3) John stands in the tradition of the prophets, although they used diverse words for it; think of Isaiah 55:7; Jeremiah 36:3; Ezekiel 33:7–9; and Hosea 5. John claims that the result of true repentance must be the bearing of fruit (Luke 3:8), which is another thought from his Hebrew Bible (2 Kings 19:29–30; Psalm 1:3; Proverbs 11:30; Jeremiah 17:8).

Isaiah 40 Fulfilled

To characterise John, you might say that he prepared the way for Jesus. This role of messenger was already foreseen in the Hebrew Bible. Before God would come, before the 'Day of the LORD,' a subordinate would get the people ready. He is mentioned in Isaiah 40:1–11 and you hear his voice in Isaiah 62. Isaiah primarily addresses the people of Israel who are in exile, to prepare them for their return to their country. This return journey will go through the wilderness. The evangelists, who all quote Isaiah 40, think that Isaiah's words find a second fulfilment in John's action hundreds of years later (Mark 1:3; Matthew 3:3; Luke 1:76; 3:4–6; John 1:23). Careful reading shows that Isaiah 40 is more about God's coming to his people than about movements of the people. The messenger asks the people to make way for God. In antiquity, such messengers would arrive before a visit from the king himself, especially to get the people to improve the roads. God's coming is announced – and he sends his son Jesus.

John the Baptist uses many ideas from Isaiah 40, but not verse 5, which says: 'And the glory of the LORD will be revealed and all people will see it together.' John apparently knows that Jesus' glory will only be fully visible after Easter and at his second coming. Again, the fulfilment of an Old Testament expectation is pulled apart: part of it is already fulfilled, part is still open.

By the way, John not only speaks *about* the wilderness, but he also speaks *in* the wilderness (Matthew 3:1; 11:7; Mark 1:4), the place where God first revealed himself to Israel (Exodus 19:1; Deuteronomy 1:31; 2:7; Hosea 13:5) and where, according to Ezekiel 20:33–37, he will once again deal with them. Isaiah 52:7–12, another passage about the messenger, also resounds in John's words. John baptises people who repent and are ready to receive the Messiah. The practice of baptism does not yet occur in the Old Testament.

The recent Christian Standard Bible prints Old Testament quotations in bold type. Yet not a single word in Luke 1 is in bold, although we have just seen that this chapter is awash with allusions to the Old Testament. Luke's use of Scripture is much more sophisticated than the use of literal quotations and it remains hidden unless you dig deeper. Absence of quotations does not mean absence of (profound) Old Testament influence!

Further Reading

Bauckham, Richard, *Gospel Women. Studies of the named women in the Gospels* (London, New York: T&T Clark, 2002).

Heer, Jos de, *Lucas/Acta 1: De oorsprongen van het geloof* (Zoetermeer: Meinema, 2006).

Riet, Peter van 't, *Lukas versus Matthew* (Kampen: Kok, 2005).

Chapter 20: The 'I Am' Sayings of Jesus

It is the evangelist John who gives us seven sayings of Jesus in which he says, 'I am....' The number seven, like much in the Gospel to John, is certainly symbolic. We usually read these sayings as beautiful symbols, and we gladly believe that Jesus is the good shepherd and the living bread; but there is much more to these sayings. Take a look at the following list:

'I am' sayings with a complement[8]	John	OT source
I am the bread of life/the living bread	6:35, 48, 51	Exodus 16:13–31
I am the light of the world	8:12	Isaiah 60:1–5
I am the gate for the sheep	10:7, 9	Ezekiel 34
I am the good shepherd	10:11, 14	Psalm 23
I am the resurrection and the life	11:25	Daniel 12:1–4
I am the way, the truth and the life	14:6	Proverbs 4:1–19
I am the (true) vine	15:1, 5	Psalm 80:9–18

You see that everything Jesus says about himself along these lines is directly based on the Old Testament. John shows how Jesus fulfils the old covenant, even taking the place of God as the shepherd of Israel. But of course, Jesus is not God's competitor – he can say these things precisely because he is one with the Father (John 10:30). For this reason, Jesus' 'I am' sayings should not primarily be interpreted as timeless and individualistic aphorisms, but in the context of salvation history. They tell us who Jesus is in the great plan of God for Israel and the nations. Only afterwards can we also apply them to ourselves. To give an example, Jesus is the good shepherd of his people Israel, a much better shepherd than previous leaders like the priestly class, and he also has other sheep than the Jewish people (10:16). In that great

---

[8] 'With a complement' means that there is another word or phrase after 'I am.' The 'I am' sayings without a complement will be discussed below.

herd, I may also find my place, but things do not start with me and do not revolve around me.

Vine

In the last of the seven 'I am' sayings Jesus claims that he is the representative of the people of Israel, because in prophetic passages of the Old Testament the vine symbolises the people of Israel (Isaiah 5:1–7; 27:2–6; Jeremiah 2:21; 8:13; Ezekiel 15; 17:1–10). However, the list above does not refer to the prophets, but to Psalm 80. This prophetic psalm not only contains a comprehensive allegory in which the vine represents Israel but also, at the end, a verse in which salvation is expected from someone called 'son of man':

> Let your hand rest on the man at your right hand, the son of man you have raised up for yourself. (Psalm 80:17)

Here 'the man at your right hand' is the king of Israel, and the psalm prays blessing over him. Christians are allowed to read the psalm as a prayer for Jesus, who both is God's vine and the saviour of the vine, Israel.

Of the seven sayings, 'I am the true vine' says most about Jesus' followers, for he immediately adds 'you are the branches' (John 15:5). In Jesus' teaching in John 15 attention gradually shifts away from himself as the vine to his followers, the branches. Verses 16 and 17 refer to two very important tasks of Jesus' followers: bearing fruit – that is, evangelism, mission, proclamation – and loving each other. This again matches Psalm 80, where the verses 10–11 already tell about the blessing that the vine spreads everywhere:

> The mountains were covered with its shade, the mighty cedars with its branches. Its branches reached as far as the Sea, its shoots as far as the River.

Free-standing 'I Am' Sayings

In addition to the seven 'I am' sayings with a complement, John's Gospel also contains seven 'I am' sayings of Jesus where these words are not followed by such a predicate and which are therefore called 'absolute' or 'free-standing' I am sayings. They occur in John 4:26; 6:20;

8:24, 28, 58; 13:19; and 18:5–8. That there are seven again is not a coincidence, for seven is the number of completeness and John loves numerical symbolism. These sayings are inconspicuous because they are very short: in the English rendering Jesus simply says, 'I am,' 'I am he' or 'It is I'; but they are not therefore less important than the previous group. And like them these sayings are deeply rooted in the Old Testament. In Exodus 3:13–15 God introduces himself as 'I am' and that is the name Israel should use to address him:

> Moses said to God, 'Suppose I go to the Israelites and say to them, "The God of your fathers has sent me to you," and they ask me, "What is his name?" Then what shall I tell them?' God said to Moses, 'I AM WHO I AM. This is what you are to say to the Israelites: "I AM has sent me to you."' God also said to Moses, 'Say to the Israelites, "The LORD, the God of your fathers – the God of Abraham, the God of Isaac and the God of Jacob – has sent me to you." 'This is my name for ever, the name you shall call me from generation to generation.'

The Hebrew text of Exodus 3 has YHWH, the Name of God that we can pronounce as Yahweh, but which is rendered as LORD in our translations.[9] In Greek, this name of God is translated as *egō eimi* and these are exactly the words that Jesus uses in these seven places in John. In other words, Jesus actually says 'I am,' 'I will be there,' or 'I am Yahweh, the God of Israel.' And that is a huge claim which no one can simply put aside!

In John 8:58, Jesus uses two words opposite each other, which are also opposites in 1:1–14: 'to be' (Greek *eimi*) and 'to become' (*ginomai*). Human beings and the rest of creation *become*, but Jesus *is*, just like God *is*. Jesus and God are eternal, creatures are not. A literal translation of 8:58 is: 'Very truly I tell you: before Abraham *became*, I *am*.'

In this light we also understand that Jesus' words in John 18:5–8 to the people who come to arrest him are saying much more than just 'I am the one you are seeking.' He again emphatically states that he is God

---

[9] See the explanation in my *Enduring Treasure*, chapter 2. There I also explain that Jehovah is an incorrect rendering of the Name.

himself. This makes clear that Jews and gentiles have come out to capture the Son of God – but they unintentionally pay him homage by falling on the ground in front of him (verse 6).

John 18:9 also illustrates that Jesus is a special person, for John says that Jesus' words were 'fulfilled.' He is referring to Jesus' promise that none of his own would be lost (John 6:39; 10:28–29; 17:12). What kinds of words are 'fulfilled?' Those of the prophets, because they are the words of God himself. Jesus is such a person.

Old Testament

The connection between Jesus and the God of the Old Testament becomes even clearer when you know that not only in Exodus 3, but later in the Old Testament as well, God refers to himself as 'I am' (*egō eimi*). These sayings occur in the Septuagint in Deuteronomy 32:39 and Isaiah 41:4; 43:10–11, 25; 45:18, 22; 46:4; and 51:12. Moreover, Richard Bauckham has rightly noted that there are seven of them! There are similar pronouncements of God in Isaiah 45:5, 6 and 21, but there the Greek words *egō eimi* are not used.

John shows us that Jesus, by adopting God's way of speaking, emphatically equates himself with God. If you want to know who God is, you must – and can – henceforth look to Jesus the Messiah. The full meaning of Yahweh's covenant name also applies to him. Thus, the Old Testament gives indispensable depth to our understanding of Jesus.

Further Reading

Bauckham, Richard, *The Testimony of the Beloved Disciple* (Grand Rapids: Baker Academic, 2007).

Porter, Stanley E., *John, His Gospel, and Jesus. In Pursuit of the Johannine Voice* (Grand Rapids: Eerdmans, 2015).

Chapter 21: Baptism and the Lord's Supper

The New Testament also uses the Old when it discusses the two ordinances of the new covenant, namely baptism and (holy) communion, which is also called the Lord's Supper (see 1 Corinthians 11:20). Even these typical New Testament practices can be better understood when you see their roots in the Old Testament.

Part 1: Baptism

The people who administer baptism in the New Testament are John the Baptist, Jesus and his disciples (John 3:22 and 4:1), and (the leaders of) the first churches. In Old Testament times, people were not yet baptised; instead circumcision was the sign that a person (well, a man) belonged to the people of God. On top of this, in the centuries before the coming of Jesus the Jews had introduced various ritual washings. It is uncertain whether during the first century AD proselytes (persons from other nations who wanted to become Jews) were already baptised, or whether this practice was introduced later, maybe even under the influence of Christian baptism.

For all these reasons it was not easy for the New Testament writers to use the Old Testament when writing about baptism. In the important passage about baptism, Romans 6, Paul nowhere refers to Scripture!

To be sure, the Old Testament does report on the washing of people and things, as in Exodus 30:17–21, but the New Testament does not pick up these passages. Neither is the well-known story about Naaman, who washed himself seven times and was thereby cured (2 Kings 5), associated with baptism in the New Testament. Psalm 51:4, where David asks God to wash away his guilt, does not echo in the New Testament either. Remarkably, even the words of Zechariah 13:1, that 'a fountain will be opened to the house of David and the inhabitants of Jerusalem, to cleanse them from sin and impurity,' are not picked up in the New Testament.

On the other hand, the important church father, Tertullian, interpreted Genesis 1:20 as saying that at the time of the creation the water had to produce living creatures and he stated that likewise the water of baptism will produce life; but he did not take this thought from the New Testament. Other writers from earlier times noted that Joshua brought the people of God through the water of the River Jordan to the promised land, and that Jesus (the same name as Joshua) brings the people of God salvation through the water of baptism; but this parallel is again not found in the New Testament.

One text from the Old Testament that is connected with baptism in the New is Ezekiel 36:25:

> I will sprinkle clean water on you, and you will be clean; I will cleanse you of all your impurities and from all your idols.

These words resound in Hebrews 10:22:

> Let us draw near to God with a sincere heart and with the full assurance that faith brings, having our hearts sprinkled to cleanse us from a guilty conscience and having our bodies washed with pure water.

This is not a quote but an echo of Ezekiel's words. In Hebrews, the cleansing of our hearts, the cleansing of our guilty conscience, and water baptism are taken together as different aspects of the same event. In the verses that follow in Ezekiel (36:26–27), the prophet speaks of the new heart and the new spirit that God gives. The author of Hebrews does not mention these promises but we can surely apply them to ourselves. It is likely that Jesus also has Ezekiel 36:25–27 in mind when telling Nicodemus that he must be born again, namely of water and spirit (John 3:3, 5). Jesus does not give a reference and because his words are at most an echo of Ezekiel, the connection is not certain; but the words of Ezekiel explain well what Jesus means.

When Jesus reproaches Nicodemus that he – a teacher of Israel – does not understand Jesus (verse 10), this suggests that Nicodemus could have known better because what Jesus says is not entirely new. If you then ask how Nicodemus could have known these things, it is reasonable to assume that Jesus bases himself on the Scriptures. In these Scriptures, Ezekiel 36:25–27 is closest to what Jesus is trying to say.

John the Baptist speaks and looks like an Old Testament prophet. Moreover, he calls the people of Israel back to the wilderness

(Matthew 3:1) and makes them go through the waters of the Jordan as at the time of the entry into the land (Matthew 3:6, compare Joshua 3–4). Thus, his work is full of old covenant symbolism which refers to the period of exodus from Egypt, the journey through the wilderness, and the entry into the promised land, as described in the books Exodus, Numbers, and Joshua. John offers the people of God a new beginning, a second chance, and they can join the revival by getting baptised. Matthew and the other evangelists do not explicitly refer to Scripture when they report these things, but the echoes are unmistakeable.

In the New Testament only two Old Testament events are explicitly connected with baptism, namely the flood and the exodus from Egypt. In both cases, the text of Scripture is not taken literally but spiritualised. The literal meaning of the events is not denied, but the writers of the New Testament have discovered a deeper meaning in them.

Peter picks up the story of the flood (Genesis 6–9) in 1 Peter 3:20–21, calling the flood an antitype (NKJV) or prefiguration (NRSV) of baptism. Peter sees the parallel between the flood and Christian baptism in that both bring salvation 'through water' (1 Peter 3:20). The people in the ark went through the water without getting wet; they were saved from and out of the water. In baptism we also go through water; a person disappears head and shoulders in water which symbolises death, depicting that God's grace saves from death. To Peter the water of the flood is thus an antitype of baptism (3:21, where the Greek has the word *antitypos*).

Part 2: 1 Corinthians 10

The difficult passage 1 Corinthians 10:1–6 can form a bridge between our discussions of baptism and the Lord's Supper thanks to the fact that Paul here applies both the passage about the escape through the sea (Exodus 13–14) and the passage about the desert voyage of the people of Israel to both baptism and the Lord's Supper. This is what he writes:

> For I do not want you to be ignorant of the fact, brothers and
> sisters, that our ancestors were all under the cloud and that

they all passed through the sea. They were all baptised into Moses in the cloud and in the sea. They all ate the same spiritual food and drank the same spiritual drink; for they drank from the spiritual rock that accompanied them, and that rock was Christ. Nevertheless, God was not pleased with most of them; their bodies were scattered in the wilderness. Now these things occurred as examples to keep us from setting our hearts on evil things as they did.

The first thing that strikes you here is that Paul addresses his audience in Corinth as descendants of the people of Israel by writing 'our ancestors.' Of course, the Greek and Roman inhabitants of the city of Corinth were not natural descendants of Abraham, Isaac, and Jacob; they only belonged to God's people in a spiritual sense. The second thing that strikes is that Paul presupposes that these new Christians with their pagan background know the biblical stories in some detail. Without much explanation, he points out how these stories apply directly to them. This is the basis for his warning that the church will fail unless it does better than Israel. What exactly went wrong with the Israelites is the subject of the verses that follow (1 Corinthians 10:7–14). They served idols (Exodus 32:1–6; Paul quotes verse 6). Israel had no reason for doing this because God was always very good to them, as Paul emphasizes. God protected them with his cloud (Exodus 13:21; 14:19–20), he led them safely through the sea and he even gave them enough food and drink in the desert.

Paul infuses these blessings with a lasting spiritual meaning by comparing them with baptism and the Lord's Supper. His comparison of the sea with baptism is a bit lame, because the exodus story emphasizes that the Israelites did *not* get wet on their journey through the sea (Exodus 14:22, 29), while the use of water is essential for baptism. The emphasis is therefore more on the effect of what happens: salvation and liberation from slavery! Paul calls this a 'baptism into Moses' because Moses was the leader of the people, in whose name everything happened.

Paul also spiritualises the manna (Exodus 16:4, 14–18) and the water from the rock (Exodus 17:6). He does not use the expression 'communion' or 'the Lord's Supper,' but it is clear that this occasion is on his mind, not least because he will say more about the Supper later (1 Corinthians 10:14–22; 11:17–34). Paul calls the gifts of God (the manna and the water) spiritual because they were given in a supernatural way.

In this context Paul makes the striking statement that the rock 'followed' (NRSV; less literally 'accompanied,' NIV) the people 'and that rock was Christ' (verse 4). Many readers have taken him to task over this sentence. How can a rock follow people? Surely it was just an ordinary rock? In our passage Paul is spiritualising every single elements of the narrative in Exodus:

Cloud	God's protection
Sea	Baptismal water
Manna	Communion bread
Water from the rock	Communion wine
Rock	Christ

Note that he does not deny the historical reality and validity of any of these things, but that he 'merely' assigns all of them an additional 'Christian' meaning. In verse 11 he draws the following conclusion:

> These things happened to them as examples and were written down as warnings for us, on whom the culmination of the ages has come.

The word 'example' here translates a Greek word related to the word *typos* (type). What happened in the wilderness at the time was a type of what is now happening to the church of Jesus. In the second place, Paul is not the first believer to give the rock a spiritual meaning. The word 'rock' is often used metaphorically in the Old Testament, as God is remarkably often called 'the Rock of Israel,' for example in Deuteronomy 32 (verses 4, 15, 18, 30 and 31), Genesis 49:24, and Psalm 18:2, 31, 46 and 19:14. The expression usually refers to his saving intervention. For Paul and for other Christians, who believe that Jesus is God, it is not a big step to say that Jesus indeed is our rock. Paul also hints at this in 1 Corinthians 10:9 by saying that in the wilderness the

Israelites tested or defied Christ. This argument implies, of course, our belief that Jesus is the eternal God. He was not merely adopted by God at the time of the New Testament but existed 'in the beginning.' It was as Trinity that God was active at the time of the old covenant. So when Paul writes that this rock accompanied or followed the people of Israel in the wilderness, it is not too difficult to understand that God/Jesus was always with the people of Israel in the wilderness.

To sum up, in 1 Corinthians 10 Paul argues that both God's blessing – in the form of baptism and the Lord's Supper – and his punishment on idolatry apply to the church as much as to ancient Israel. He does not discuss the deeper meaning of baptism and communion. At most, you can deduce that baptism – which Paul mentions first, verse 2 – is a one-off event of initiation, just as Israel went through the sea once at the beginning of its existence, while communion – in verses 3 and 4 – is repeatable, just as Israel regularly received manna and water from the LORD.

Part 3: The Lord's Supper

Unlike baptism, the Lord's meal does have a direct precursor in the Old Testament: the Passover meal. It was the Lord Jesus himself who celebrated this Passover with his disciples just before his crucifixion, transforming its meaning in such a way that it became our 'Holy Communion.' The meal commemorating the exodus from Egypt henceforth became the meal of the new covenant, which recalls Jesus' sacrificial death. Which material from the Old Testament do the writers of the New use when they discuss this meal?

The description of the institution of the Lord's Supper can be found in Matthew 26:26–29, Mark 14:22–25, and Luke 22:14–20. The last part of it in Luke goes as follows:

> And he took bread, gave thanks and broke it, and gave it to them, saying, 'This is my body given for you; do this in remembrance of me.' In the same way, after the supper he took the cup, saying, 'This cup is the new covenant in my blood, which is poured out for you.' (Luke 22:19–20; see also Matthew 26:27–28 and Mark 14:24)

The expression 'pouring' or 'shedding' blood alludes to the Old Testament expression 'shedding blood,' which never denotes a regular sacrifice, but always the use of violence (see Genesis 9:6; Isaiah 59:7; Ezekiel 18:10). Jesus's use of this expression shows that he knew he would be murdered. Jesus and Luke do not directly quote from Scripture in this report, but they clearly echo two passages. The first of these is the story of the ratification of the covenant between God and Israel in Exodus 24, where you read:

> Moses then took the blood, sprinkled it on the people and said, 'This is the blood of the covenant that the LORD has made with you in accordance with all these words.' Moses and Aaron, Nadab and Abihu, and the seventy elders of Israel went up and saw the God of Israel. … they saw God, and they ate and drank. (Verses 8–11)

Both covenant ceremonies involve the flowing of blood and a joint meal.

The second passage that resonates in Luke's words is Jeremiah 31:31–34, in particular the expression 'the new covenant' which Jesus uses. The Lord explains the supper as the meal of the new covenant which had been promised in Jeremiah 31. By means of Jesus' death on the cross, God now makes this new covenant with the people.

You can also hear Scripture in a few details of Jesus' words. The command to celebrate this meal regularly recalls the instruction regarding the Passover in Exodus 12:14 and Deuteronomy 16:3. The emphasis on remembrance of what God did for people, especially in the exodus, can be found, for example, in Exodus 13:3, Deuteronomy 5:15 and 16:3, and Psalm 77:11–12. Finally, Jesus' expression 'for you' makes it clear that he consciously sacrifices himself on behalf of the people, a thought particularly evident in Isaiah 53:10–12 and Zechariah 9:11. All these things together show that in Jesus God is adding a new, superlative act of salvation to everything he had already done for Israel. Now the redemption of his people is complete. You can only fully understand the new covenant once you understand the old one.

The only letter in which Paul writes about the Lord's Supper is 1 Corinthians, but this letter has much to say about it. Yet after 1 Corinthians 10:1–6 Paul no longer quotes the Old Testament on the subject. His rendering of the institution of the meal in 1 Corinthians 11:23–26 is very similar to Luke's version. In the surrounding passage, verses 17–34, there are not even any allusions to the Old Testament, but in 1 Corinthians 10:16–22 Paul does refer to ancient Israel in general. In verse 18 of this passage he probably thinks of rules regarding the eating of sacrificial meat as in Leviticus 7:6 and 10:12–15, and Deuteronomy 18:1–4:

> Consider the people of Israel: do not those who eat the sacrifices participate in the altar?

The Gospel of John does not describe the institution of the Lord's Supper, so it does not have the words of the institution. Instead John (13:1–20) tells how Jesus washes his disciples' feet. Washing someone's feet on arrival was a custom among many nations and also in Israel, but people usually did it themselves (Genesis 18:4; 19:2; 24:32; 43:24; Judges 19:21; differently 1 Samuel 25:41). The rabbis had determined that Jewish servants were not required to wash their masters' feet because it was such humiliating work. Jesus takes on this labour voluntarily! I do not find references to Scripture in this passage in John.

John does see Jesus as the Passover lamb. At the exodus from Egypt the Israelites had to smear the blood of a lamb or goat on their doorposts and to eat the rest of the animal (Exodus 12). Since then they had been celebrating the Passover each year, slaughtering and eating a lamb (12:43–50; Leviticus 23:5–8). God told them that they would be safe if they were protected by the blood of a lamb (Exodus 12:23). Just as the blood of the lamb at the exodus took the place of the blood of the firstborns, the blood of Jesus comes instead of ours. The Passover meal was thus a type, a prefiguration, of the death of Jesus. The first reference to Jesus as the Passover lamb is in John 1:29, where John the Baptist calls him 'the Lamb of God, who takes away the sin of the world.' In Jesus God provides himself with the lamb that dies for the sins of the people; Isaac in Genesis 22 is a type of Jesus. But John 1:29 also reflects the image of the innocent lamb of Isaiah 53. In that chapter

Isaiah compares the servant of the LORD to a lamb, making it clear that his suffering will be vicarious. This is possible because with God innocent blood has a forgiving and reconciling effect (Leviticus 17:11; Romans 3:25; Hebrews 9:22).

John again designates Jesus as the Passover lamb in John 19:36, yet this time without using the word 'lamb.' The verse says that none of Jesus' bones was broken despite being him being crucified. In the preceding verses 31–32 John had just explained that normally the legs of crucified people were broken to hasten their dying; but with Jesus this did not happen because he had already died (verse 33). In his comment on this striking event John argues that this was a fulfilment of Scripture:

> These things happened so that the scripture would be fulfilled: 'Not one of his bones will be broken.' (John 19:36)

The evangelist is not here literally quoting Scripture, but he combines Exodus 12:46 (see also Numbers 9:12) with Psalm 34:20 because the form of the verb he uses for 'break' comes from the psalm. You can also hear an echo of the previous verse in this psalm:

> The righteous person may have many troubles, but the LORD delivers him from them all.

Because according to the law the bones of the Passover lamb were also not allowed to be broken, this detail of the description shows that Jesus has the quality of a Passover lamb.

That Jesus is indeed the true Passover lamb is also clear from the fact that John draws attention to the fact that the time of his crucifixion coincided with the time when the Jews were slaughtering their Passover lambs (John 13:1 and 19:31) – something that would no longer be necessary from that moment on. Jesus thus stands in the line of Scripture as the Lamb of God for the last days.

When John does write about Communion, he does so in a very different way from the other evangelists. In John 6 he makes no connection with the Passover and the Passover lamb, but rather with the manna (verses 31, 49 and 58). The direct reason for Jesus' teaching in this chapter is his feeding of the 5,000 men (6:1–13). Even though it is not explicitly mentioned, in John 6:52–58 Jesus has clearly brought the conversation to the topic of the Lord's Supper. When you look back through John 6 from the end, you see that he has been working towards this point from verse 25 onwards. His famous statement 'I am the bread of life' (verses 35 and 48) must be understood in this light.

Jesus does not give his audience an easy time. His command that we should eat his body and drink his blood (verses 53 and 56) is both strongly worded and starkly realistic. Jews who took these words literally would have been even more offended than we are, for they had been given the explicit prohibition of blood (Genesis 9:4; Leviticus 17:10–14). In this case we must take Jesus' words seriously but not literally. He means to say that he is giving his body and blood so that the world may live. The salvation of humanity depends on him – and our personal salvation depends also on our faith in him. We express ourselves similarly when we say that we devour a book or that we drink in someone's words. Jesus finishes his teaching by saying that whoever eats his flesh receives better food than the manna (verse 58). People who ate manna remained mortal, but whoever eats him, the manna for the end times, will live forever. To say this in plain language: if you believe in Jesus and you act on this by sitting at his table with his community, then for time and eternity you are on God's side. In the past salvation was only for Israel, but now it is for everybody. The Jews protest against this thought, they 'grumble' (verse 41) just as they had in the past 'grumbled' in the wilderness (Exodus 16:2, 8–9; 17:3). John deliberately uses the same word as Scripture.

Further Reading

Beasley-Murray, George R., *John*. Word Biblical Themes (Dallas: Word, 1989).

Hays, Richard B., *The Conversion of the Imagination: Paul as Interpreter of Israel's Scripture* (Grand Rapids: Eerdmans, 2005).

Hays, Richard B., *Echoes of Scripture in the Gospels* (Waco: Baylor University Press, 2016)

Reiling, J., *Gemeenschap der heiligen. Over de gemeente van Jezus Christus naar het Nieuwe Testament* (Amsterdam: Ten Have, 1964).

Chapter 22: Babel

The city of Babel and the surrounding country of Babylon occur frequently in the Bible. The heartland region of Babylon lay in the middle and south of present-day Iraq; its capital city Babel was situated on the Euphrates River. Babel is the first city to receive attention in the Bible, and also the penultimate. (The last is the New Jerusalem.) Against the backdrop of all kinds of historical information, the city is often represented as an anti-godly power. Babel occurs in very different places; it is a power that comes up, disappears, and yet makes a comeback. As a connecting thread through the Bible, Babel shows that humanity is always 'inclined to all evil,' but it also shows God's sovereignty and eventual victory.

The Tower

Genesis 10:10 states that Babel owed its existence to the great Nimrod, the first ruler on earth. That does not bode well! Genesis 11 then tells that in prehistoric times Babel was the central city of humanity. Even after the flood humanity did not have the intention to do God's will. They rather wanted power at God's expense; the position under God was too low for them. In their desire to be independent of God they refused to spread across the earth as he had instructed (Genesis 1:28; 9:1, 7), hence they built a huge city and a tall tower. (A more cynical approach is to say that they were afraid of being scattered over the big empty earth and thus anxiously clung together.) What the people say in verse 4, that they want to make a name for themselves, is similar to what people without God have been saying or thinking for centuries. Life centres on their own fame and power. The tower of Babel symbolises human pride and ambition.

In Genesis 11:5, the perspective in the narrative shifts to God the LORD. While the people below are convinced that they are busy building a skyscraper, he has to descend to earth — and to put his glasses on his nose, so to say – in order to be able to see their construction work at all. It is therefore easy for him to scatter the people. God leaves the city and the tower as they are for they are no longer a threat to him. The whole enterprise ends in abject failure. The story shows that God wants people's lives to be primarily focused on him. The human pursuit of autonomy is a serious form of idolatry.

The Prophets

But Babel returns. When the book of Kings mentions Babel or Babylon, it primarily has the New Babylonian Empire in mind, which existed from 625 to 539 BC and which was a constant threat to the small kingdom of Judah. In 597 BC, King Nebuchadnezzar conquered Judah and brought a number of Judeans as exiles to Babel (2 Kings 24); ten years later he returned and destroyed Jerusalem and the temple (587 BC, 2 Kings 25). This was the punishment for the persistent sin of the people. The prophets had seriously warned them against this possibility, but they had not repented. These are the bare facts; but the spiritual importance of Babel goes deeper, as you can see from the level of attention that Babel receives from the prophets of Israel. In the series of prophecies against gentile nations in Isaiah (Isaiah 13–23), Babylon comes first (Isaiah 13–14), while in his series Jeremiah has Babylon in the last place and pays much attention to it (Jeremiah 50–51). Ezekiel 30:10–11 shows what a terrible reputation the Babylonians had. These three prophetic books also mention Babel in many other places. Their descriptions of Babel are much rougher, more realistic, than those in Genesis; some passages are decidedly bloody. The prophets especially suggest that Babel is an irresistible power. At the same time, it is also the epitome of idolatry and opposition to the God of Israel. Only Isaiah 46 is somewhat light-hearted as it mocks the idols of Babel.

Yet the world-domination of Babel would not last for ever. Already Isaiah 21:1–10 contains the exclamation, 'Babylon has fallen, has fallen!' (verse 9) This is an announcement of the conquest of the city by King Cyrus of Persia in 539 BC, which suddenly brought an end to the Babylonian Empire. The same double exclamation 'fallen, fallen' is later used in Revelation 14:8 and 18:2.

Sometimes the name Babel no longer refers to the concrete city on the Euphrates but it has become a symbol of earthly power in general. You see this in Isaiah 13:9–13 and 14:3–23, where the demise of anti-divine powers at the end of time is in view. This shift in significance is also gratefully used by John in Revelation.

Revelation 17–18

Babel is a power that keeps returning. The Bible shows us patterns and repetitions in history. The prophet John opposes a world power that he calls Babylon or Babel, expressing himself with the help of the Old Testament. Revelation 17–18 is so heavily based on the Scriptures that you could wonder which elements of these chapters do *not* come from the Hebrew Bible! I could provide two long parallel columns of phrases from the prophets next to phrases from Revelation 17–18; but the case is clear, and I shall limit myself to some examples.

The first reference to Babel in this passage (Revelation 17:1) calls it a city which 'sits by many waters'; this expression is derived from Jeremiah 51:13:

> You who live by many waters and are rich in treasures, your end has come, the time for you to be destroyed.

After this reference to a lot of water you might be surprised to see that John is taken to a desert (17:3); that element is probably derived from Isaiah 21:1, where it says that the doom for Babel, 'the Desert by the Sea,' will come from 'the desert, from a land of terror.'

The title awarded to Babel, 'Babylon the Great' (17:5), is taken from the book of Daniel, where King Nebuchadnezzar refers to his capital city as 'the great Babel I have built ... by my mighty power and for the glory of my majesty' (Daniel 4:30).

Below is a list which shows how Revelation makes use of the description of the humiliation of Babel in Isaiah 47:

	Isaiah 47	Revelation
The city emphatically seen as a woman	1–3, 5	17:1–7, 18:7
Royal titles	1, 5, 7	18:7
Persecution of God's people	6	17:6; 18:24
Denial that she is a widow	8	18:7

Unexpected downfall	7, 11	18:10, 17–19
… in one day	9	18:8 (even hours, verses 10, 17)
Fire	14	17:16
The importance of trade for the city	15	18:11–16, 23
Abandoned / betrayed by allies	15	17:16–17

Isaiah 47 and Revelation 17–18 are both laments, or better parodies on laments. This brings us to the use of Ezekiel in Revelation 17–18 because Ezekiel 26, 27 and 28:1–19 contain real laments about a trading power that perishes, and these passages can be recognised as the backdrop of Revelation 18:9–19. However, Ezekiel is describing the city of Tyre, which was situated by the sea and was eventually plunged into the sea (26:3, 12, 17; 27:3–4; 28:2, 8). By adopting much from Ezekiel, John combines elements of the cities of Babel and Tyre in his description of the anti-divine power, even though Babel was, of course, not at all situated by the sea (18:17, 19, 21). In Ezekiel it is the rulers of the sea who complain about the downfall of the trade city (26:16; 27:28–31) and John includes similar groups of lamenters (18:9, 11, 15). John's list of merchandise (Revelation 18:11–14) is an adaptation of Ezekiel 27:12–25; and the complaint in Revelation 18:17–19 exhibits strong agreement with the way of mourning in Ezekiel 27:26–32.

It was also Ezekiel who gave a detailed description of prostitution as a symbol of sin (Ezekiel 16 and 23), but according to him Jerusalem is the guilty party. It is remarkable that John is not negative about Israel and Jerusalem, using the ugly imagery with reference to Babel.

Rome

Although John uses the name Babel, in fact he has the city of Rome and the Roman Empire in view, as in Revelation 13. Can we be sure of this? Yes, for several reasons. In 17:9 John calls his subject a city situated on seven hills. Babel lies in the plain of the River Euphrates, but Rome was and is known as the city on seven hills. In 17:6 John accuses 'Babel' of murdering Christian martyrs, and he probably means (among others) Peter and Paul, who had died for their faith in Rome. In 17:18, the city is called 'the great city that rules over the kings of the earth.' Again, in the time of the New Testament this description only fitted the city of Rome; at that time Babel was an insignificant town. If you still have doubts, do consider that 1 Peter 5:13 also uses the name Babylon to refer to Rome. The tradition of the church connects the apostle Peter emphatically with Rome, never with the literal Babylon.

Revelation contains the same hard, realistic descriptions of Babel as the books of the prophets because John makes use of their words. Central to Revelation 17 is a prostitute who sits on a beast; these metaphors represent the city of Rome and the Roman Empire which sustains it. The anti-Christian powers are openly exhibited: desire, money, sex, and power. Prostitution is often a metaphor for idolatry, but of course it also takes place literally. The combination of prostitution and economics already occurs in the criticism of the prophet Nahum (3:4, 16) on another powerful city, Nineveh. So in his description of Rome, John combines characteristics of Tyre, Nineveh, and Babel.

The world in which John and the early Christians lived was dominated by the Roman Empire, which occupied the entire Near East including Egypt. The Gospels make clear that the Romans were a cruel occupying force. However, surprisingly, many people in the area to which John is sending the book of Revelation, the west of present-day Turkey, were pleased with the Romans because they had brought the region peace and prosperity. The economy was flourishing, and the Asians were happy to worship Romans gods including the emperor. No wonder that in Revelation 17–18 John describes Rome as a very attractive, seductive prostitute, who promises a good life and is befriended with the powerful and wealthy people. (On the other hand, Revelation 13 is more about the ideology of the anti-Christian power.) The long list of trade goods in 18:12–13 shows how strong and attractive the commercial life of Rome was. When Rome perishes her trading partners no longer have access to all that wealth. The Christians are warned against the tempting power of all these things.

All these things show that Revelation is a political text, just as political as the prophets of the Old Testament. John criticises the government and predicts the end of the current administration. At the same time, he shows that there is nothing new under the sun. Babel has popped up again and its new incarnation is once again a threat to the people of God. This has happened before, and it is likely to happen again.

It Once Was, Now is Not, and Yet Will Come

Like the rest of Revelation, the prophecy concerning Rome does not only speak about John's own time. His book covers all of history until the end of time. In Revelation 17:8 John emphasizes that the beast was, is not, and yet will be again. The anti-Christian power Babel-Rome later reappeared in the form of the Muslims who conquered almost all of Europe, in the form of the medieval papacy, Napoleon, Stalin, Hitler, and Pol Pot, and it will once more emerge elsewhere if the Lord Jesus does not return very soon.

For contemporary readers of Revelation, the central statement about Babel is the warning in 18:4:

> Come out of her, my people, so that you will not share in her sins, so that you will not receive any of her plagues.

This warning was necessary for the congregations to which John was writing because many people were quite comfortable with the social and economic power of Rome. It is also very relevant to us. And we need each other to become pure and holy, and to remain so, for it is difficult to resist temptation.

It is striking that the book of Daniel plays virtually no role in John's description of Babel. That book is set in the city of Babel and describes the kings of Babel as apexes of pride, power, lust, and stupidity, but John does nothing with it. I think that this is because in his day Daniel was still able to live at the court and even to have an important role in government, whereas John is convinced that this is no longer possible in his time.

We see that John uses images and statements from the Old Testament to describe the anti-Christian powers; this tells us that there is something predictable about the powers which threaten the church of Jesus Christ in the past, present, and future. Am I going too far when I suggest that this is because God's opponent has only a limited number of tricks and

154

masks available, and that these have already been played, revealed, and exposed in the Old Testament?

Further Reading

Arnold, B.T., 'Babylon' in Mark J. Boda and J. Gordon McConville (eds), *Dictionary of the Old Testament Prophets* (Downers Grove, Nottingham: IVP, 2012) 53–60.

Ryken, Leland, James C. Wilhoit and Tremper Longman III (eds), *Dictionary of Biblical Imagery* (Leicester: IVP, 1998).

Tõniste, Külli, *The Ending of the Canon: A Canonical and Intertextual Reading of Revelation 21–22*, LNTS 526 (London: Bloomsbury T&T Clark, 2016).

Chapter 23: Matthew

Of the New Testament writers, Matthew is the one who refers to Scripture most clearly. That will also be the reason why his book opens the New Testament, for Matthew makes the most obvious connections with the preceding, Old Testament. I have no doubt that you know his stock phrase that something happened so that the words of the prophet were fulfilled, followed by a reference to a prophetic book. Variations on this formula occur thirteen times in this Gospel, namely in 1:22; 2:15, 17, 23; 4:14; 8:17; 12:17; 13:14, 35; 21:4; 26:54, 56; and 27:9. This frequency immediately shows how important the fulfilment of Scripture is for Matthew. In Matthew 27:35, the NKJV has a whole extra sentence compared to modern translations. This phrase also mentions a fulfilment, but the best manuscripts do not have these words: a diligent scribe borrowed them from John 19:24 and they do not originally belong in Matthew. Later in this chapter, I will comment on these 'fulfilment quotes' but I will begin with other things.

Boring Beginning?

It is striking that Matthew does not start with a *story* about Jesus but with a genealogy. On this list many names from the Hebrew Bible make an appearance and it would be hard to write a more outspoken connection between 'old' and 'new.' Matthew means to say that the Lord Jesus did not come out of a vacuum, but that he stands in the line of God's history with the people of Israel and he is descended from the great King David. Matthew seems to have written his book mainly for Jewish readers, but for us this is good to remember as well.

The first two words of the Greek text of Matthew's book are *biblos geneseōs*. In *biblos*, which means 'book,' you may recognise our word Bible, which simply means 'books.' In the second word you may recognise 'Genesis.' This word can mean various things, dependent on the context: origin, beginning, becoming, or descent. The choice of this word is, of course, the evangelist's bold allusion to the beginning of the Old Testament, where we find Genesis, the 'book of the beginning.' At the beginning of the New Testament we find Matthew, the book about the 'genealogy of Jesus the Messiah.' The term *biblos geneseōs* occurs literally in the Septuagint in Genesis 2:4 and 5:1.

When you look at Matthew's list of names in more detail, you will recognise that it has a clear structure. The list begins and ends with the same names, but in reverse order: Jesus the Messiah, David, Abraham (verse 1) – Abraham, David, the Messiah (verse 17). The evangelist emphatically states that his list contains three times fourteen generations (verse 17), but when you turn to the Old Testament you will notice that quite a few persons are missing from Matthew's list. (I will spare you the details.) Matthew has clearly not included all the names of all intermediate persons, but he has rather made a selection. The number of three times fourteen that he presents is the artificial result of his omissions. But why fourteen? When you count the Hebrew letters of the name David in the Jewish way (a = 1, b = 2, etc.), you see that in the Hebrew alphabet, d = 4 and v or w = 6; the numerical value of the name David is therefore fourteen. (In Hebrew the vowels, here, the 'a' and the 'i,' were not written.) Thus Matthew's selection emphasizes that Jesus is the promised king in the lineage of King David.

Another striking feature of the genealogy in Matthew 1 is that four women are mentioned, three of them by name: Tamar, Rahab, Ruth, and 'the wife of Uriah' (NRSV), Bathsheba. Normally genealogies contain no or hardly any women, so Matthew must have added these four especially. That is an important decision in itself, because he shows much more respect for women than most other Jews of the time. The women he mentions have something special. In the Old Testament you see that with all four of them 'something is going on.' Tamar's story is in Genesis 38; it is a seedy story in our eyes, in which Judah is criticised for his treatment of Tamar. Rahab was a prostitute (Joshua 2); Bathsheba became pregnant as a result of David's adultery (2 Samuel 11). The four women all deviate from the norm. Three of the four are foreign women: Tamar and Rahab from Canaan, Ruth from Moab; Bathsheba was married to a foreigner, the Hittite Uriah. These four women were therefore on the margins of society. By mentioning them specifically, Matthew probably wants to give evidence that the promise is being fulfilled that in Abraham *all* nations will be blessed

(Genesis 12:2). Women from other nations are included in the list of ancestors of the Messiah!

The Structure of the Gospel

Now let us take a look at the big picture of this Gospel, the structure of the book. In comparison with the other Gospels, Matthew has organised things quite tightly. While in Mark and Luke stories about Jesus' deeds and teaching continually alternate in what might appear to be no particular order, Matthew includes the teaching of the Lord in five large blocks. I have numbered these teaching blocks for convenience:

Matthew 1–4: Stories

      5–7: Teaching block 1

      8–9: Stories

      10: Teaching block 2

      11–12: Stories

      13: Teaching block 3

      14–17: Stories

      18: Teaching block 4

      19–22: Stories

      23–25: Teaching block 5

      26–28: Stories

A comparison with Mark and Luke shows that it must have been Matthew who systematically ordered the contents of his book and thus brought the teaching of Jesus together into five rather artificial blocks. Why would he have done that? Early on, the church already supposed that the number of five blocks of teaching must refer to the five books of Moses in the Old Testament, Genesis to Deuteronomy. This means that Jesus is the new teacher of Israel and that the story of his life is Scripture. Matthew underlines the parallel between Jesus and Moses by concluding every block of teaching with words such as 'When Jesus had finished saying these things' (7:28; 19:1; see also 11:1; 13:53; 26:1). In Greek, these five concluding phrases are very similar, which gives them great emphasis. But they also closely resemble the way in which the Septuagint concludes the words of Moses in Deuteronomy 31:1 and 32:45. For example, in Deuteronomy 31:1 (NRSV) it says:

> When Moses had finished speaking all these words to all Israel...

The structure of Matthew's book thus suggests that Jesus is the new Moses; the evangelist is more or less saying, 'Here is Moses II.' For his Jewish readers as well as for us this means that Jesus' teaching has the same authority as – or even more than – that of Moses. And Matthew probably also claims that his book, which contains this inspired teaching, deserves to be included in the collection of sacred books. Which is exactly what the church has done.

Types of Jesus

Matthew shows who Jesus is by describing various people from the Old Testament as his forerunners. We call such persons types of Jesus. Here are the most important ones:

Moses

Not only does the structure of the Gospel show that Jesus is the new Moses, the evangelist also makes this clear in other ways. There are striking parallels between the biographies of Moses and Jesus:

- Both are 'welcomed' on earth by a murderous king who kills countless children (Exodus 1 and Matthew 2:1–12). There is even a Jewish tradition that adds the following to the narrative of Exodus 1: someone had predicted to the pharaoh that a boy would be born who, once grown up, would humiliate the Egyptians, who would be more just than any other person and who would be remembered forever. To eliminate *that* child, pharaoh killed all Jewish boys.

- Both of them go into exile to escape persecution (Exodus 2 and Matthew 2:13–23).

- Both are called upon to return by God himself when the situation is safe to do so (Exodus 3:7–10; 6:2–8; Matthew 2:15, 19–21); in addition, the Greek text of Exodus 4:19b, 'for all those who were seeking your life are dead' (NRSV), served as model for Matthew 2:20b, 'for those who were seeking the child's life are dead' (NRSV).

- Both go through the water (Exodus 14 and Matthew 3:13–15).

- The role of the number forty in their lives. Moses lived in Egypt for forty years and spent forty years in the wilderness in preparation for his task (Acts 7:23, 30); later he travelled through the wilderness with the people of Israel for forty years (Numbers 14:33–34; Deuteronomy 1:3; 2:7); he also spent forty days and nights on Mount Sinai without eating or drinking (Exodus 24:18; 34:28; Deuteronomy 9:9). Jesus was forty days and nights in the wilderness in preparation for his work, even fasting (Matthew 4:1–11).

- The teaching of both is linked to a mountain (Exodus 19:3; 24:1–3; 34:28–29; Matthew 5:1 and 8:1).

- As God appeared to Moses (Exodus 24 and 34), the glorified Jesus appears to his disciples (Matthew 17:1–8). The similarities are in the mountain, the cloud, the radiant face (Exodus 34:29–30, 35; Matthew 17:2), the voice from the cloud, and the period of six days (Exodus 24:16 and Matthew 17:1).

- Both compare the people of Israel to a flock of sheep without a shepherd (Numbers 27:17 and Matthew 9:36).

These parallels gain in importance when you realise how important Moses was for the then Jews. We hear something of this in the words of Stephen:

> He [Moses] was sent to be their ruler and deliverer by God himself … He led them out of Egypt and performed wonders and signs … and he received living words to pass on to us. (from Acts 7:35–38)

David

According to Matthew, Jesus is the son of David, both according to legal descent and in a spiritual sense. Jesus is legally a descendant of David because his mother Mary married a descendant of David (1:1–

17); this Joseph, himself a 'son of David' (1:20), gave him his name and adopted him as his legitimate son (1:18–25). Besides, Jesus was born in the city of David (2:1–12). But the Lord Jesus is also spiritually the successor of David, the great king of Israel who was remembered with nostalgia. For hundreds of years no king from David's house had ruled over Israel, but there were high expectations of the coming of such a person, based on promises such as 2 Samuel 7:12–16. Therefore, the Pharisees can be quoted as saying that the Messiah they are expecting will be a son of David (22:42). And Matthew's good news is that Jesus is indeed this new David, the great king of Israel. Matthew begins his book with this statement (1:1), the impression is reinforced by the visit of the magi from the East (2:2), and it is later confirmed during the trial of Jesus (21:5; 27:11, 29, 37). Finally, there are people who meet Jesus and who address him or speak about him as 'Son of David' (9:27; 12:23; 15:22; 20:30–31; 21:9, 15; 22:42). Jesus thinks it is fine to be addressed in this way.

You can hear the combination of astonishment and expectation among the people in 12:23: someone who can performs healings like Jesus must be the expected son of David; and if so, things will naturally change fundamentally! Jesus is the one who revives the history of Israel, and who brings it to completion and fruition, even though this happens in a different way from what people had expected.

Son of Man

You may not have thought about it, but the strange title 'Son of Man' can also be understood from an Old Testament perspective. The explanation is not in the fact that God often calls the prophet Ezekiel 'son of man' (e.g. 4:1; 5:1; 6:2; 7:2; NRSV: 'mortal') or in the fact that everyone, well-regarded, is a child of other humans. No, the title stems from the following vision of the prophet Daniel:

> There before me was one like a son of man, coming with the clouds of heaven. He approached the Ancient of Days [= God] and was led into his presence. He was given authority, glory and sovereign power; all nations and peoples of every language worshipped him. His dominion is an everlasting

dominion that will not pass away, and his kingdom is one that will never be destroyed. (Daniel 7:13–14)

This vision is clearly a messianic prophecy; by calling himself Son of Man (for example, in Matthew 8:20; 11:19; 25:31; 26:64) Jesus is therefore claiming that he is the fulfilment of this prophecy, so the one who receives eternal dominion from God. Without knowledge of Daniel 7 you would not know this.

The Servant of the LORD

Jesus is also the servant of the LORD about whom Isaiah had spoken, especially in Isaiah 42; 49–53; and 61; in Matthew's Gospel this is evident in the following verses:

- 8:16–17, where the evangelist cites Isaiah 53:4, 'he took up our pain and bore our suffering.'

- 12:15–21, where he quotes Isaiah 42:1–4; this is probably the longest quotation in the Gospel.

- 20:28, where Jesus says that 'the Son of Man did not come to be served, but to serve, and to give his life as a ransom for many.' This is a summary of the prophetic words in Isaiah 53:10–12, which Jesus applies to himself.

- 27:57, where Josef of Arimathea is called 'a rich man.' These words show that Jesus was with the rich in his death, fulfilling Isaiah 53:9.

And More...

Moses, David, the servant of the LORD – Matthew combines them all. In this way you see that Jesus unites in himself all these different identities from the Hebrew Bible. Hence to understand the Lord Jesus, you must always return to the Old Testament. In the middle part of his book Matthew compares Jesus to even more people and things: he is not only better than Moses (implicitly in 11:28–30) and David (12:3), but he also surpasses the temple (12:6), Jonah (12:41), the mighty King Solomon (12:42), and John the Baptist, who is seen here as the last prophet of the old covenant (11:11).

Son of God

And yet Jesus is more than all these Old Testament persons combined: He is the Son of God. In the Old Testament, the people of Israel are occasionally called 'son' or child of God, namely in Exodus 4:22, Psalm 80:15, and Jeremiah 31:9, as well as in Hosea 11:1:

> When Israel was a child, I loved him, and out of Egypt I called my son.

Matthew cites these words because they have now been realised in Jesus (2:15). Words that in Hosea refer to a fact from the past turn out to have a prophetic layer in the light of Jesus' coming. Matthew 2:15 is therefore not an assertion about the literal meaning of Hosea 11:1, but it shows that the evangelist sees a deep connection between Israel as God's son and Jesus. (It is also interesting to see that this son of God is taken to Egypt by a Joseph, just as in Genesis 46 another Joseph took Israel to Egypt; in both cases, Joseph saved his family in this way.) As the Son of God, Jesus is now also the representative of the people of Israel, both in his exemplary life and in his death. Matthew tells about Jesus on the cross:

> Those who passed by hurled insults at him, shaking their heads. (27:39)

This is an echo of an Old Testament verse about the suffering of the people which also combines the shaking of heads and hurling insults:

> All who pass your way clap their hands at you; they scoff and shake their heads at Daughter Jerusalem. (Lamentations 2:15a)

The parallel between Lamentations and Matthew is clear, not least because both verses are about passers-by. In this way Matthew applies the words from Lamentations about the demise of Jerusalem to Jesus on the cross. In his suffering and death, he is representing the whole nation.

Jesus and the Law

The entire Sermon on the Mount is full of Jesus' explanation of the Scriptures and especially in Matthew 5 you can see how the Lord is constantly in dialogue with his Jewish roots. It is also striking that throughout the Gospel Jesus continually cites the Scriptures, whereas the Pharisees never do this and the Sadducees only once (in 22:24). If you look up this verse, you will see that in their quotation the Sadducees are merging two passages, because they add a tad of Genesis 38:8 to Deuteronomy 25:5. The Pharisees rely solely on later traditions and thus have no divine authority (15:1–6).

Those Awkward Quotes

Sometimes Matthew does not quote at all despite using the Hebrew Bible, leaving it to his audience to hear the echoes. One example of this is found in Matthew 11:5, where Jesus is alluding to the beautiful prophecy in Isaiah 35:5–6a. Another is found in 25:35–36, where he is not inventing new guidance for his followers but rather applying Isaiah 58:6–7.

However, Matthew is an evangelist who quotes frequently. Fortunately, many of these quotes do not cause any problems. Even though he does not always quote literally, we can understand, for example, that Matthew 4:14–16 contains words from Isaiah 8:22 to 9:1 and that Matthew 8:17 indicates the fulfilment of Isaiah 53:4. I will discuss a few striking, complicated quotations and a couple of allusions.

Matthew 1:22–23: Immanuel

I wrote above that Matthew regards Jesus as the Son of God and the true representative of Israel. I also mentioned Matthew 3:17 and 17:5 in the discussion of Psalm 2, because the title Son of God is used for Jesus in the psalm. It remains to discuss the name Immanuel. This name consists of the elements *imma-nu-el* and it literally means 'with-us-God (is).' Matthew finds this name in Isaiah 7:14. In chapter 9 I explained the meaning of the promise of Immanuel in Isaiah 7 and how the Septuagint has added a prophetic layer to the text by using the Greek word *parthenos*, which means 'virgin.' It is no wonder that Matthew hears the words of the angel to Joseph as a promise of further fulfilment of Isaiah's promise. At the same time, Jesus is more than the first Immanuel. He is not just a sign of God's help, but God himself. The LORD God himself is now with his people.

Joseph gives the promised baby the name Jesus (1:21), but his presence means that one can speak about Immanuel (1:23). In this first fulfilment quote Matthew claims that in the human Jesus of Nazareth we meet God himself, the God of Israel. Matthew uses the name Immanuel not only at the beginning of the Gospel, but also – a bit hidden – at the end (28:20, 'I am with you'). As a result, the name encloses the whole book and determines its interpretation. Moreover, you may be able to hear this beautiful name in 17:17 (NRSV) and 18:20 as well.

Matthew 2:6: Micah and Samuel

King Herod summons Jewish scholars to tell him where the Messiah will be born (Matthew 2:4). In their answer they refer to 'the prophet' in the singular (verse 5), but what they say is a combination of words from the prophet Micah with statements from the book of Samuel:

> But you, Bethlehem, in the land of Judah, are by no means least among the rulers of Judah; for out of you will come a ruler who will shepherd my people Israel.

Most of this verse comes from Micah 5:2 – although the scribes do not quote verbatim – but the element 'shepherd my people Israel' derives from 2 Samuel 5:2. These are words that were spoken directly to David and which now receive a second fulfilment in David's great Son. The context in 2 Samuel 5 is that the people had hitherto obeyed King Saul, a bad king, but now prefer to obey David. You can hear a stab at the bad King Herod here as well: your government will not last much longer!

Matthew 2:23: Nazarene

Much has been written about Matthew's remark that 'the prophets' had said that Jesus 'would be called a Nazarene' (2:23). There is no prophecy like this in the Hebrew Bible, at least not in these words, but when you look closely, you see that Matthew is not really suggesting this. In most of his fulfilment quotations he refers to 'the prophet' in the singular. In these cases, he has his sight on a particular passage in a prophetic book. But here in 2:23 he refers more generally to 'the prophets' and not to one passage. So what does Matthew mean? Does he see a link between the name of the town of Nazareth where Jesus grew up and the institute of the Nazirite about which you read in Numbers 6? Apart from agreements in sound between Nazareth and Nazirite, in Hebrew and Greek as well as in English, there is nothing to suggest so. Nazirites were not allowed to drink wine or to come close to dead people, things Jesus frequently did; see, for example, Matthew 11:19. It is therefore more likely that Matthew plays with the Hebrew word *netser*, which means branch. It is used for a small, insignificant twig. Just as Nazareth (*Natsaret* in Hebrew) was an insignificant town (see John 1:46), so a *netser* was an insignificant branch – from which God would bring forth something big. This word *netser* is used for the Messiah in Isaiah 11:1, where it opens the rich messianic passage Isaiah 11:1–10:

> A shoot shall come out from the stock of Jesse, and a branch shall grow out of his roots. (NRSV)

Some of the Dead Sea Scrolls, which give us insight into Jewish thought in the time of Jesus and Matthew, also use the term *netser* to express the humility of the expected Messiah.

Matthew may also have had other prophetic passages in mind, such as Isaiah 4:2; Jeremiah 23:5–6; 33:15; Zechariah 3:8; 6:12, in which a similar word for sprout or twig is used; I quote two of these verses:

> In those days and at that time I will make a righteous Branch sprout from David's line; he will do what is just and right in the land. (Jeremiah 33:15)

> On that day the branch of the LORD shall be beautiful and glorious, and the fruit of the land shall be the pride and glory of the survivors of Israel. (Isaiah 4:2 NRSV)

In all these passages the branch is a descendant of King David. Some English translations even use a capital B in branch in these places, so that readers will not miss the messianic overtones of the word. I think that the evangelist Matthew is taking all these prophetic references to the branch together in 2:23. His use of the Bible is freer than ours often is, but by our faith in the Lord Jesus as the one who 'fulfils' the Scriptures we understand his way of thinking. A free rendering of Matthew 2:23

can therefore be: 'He will be called Branch, an insignificant twig, and he will descend from the family of David.'

A closing remark: now that you have seen Matthew using Isaiah 11, you may also read the remainder of that passage as the background to his Gospel. Thus, the coming of 'the Spirit of God' on Jesus at his baptism (Matthew 3:16) is clarified by Isaiah 11:2, where 'the Spirit of the LORD' is mentioned:

> The Spirit of wisdom and of understanding, the Spirit of counsel and of might, the Spirit of the knowledge and fear of the LORD.

Matthew 4:1–11: Answer to the Devil

The story about Jesus' temptation in the wilderness gains depth when you see that both the devil and Jesus himself take their words from Scripture; but the devil does so superficially and only his second question to Jesus comes from the Word. Jesus' actions bring Deuteronomy 6–8 to life.

Jesus responds to the devil's first question with words from Deuteronomy 8:3. The link between Deuteronomy 8 and Matthew 4 is that both passages are about hunger. Moses reproaches the people of Israel because they have not passed God's test. Like Israel, Jesus is now also being put to the test. Will he be obedient to God's will? Israel did not really trust God, but Jesus does put all his trust in him!

Apparently, the devil thinks, 'I can do this too,' and in his second question to Jesus he quotes from Psalm 91:11–12. He duly uses the words 'it is written' and he adheres to the text (in the Septuagint translation). His reasoning will be that if the promise of this psalm already applies to a pious Israelite, then it surely applies to Jesus, the Son of God. We call this an argument *a fortiori*. The devil says '*If* you are the Son of God,' but the word 'if' does not express doubt here – he knows his opponent! Jesus finds his second answer a little earlier in Deuteronomy (6:16; see also Exodus 17:1–7); the connection is again about temptation, for it recalls how the people of Israel tempted God. Jesus is doing better than the people and he does not want to tempt God by performing a spectacular stunt. The devil's use of Scripture is a farce.

For his third answer, the Lord goes back even further in Deuteronomy, to 6:13. The devil invites Jesus to worship him, but only God is worthy of worship – and Jesus, his Son. Matthew uses the same word 'worship' more often, for example in 2:2, 8, 11; 14:33; and 28:9, 17.

This story not only shows that Jesus successfully resisted the devil; the deeper message is that he was successful where the people of Israel had failed and that he is the obedient Son of God. The Lord Jesus knows the Scriptures, he fulfils the command of Deuteronomy 8:1–6, and he observes the great commandment of Deuteronomy 6:1–5.

Matthew 12:1–8: Sabbath or Mercy?

During one of Jesus' conflicts with the Pharisees over the Sabbath, they point him to the command regarding the Sabbath (Matthew 12:2), but by contrast Jesus refers to the behaviour of David (verses 3–4). At a certain moment this great king did not obey the rule that consecrated bread, the bread of the Presence (verse 6), was only meant for consumption by the priests (1 Samuel 21:2–7; for the rule see Leviticus 24:5–9). Jesus also argues that the priests do perform duties even on the Sabbath (verse 5). He then claims that he is more important than the temple (verse 6). One would think that this settles the matter. Jesus' authority surpasses the laws and regulations of the old covenant. But it is not so simple. Jesus does not abolish the law without more ado. That is why in verse 7 he quotes words of God from the Old Testament which show that already under the old covenant good intentions were more important than strict adherence to the law: 'I desire mercy, not sacrifice.' These words come from Hosea 6:6 but they also resemble 1 Samuel 15:22.

Further Reading

August, Jared M., '"He shall be called a Nazarene." The non-citation of Matthew 2:23,' *Tyndale Bulletin* 69.1 (2018) 63–74.

Hays, Richard B., *Echoes of Scripture in the Gospels* (Waco: Baylor University Press, 2016).

Chapter 24: Mark

A Strange Beginning

At first glance, the evangelist Mark does not seem to do much with the Old Testament, but this impression is deceptive. Mark uses it right at the beginning, but in a rather problematic way. He first calls his book a 'gospel' (1:1), which means 'good news' (I will come back to that). But already in Mark 1:2–3 it becomes clear that the coming of Jesus Christ into the world is not only *good* news. Something strange is going on in these two verses. Mark writes, 'it is written in Isaiah the prophet,' so you expect a quotation from Isaiah, yet in reality Mark combines words from Isaiah 40:3 with words from Malachi 3:1 and Exodus 23:20. That is, of course, not an error of the evangelist, because Mark knew very well what he was doing. We have seen such combined quotations elsewhere in the New Testament. They were common at the time because people were not as obsessed with accuracy in the use of sources as we are. Moreover, here in Mark 1:2–3 most words do indeed come from Isaiah, as you can see:

> I will send my messenger ahead of you, (Exodus 23:20) who will prepare your way – (Malachi 3:1) a voice of one calling in the wilderness, 'Prepare the way for the Lord, make straight paths for him.' (Isaiah 40:3)

Thus, Mark is correct according to the customs of the time when he only mentions Isaiah as the source of his combined quote.

There is more to say about these verses, which takes the form of an important rule: always pay attention to the Old Testament context of any New Testament quotations and references! Because Mark quotes in the Jewish way, he is assuming that his readers will take the context of the quoted words into account. The context of Malachi 3:1 is a warning against God's judgement over Israel in Malachi 3:1–5. In this way the first readers of Mark and we also receive a warning: God's messenger will also bring judgement. On the other hand, Exodus 23 and Isaiah 40 are texts about God's salvation. Exodus 23 is about the departure of Israel from Egypt while Isaiah 40 is about a new exodus, namely the return of the people of Israel from the exile in Babel to the promised land. By means of this combination of Old Testament references Mark characterises John the Baptist as the person who introduces a major intervention of God in Israel. God is going to do new things, there are new possibilities, but at the same time he will not let sin go unpunished. Good news? Yes, but it will not be accepted by everyone.

More Judgement

In the second story of the Gospel the threat of judgement increases. What does Jesus mean when he wants to send Simon and Andrew 'to fish for people' (Mark 1:17; 'I will make you become fishers of men,' ESV)? Perhaps not what we may hear about it on Sunday! Those who read their Old Testament will see that the expression 'catching people' points to God's judgement (Jeremiah 16:16–18; Amos 4:1–2; Habakkuk 1:14–17)! For this reason alone, it may mean the same here in the Gospel. This explanation of Jesus' words is in line with the fact that it is no fun for a fish to be caught. Jesus' words therefore express that his followers, like John the Baptist, must announce God's impending judgement over Israel. You see that Mark's Gospel begins in a rather threatening way.

Even more menace follows in Mark 4:29, where the image of the farmer using a sickle for the harvest echoes Joel 3:13, another text about God's judgement. Once again the context, that is all of Joel 3, can also be heard. (See also Revelation 14:14–19 for this image.) Other menacing echoes of the Old Testament are in Mark 9:48, where Jesus alludes to Isaiah 66:24, and in Mark 12:38–40, an allusion to God's care for widows and orphans according to Exodus 22:21–24.

Modes of Using Scripture

In this chapter, as in the book as a whole, I am using the words quotation, reference or allusion, and echo frequently. They indicate the various ways in which Jesus and Mark – and the other authors of the New Testament – make use of the Old Testament. The present chapter is ordered according to these modes of use of Scripture and I will give examples of each, beginning with the quotations.

Quotations

The clearest way to connect Old and New Testament is by a *quotation*, which normally looks as follows: colon, open quotation marks, text, close quotation marks. (Older translations such as the King James do not use quotation marks.) Mark gives such a quote in 7:6–7, where you find the following words of Jesus:

> 'Isaiah was right when he prophesied about you hypocrites; as it is written: "These people honour me with their lips, but their hearts are far from me. They worship me in vain; their teachings are merely human rules."'

Jesus here *quotes*, as is clear from his introductory words 'it is written.' For the convenience of the hearers, Jesus adds that he is quoting from Isaiah. (In the later division of the text into chapters and verses, this is Isaiah 29:13.) By quoting, people usually express agreement with the words they are using, and so does Jesus. Quotation often points to an element of the Old Testament that is fulfilled in the New. In this case, Jesus reinforces his criticism of the Jewish leadership by quoting words from Isaiah, the greatest prophet of Israel. In what follows (Mark 7:8–13), he explains why he thinks Isaiah's prophetic words are indeed applicable here. He criticises the contradiction between what the people say and what is in their hearts, a contradiction not unknown in our own time.

Quotations in the New Testament put an 'equals' sign between something in the Scriptures and something in the time of the New Testament. Strictly speaking, the words of Isaiah were not predictions: they were spoken to his contemporaries. Yet his prophetic criticism also applies to the people in Jesus' time. In this quotation, Mark uses the Septuagint of Isaiah, which is sharper than the Hebrew text. He quotes only one verse, but the context in Isaiah 29:9–12, which is prophetic criticism of the sin of God's people, resounds – just like God's promise in Isaiah 29:14 that he will again do miracles for his people.

The last quotation in Mark's Gospel, namely 14:27, is also very clearly indicated:

'You will all fall away,' Jesus told them, 'for it is written: '"I will strike the shepherd, and the sheep will be scattered."'

This time Jesus does not say from which book of the Old Testament he quotes, but it is Zechariah 13:7.

Combined Quotations

When I started this chapter with the combined quotation in Mark 1:2–3, I stated that Jewish texts from the time of Jesus often merged words from different parts of the Bible into one quotation. In this case, by mentioning only Isaiah as a source Mark is leaving it to his readers to figure out that not all words in the quotation are from Isaiah, and where they come from.

He does this more often. At his baptism Jesus is addressed by God with words that all come from the Old Testament, even though Mark does not indicate this. 'A voice' comes from heaven saying:

> You are my Son, whom I love; with you I am well pleased. (1:11)

It seems that this short sentence combines three verses from the Old Testament:

- 'You are my Son' from Psalm 2:7.

- The words 'whom I love' or 'the Beloved' (NRSV) from Genesis 22:2, 12, 16 in the Septuagint.

- 'With you I am well pleased' from Isaiah 42:1.

In this case it is obvious that the contexts of these Bible passages resonate in the quotation, and therefore you may see Jesus as the one coming to fulfil the messianic expectations of Psalm 2 and Isaiah, and as the willing only son who resembles Isaac. He is both the descendant of David expected in Psalm 2 and the servant of the LORD from Isaiah 42, and his baptism confirms him in this combined role. Please note that Isaiah 42 also says that God's servant will be filled with God's Spirit.

By using this combined quotation right at the beginning of his book, Mark immediately gives readers high hopes of Jesus, especially those who turn to their copy of the Scriptures (or remember them from memory). No wonder that according to the following passage Jesus begins by announcing that the kingdom of God is near (Mark 1:15)! He demands his rightful place as king over Israel. What the kingdom entails you find in Isaiah 42 and Psalm 2, among other passages; readers who ignore the Old Testament are missing most of the meaning of the kingdom.

In the story about the transfiguration of Jesus on the mountain (Mark 9:7), the same voice from heaven speaks almost the same words as in 1:11, so that during Jesus' ministry his identity is confirmed: he is the one who fulfils both Isaiah 42 and Psalm 2.

There is another passage in which Mark, or actually Jesus himself, combines two passages of Scripture:

> And as he taught them, he said, 'Is it not written: "My house will be called a house of prayer for all nations"? But you have made it "a den of robbers".' (11:17)

Compare this with the following two places:

> 'For my house will be called a house of prayer for all nations.' The Sovereign LORD declares – he who gathers the exiles of Israel: 'I will gather still others to them besides those already gathered.' (Isaiah 56:7d–8)

> Has this house, which bears my Name, become a den of robbers to you? But I have been watching! declares the LORD. (Jeremiah 7:11)

You see that Jesus is asking his question with words taken from Isaiah and answering his question with words from Jeremiah. In Greek he actually uses only two words from Jeremiah, for 'den of robbers' is two words in Greek. As an aside, here again the context of both prophetic verses should be read as well: Isaiah 56 has a lot to say about everyone's access to God, which is about to become reality in Jesus. God will no longer only be accessible to Israel. And Jeremiah preaches an entire sermon against the injustices in the temple, announcing its destruction (7:1–8:3). You see that Jesus *quotes* only a few words but *alludes* to the wider context in which they occur.

Allusions

At university one of my professors would say that he was making a certain remark 'in the presence of a great cloud of witnesses.' Some in our group would smile at this, because they understood that he was *alluding* to an expression in Hebrews 12:1. But students who did not know Hebrews missed the allusion completely. A similar situation is common in the Bible itself. I showed above that Jesus's words 'fishers of people' allude to Jeremiah 16:16–18, among other passages. But if you don't know these verses and do not investigate, you will never know this! This makes allusions rather insecure: have we discovered all the allusions in a particular text? It is easy to see that computers have helped us in this respect, because word study has become both much simpler and more reliable. Much biblical research now takes place on screen. Initially the labour of monks and others during many centuries was confirmed, subsequently we can discover even more – and faster!

The term allusion is used for a combination of two or more important words in a younger text, which also appear in an older text and which call the older text to mind. A good example of an allusion of Mark is 2:7, where Jesus' opponents express the view that only God can forgive sins. This comment is an allusion to Old Testament places where this is stated explicitly, such as:

> I, even I, am he who blots out your transgressions, for my own sake, and remembers your sins no more. (Isaiah 43:25)

> Who forgives all your sins, and heals all your diseases. (Psalm 103:3)

> The LORD, the LORD, the compassionate and gracious God, slow to anger, abounding in love and faithfulness, maintaining love to thousands, and forgiving wickedness, rebellion and sin. (Exodus 34:6–7a)

Jesus' opponents are right that ordinary people cannot forgive sins, for the Bible says so. The fact that Jesus does forgive sins can only mean that he is God.

Another allusion, referring more to an idea than to one specific verse, is the expression 'sheep without a shepherd' (Mark 6:34) which we find

174

in Numbers 27:17, Ezekiel 34:5, and other places. In Ezekiel 34 the entire passage of Ezekiel resounds, in which God promises a new David as shepherd of the people (Ezekiel 34:23). Jesus is this person who has heart for the sheep: he is the good shepherd.

Have you ever noticed that the translators of Mark 13:14 have put the words 'the abomination that causes desolation' in quotation marks? They did so because Jesus is alluding to a well-known term here. The weird expression 'abomination that causes desolation' occurs three times in Daniel (9:27; 11:31; 12:11), where it refers to the pagan king Antiochus IV who conquered Jerusalem in the second century BC and deconsecrated the temple. He halted the regular sacrifices to God, instead sacrificing pigs – animals unclean for the Jews – to the Greek god Zeus on the altar.[10] Antiochus' reign of terror, torture, and oppression lasted for three years. It was such a terrible period for the Jewish people that they had not forgotten it in Jesus' time. Yet now Jesus predicts that just such a terrible time of suffering will happen again! However, it is not clear exactly what Jesus is referring to: is it the conquest of Jerusalem by the Romans in AD 70 or something that will happen later?

Another allusion to Daniel in Mark 13 can be seen in the fact that 13:19 sounds similar to Daniel 12:1. In this way Jesus indicates that in the future the church will be oppressed in the same way as the people of Israel at the time. In many countries this is a terrible reality for Christians.

Combinations of Allusions

Mark's Gospel also contains combinations of allusions, as in 14:62 where Jesus is quoted as saying:

> 'I am,' said Jesus. 'And you will see the Son of Man sitting at the right hand of the Mighty One and coming on the clouds of heaven.'

Jesus is not quoting Scripture here, but combining elements from the following texts:

---

[10] This is described in the apocryphal book 1 Maccabees 1.

The LORD says to my lord: 'Sit at my right hand until I make your enemies a footstool for your feet.' (Psalm 110:1)

In my vision at night I looked, and there before me was one like a son of man, coming with the clouds of heaven. He approached the Ancient of Days and was led into his presence. (Daniel 7:13)

It is clear that 'the right hand' is taken from Psalm 110, but 'the clouds of heaven' and the title 'Son of Man' from Daniel 7. Both prophetic passages are fulfilled in Jesus, as his allusion suggests.

Echoes

Sometimes an element of the Old Testament resounds so softly in the words of the New Testament that we no longer speak of an allusion but of an echo. Take for example Mark 1:15:

The time has come … The kingdom of God has come near. Repent and believe the good news.

If you listen carefully to these words you can hear the echo of Daniel 7:22:

Until the Ancient of Days came and pronounced judgment in favour of the holy people of the Most High, and the time came when they possessed the kingdom.

Jesus announces the coming of God's kingdom using expressions that remind us of Daniel: 'The time has come' and 'kingdom.' With an echo it is always possible to say, 'I do not hear this,' or in modern terms, 'I do not get this.' There is thus an element of uncertainty in echoes; much depends on the context and on the position of the hearer.

Mark 1:10 contains a rare, strong expression: when Jesus was baptised, the heavens were 'torn open.' This is an echo of Isaiah 64:1, where the prophet asks God to tear (NRSV) or rend (NIV) the heavens to come to the rescue of his people. In this way Mark indicates that the important moment has come when God is doing this, through Jesus of Nazareth who receives the Holy Spirit that will give him power for his work.

Another example of an echo is in Mark 4:35–41, the story of the storm at sea, in which Psalm 107:23–32 resounds:

> He stilled the storm to a whisper; the waves of the sea were hushed. They were glad when it grew calm, and he guided them to their desired haven. (Psalm 107:29–30)

In both situations the point is that God (Jesus) is more powerful than the primal force of the water. The echo of the psalm therefore expresses – without the need for explanation – that in Jesus the power of God is present. Mark closes this narrative with the open question, 'Who then is this, that even the wind and the sea obey him?' Any readers with knowledge of the Old Testament are well-placed to answer this important question correctly, even more so if they also hear the echoes of Job 38:8–11 and Psalm 65:7.

An important echo in Mark 6:45–52 enables us to hear more about who Jesus is. This passage describes that he walks on the sea, without any apparent connection with the Old Testament, as there is no quotation or allusion. Yet it contains echoes of Job 9:4–11 and Exodus 3:14. First listen to Job 9:8:

> He [God] alone stretches out the heavens and treads on the waves of the sea.

Was Mark aware of this echo when he described Jesus' walking on the sea? Perhaps not – that is not important in an echo. The Bible is such a good book that we may be hearing things which the writers themselves did not yet hear. In such a case the Holy Spirit brings out even more than the writers were aware of, pointing us to Jesus.

This echo tells us that like the power of Yahweh (the LORD) in the Old Testament, so is the power of Jesus according to the New Testament. He walks on the sea for he has power over all creation because it is *his* creation.

Perhaps Mark has put another echo in this story on purpose. He writes that when Jesus arrives at the disciples' boat, he 'wants to pass by them' (Mark 6:48). How strange! Why does he not go to them? Or not so strange, if you can hear that the same Greek word for 'pass by' that Mark uses occurs in Exodus 33:17–23 and 34:6 with reference to the God of Israel. It indicates the way God appears to Moses: very real, yet elusive. He passes by Moses. That Jesus is walking on the sea is therefore much more than a trick or an exciting story. It shows readers of the Old Testament that he is God, a God who passes by beyond our grasp.

I make one more comment on this story, because it also contains a real quotation, albeit a very short one. Jesus says to his terrified disciples, who think that he is a ghost: 'It is I.' In the Greek it only says 'I am' – the same words that God spoke to Moses in Exodus 3:14. Yet these few words are enough to show that Jesus equates himself with God.

I return to Mark 11:17, where Jesus cleans the temple whilst accusing its leaders that they are to blame for the fact that God's house is no longer a place of worship but a den of robbers. His radical action is clearly a strong warning of the coming destruction of the temple which – because the Jews did not listen – indeed took place in the year AD 70. At the same time, Jesus's action briefly realises the situation which will arise at the end of time, according to the last words of Zechariah (14:21 NRSV):

> And there shall no longer be traders in the house of the LORD of hosts on that day.

Although Mark does not mention Zechariah at all, the echo of his words is clearly audible. The Hebrew Bible thus enables us to see that Jesus' activity in the temple is prophetic in two ways: it is a serious warning to sinners and it temporarily displays God's final salvation.

Mark and the other books of the New Testament not only contain echoes of the Old Testament, but also of some other Jewish writings and of the culture of the time. These echoes are not the subject of this book, but some of them deserve to be mentioned. First of all, Mark's use of the word 'gospel.' This Greek word (*euangelion*) means 'good news' and it was originally not a 'Christian' word. On the contrary, it was used by the Romans to describe the achievements of their emperors. Thus, an inscription in honour of emperor Augustus (see Luke 2) praises him as saviour and says that his birth was the beginning of gospel for the whole world. Quite a pretence, yet Roman emperors were often called 'son of god' as well.

Mark puts things on edge by starting his book with the words, 'The beginning of the gospel of Jesus Christ, the Son of God' (CSB, ESV). The reader will have to choose what the real gospel is: the promises and pretences of the emperor or the word of Jesus. Later in his book, Mark again implicitly asks, 'who is more powerful, Jesus or the Roman emperor?' In Mark 5:9, Jesus liberates a man from a demon calling himself Legion. The same word was used for a group of Roman soldiers! So the narrative implies that, with force majeure, Jesus chased a Roman legion back into the sea. This scene resembles a political cartoon! Such an echo is not to be missed.

Model

As final mode of use of the Scriptures I will discuss the use of the Old Testament as a *model* for the description of a person, a case or an event. This use is also common in the New Testament, including in the shortest Gospel. For example, Mark characterises John the Baptist as the new Elijah by describing his ministry in the wilderness (1:4), his clothing (1:6), and his radical message. A second example is that Jesus is just as critical of the temple as the prophet Jeremiah (see esp. 7:1–8:3) was in his time, so that we can see Jeremiah as a model for Jesus in Mark 11–13.

Mark's Gospel does not contain many parables of Jesus, most of which are clustered in Mark 4. Much later, Mark 12:1–12 still offers 'the parable of the vineyard.' This has many similarities with 'the song of the vineyard' in Isaiah 5:1–7, but Jesus does not openly refer to Isaiah and Mark does not think it is necessary to be explicit either. The two passages start in similar fashion:

Isaiah	Mark
My loved one had a vineyard on a fertile hillside. He dug it up and cleared it of stones and planted it with the choicest vines. He built a watchtower in it and cut out a wine press as well.	A man planted a vineyard. He put a wall round it, dug a pit for the winepress and built a watchtower. Then he rented the vineyard to some farmers and moved to another place.

Despite these agreements, however, the passages have different applications. In Isaiah, where God is the speaker, the vineyard is the problem. It does not bring fruit and finally God clears it out. The vineyard is an image for Israel, as often in the Old Testament (esp. Isaiah 27:2–6; Jeremiah 2:21; 12:10; Ezekiel 19:10–14; and Psalm 80:8–18). Isaiah criticises the people for their sins, especially in Isaiah 5:7, and announces God's judgement.

In Jesus' parable the tenants of the vineyard are the problem; these people stand for Israel's leaders, who are called 'the chief priests, the teachers of the law and the elders' (Mark 11:27). They understand that Jesus is speaking about them and react furiously (Mark 12:12). Please note that the new owners of the vineyard, called 'others' by Jesus, are not the church but *Jews and* gentiles who follow Jesus, a group led by Jews such as Peter, Paul, and James.

So what is the value of recognising Isaiah 5 as the *model* for Jesus' parable? First, it makes clear that Jesus gives the people of Israel hope for a new beginning. God will not clear out the whole vineyard, as in Isaiah's time, but only punish the leaders of the people and give the vineyard to others (verse 9). The leaders should have cared for the people, but they failed. This shows that in every period of history, leaders bear a heavy responsibility!

Secondly, and much more subtly, light falls backwards on Isaiah's text. His song mentions the enigmatic person 'my loved one' as initiator of the vineyard, and his identity remains hidden. The parable refers to the son of the owner – recognisably Jesus – as the one 'whom he loved' (verse 6). Twice before in Mark the voice of God has called Jesus the Son 'whom I love' (1:11 and 9:7). The use of these words shows that the loved one in Isaiah is also Jesus, that he is the one who constructed the vineyard in Isaiah. He is the actual owner of the vineyard.

Less important for the application is a nice parallel between both texts. In Isaiah 5:3–4, God asks the opinion of the hearers of his song; in the same way, Jesus asks his audience, 'What then will the owner of the vineyard do?' (Mark 12:9). In both cases, the speaker answers his own question.

Jesus' parable contains yet more, because apart from Isaiah as model, an echo of Jeremiah is also audible. Just before Jesus told this parable, he had spoken critically of the temple and cleansed it (Mark 11:15–18). Taken together, Jesus' words in Mark 11 and 12 strongly resemble Jeremiah's great speech in and against the temple in Jeremiah 7, in which the prophet says, 'until now, day after day, again and again I sent you my servants the prophets.' (Jeremiah 7:25). Jesus echoes these words and seems to add some details in Mark 12:2–5. So can you say that there is also an agreement between the temple and the vineyard? Yes, especially when I tell you that contemporary Jewish interpreters saw the tower in the vineyard (Isaiah 5:2; Mark 12:1) as a symbol of the temple.

Finally, the story of Joseph is also audible in the parable. 'Come, let's kill him,' say the tenants of the vineyard to each other (Mark 12:7). Exactly the same words occur in the Septuagint of Genesis 37:20, spoken by Joseph's brothers when they see him coming, so they form a quote rather than an echo. This combination of words does not occur anywhere else in the Bible. Jesus is a second Joseph, Mark suggests. And the similarity between Joseph and Jesus has prophetic value, for after much misery Joseph was given a new, better life – and Jesus will die but also arise. This is also the thrust of the words from Psalm 118 which Jesus cites at the end of the parable.

All Together

All modes of use of Scripture that I have distinguished occur together in Mark 11:1–10, but I only point this out in brief:

- Verses 9–10 contain a *quotation* from Psalm 118:25–26.

- The crowd mentions the reign of David, which is an *allusion* to Old Testament expectations like 2 Samuel 7:16, Isaiah 8:23–9:6, Jeremiah 23:5, and Psalm 89, and also to the words of Bartimaeus in the previous story (10:47–48).

- The *echo* of Zechariah 9:9 resounds in verses 2 and 7.

- The *model* for the description of Jesus' entry is the triumphant entry of a ruler or an army commander. The Romans had such processions and Psalm 24:7–10 describes one.

Finally

I have shown that Mark uses the Old Testament everywhere, in various ways, to make clear who Jesus is and what his ministry means to people then and now. Of the Old Testament books, Mark uses Isaiah most.

Yet we need to look at what Jesus is doing in Mark 7:14–15 and 10:3–9, where he seems to go against the Old Testament. Mark 10:1–12 is about the question whether divorce is permissible. From the rules in Deuteronomy 24:1–4 the Jews concluded that divorce was indeed allowed; on the contrary, Jesus states that God's plan in Genesis 2 is undeniably that divorce is wrong. Jesus actually pitches one part of Scripture against another, opting for the radical strict rule over against the accepting attitude of his Jewish contemporaries. He thus lays the bar pretty high. For him the arrangement in Deuteronomy 24 is a mere concession, a provision for certain situations, but not a generally applicable principle. The principle, God's original plan with the good creation, is in Genesis 2.[11] Jesus ranks the scriptural statements, with Genesis above the later legislation, but he does not attack the authority of Scripture. We do not need to explain the verses 11–12 too rigorously: Jesus states that you may not leave your spouse for another; that he calls adultery. He criticises situations when a third person is involved but he does not say that divorce is never allowed.

Mark 7:14–15 is a different case. Here Jesus draws the conclusion from what was discussed in 7:1–13: cleanliness is an inner matter because food makes no one unclean. Mark himself underlines this radical statement again in verse 19: Jesus simply abolishes the food laws of Leviticus 11 and 17 and other passages. In this way he enables his followers to eat together with non-believers; Christians do not have to live in the social isolation imposed on the Jews by the laws of purity. Acts 10–11, Romans 14, and Galatians 2 tell you about the laborious reception of, and reflection on, Jesus' radical pronunciation.

So Jesus declares part of the law obsolete! You can understand this when you accept that Jesus is himself God and therefore has the right

---

[11] On the good creation and on sexuality, see also my *Enduring Treasure*, chapters 1 and 3 respectively.

to abolish (certain elements of) the law of Moses. He is allowed to bring the stipulations of the covenant between God and humanity back to how they were before the legislation on Sinai. In this way he grounds the life of his followers on God's earlier covenants with the people, namely the covenants in creation and with Abraham. Many aspects of the later Sinai covenant are no longer valid as a result of the advent of the Messiah. In Hebrews this thought is developed further. But which stipulations are no longer valid, and which still are, is a decision of Jesus as the Son of God, not our decision. God alone is the giver of the law – he alone can repeal and retract it. The law, which was intended to bring people to God and to keep them close to him, is now subordinate to Jesus.

Further Reading

France, R.T., *The Gospel of Mark. A Commentary on the Greek Text*, NIGTC (Carlisle: Paternoster, 2002).

Hays, Richard B., *Echoes of Scripture in the Gospels* (Waco: Baylor University Press, 2016).

Chapter 25: Luke

More than the other evangelists, Luke tells a story, the life story of Jesus. His way of storytelling resembles that of the Old Testament. The same kind of people are depicted, and similar events happen. Yet there is a clear difference: the existing story of Israel – Luke's source of inspiration – is one great promise, the story of Jesus is its fulfilment. Luke quotes Jesus as using the word 'fulfilled' (from the Greek verb *pleroō*) in 4:21, 22:37 and 24:44. Matthew uses the word more often, usually in his own commentary on events.

In Luke 4, Jesus fulfils Scripture by reading it in public. The 'year of the Lord's favour' begins when Jesus proclaims it in Nazareth. In Luke 18:31 Jesus uses another Greek word for 'fulfil' (*teleō*), but its meaning is the same:

> Everything that is written by the prophets about the Son of Man will be fulfilled.

Luke 24

Luke's penultimate story is about reading and explaining the Scriptures. The risen Lord meets two of his disciples on the road to Emmaus and, 'explained to them what was said in in all the Scriptures concerning himself,' 'beginning with Moses and all the Prophets' (Luke 24:27). Moments later, Jesus repeats the same teaching for a larger group of followers (24:44–47). Luke's wording suggests that the entire Old Testament is about Jesus, that you can discover him everywhere in the sacred Books, but also that some explanation is needed in order to see this. How I would have liked to listen in to this teaching of the Lord! Would my book have been much different?

In Luke 24:44 Jesus says that everything that was written about him has now been fulfilled. His words leave it to Luke's readers to discover exactly *what* in the Scriptures relates to him and *how* it is fulfilled. In fact, Luke here presents Jesus as an example and inspiration for the authors of the New Testament, who each in his own way attempt to show that Scripture is fulfilled in Jesus.

The effect of the Emmaus story is that at the end of his Gospel Luke refers his readers back to the Scriptures: read them and find out that they are about Jesus. When they do so, the readers will also see that Jesus was indeed 'the one to set Israel free' (24:21 NRSV note). This word 'free' or 'redeem' echoes the repeated promises of Isaiah that God would become the Redeemer of Israel (41:14; 43:14; 44:6, 24; 47:4; 49:7, 26; 54:5; 59:20; 60:16), promises which were fulfilled in Jesus. Luke does much more with Isaiah than I can show here, but also see chapter 27 on Acts.

Jesus' Freedom

You see that Luke and Jesus have great respect for the Scriptures, but they do not handle them overly literally. Let me give two examples which illustrate their approach.

The words of Jesus' 'manifesto' in Luke 4:18–19 are perhaps the most famous quotation from the Old Testament in the New. Jesus reads from Isaiah 61 and declares that these words are about him as he is fulfilling them. I am not the first to point out that Jesus handles the words of the prophet rather freely, because to Isaiah 61:1–2a he adds a few words from another passage, namely from the middle of Isaiah 58:6: 'to set the oppressed free.'

The second example of Jesus' freedom is Luke 10:25–28, which tells that 'an expert in the law' puts Jesus to the test by asking how he should live.

> He [Jesus] said to him. 'What is written in the Law? What do you read there?' He [the lawyer] answered, 'You shall love the Lord your God with all your heart, and with all your soul, and with all your strength, and with all your mind; and your neighbour as yourself.' And he said to him, 'You have given the right answer; do this, and you will live.' (NRSV)

Mark, Luke's model, writes that it is the lawyer who asks Jesus what the most important commandment is, to which Jesus himself gives the answer (12:28–34). I am not concerned about the fact that Luke swaps the roles. In Luke, it is the legal expert who quotes from Scripture, while in Mark it is Jesus. Much more interesting is the fact that in Mark the two commandments are distinguished: the principal commandment to love God, cited from Deuteronomy 6:5, and the second most important commandment, to love the neighbour, which is taken from Leviticus 19:18. Yet Luke reports that the lawyer combines these two commandments into one great commandment, and that Jesus expresses his approval of this blending! Both the lawyer and Jesus thus handle Scripture freely, combining a text from Deuteronomy with one from Leviticus.

Moreover, the lawyer adds a fourth part to 'heart,' 'soul,' and 'strength' – 'your mind'; these words are also in Matthew 22:37 and Mark 12:30. This addition was common at the time, and again this shows a certain freedom in quoting Scripture. Is Jesus here putting the words of Paul into practice, 'the letter kills, but the Spirit gives life' (2 Corinthians 3:6)?

Luke 1–2

1. What you can hardly hear in a modern translation is how Luke deliberately varies his language. In 1:1–4 he begins with one long, complicated Greek sentence, just as Greek readers loved, as if to say: I can do this! (NRSV and ESV do indeed render this as one sentence.) Starting from chapter 3, Luke writes correct but much simpler Greek. In between, in the birth stories of chapters 1 and 2, he uses simple Greek that sounds much like Hebrew. This style is one of the ways in which he establishes the connection between his book and the Jewish Scriptures. Luke's style is a claim that the story of God and his people continues.

2. Luke shows how the legal requirements of the old covenant are kept in the cases of John and Jesus:

Old covenant	John	Jesus
Circumcision according to Genesis 17:9–13 and Leviticus 12:3	Luke 1:59	Luke 2:21
Dedication (and purification) with sacrifice according to Leviticus 12:6–8	–	Luke 2:22–24, 39

Attending Passover festival according to Deuteronomy 16:1–8	–	Luke 2:41–42

If you did not yet know, the events are taking place in Israel and all characters are pious Jews.

3. According to 1:17 John the Baptist has some traits of the prophet Elijah, but Luke does not develop this. He rather models the description of John on the prophet Samuel. The agreements between 1 Samuel 1 and Luke 1:5–25 are enormous. The two stories begin in identical ways because the wording of Luke 1:5 closely resembles 1 Samuel 1:1. In both situations there is the problem of childlessness, the main location is the house of God, and the return home is mentioned separately. In both stories people pray to have a child, and someone else announces that this prayer is answered. For both sons a special vow is made (1 Samuel 1:11 and Luke 1:15) and both receive their name from their mother.[12] Both sons reach the whole nation with their ministry (1 Samuel 3:20; Luke 1:80; 3:7, 15, 21), but they make way for the person who comes after them: David in the case of Samuel, Jesus in the case of John. This is linked to the fact that the birth of John is heralded as that of a prophet (Luke 1:17), and that of Jesus as a king (Luke 1:32–33) – yet both of them will follow Old Testament models. Later in the story Luke also describes Jesus as prophet, calling him prophet in 7:16, 13:33 and 24:19. Jesus is both.

4. One simple phrase puts John's mother, Elizabeth, right alongside Rachel. When Rachel was finally pregnant after a long period of childlessness, she said, 'God has taken away my disgrace' (Genesis 30:23). According to Luke 1:25, Elizabeth uses exactly the same words in a similar situation.

5. When the angel Gabriel announces to Mary the birth of Jesus, he does not refer to the Scriptures with their many messianic promises and he does not use the word 'fulfil,' but his words are equally steeped in them:

---

[12] The vow regarding John is the vow of a Nazarite, that was someone who dedicated himself specifically to God, see Numbers 6:1–5.

He will be great and will be called the Son of the Most High. And the Lord God will give to him the throne of his father David, and he will reign over the house of Jacob for ever, and of his kingdom there will be no end. (Luke 1:32–33)

These words are mainly based on 2 Samuel 7:11–16, but you can also hear Isaiah 9:6; Ezekiel 37:25; Daniel 7:14; Micah 4:7; Psalm 2:7; and Psalm 89:27–30.

6. Mary, Zechariah, and Simeon interrupt the storyline by singing a messianic psalm that would fit well in the Old Testament. Mary's song closely resembles the hymn of Hannah, another new mother (1 Samuel 2:1–10), but many other passages of Scripture also resound, as this list shows:

Mary's song	Hebrew Bible
Verse 46 My soul glorifies the Lord	Exodus 15:1 I will sing to the LORD Psalm 34:3 glorify the LORD with me
47 My spirit rejoices … my Saviour	1 Samuel 2:1 My heart rejoices in the LORD Psalm 35:9 My soul will rejoice in the LORD; see also Habakkuk 3:18
48a the humble state of his servant	1 Samuel 1:11 look on your servant's misery
48b all generations will call me blessed	Genesis 30:13 The women will call me happy
49 has done great things for me	Psalm 70:19 you have done great things; see also Deuteronomy 10:21
50 His mercy … from generation to generation	Psalm 103:17 (NRSV) the steadfast love of the LORD is from everlasting to everlasting

51 Mighty deeds with his arm … scattered those who are proud	Psalm 89:10 with your strong arm you scattered your enemies; see also Exodus 15:6
52 brought down rulers from their throne … lifted up the humble	Job 12:19 overthrows officials long established Ezekiel 21:26 (NRSV) Exalt that which is low, abase that which is high
53 filled the hungry with good things	Psalm 107:9 fills the hungry with good things
54a helped his servant Israel	Isaiah 41:8, 10 Israel my servant … I will strengthen you and help you
54b remembering to be merciful	Psalm 98:3 He has remembered his love and his faithfulness to Israel

A list like this could also be made for the songs in Luke 1:68–79 and 2:29–32. Sometimes the similarities with the Septuagint are larger than those with the Hebrew text, but English translations tend to minimise the differences.

Not only are many thoughts the same, the songs of Hannah and Mary also have the same role in the narrative of which they are part: in both songs a woman thanks God for her child, but actually she sings of what God will do for all of Israel via that child; they sing of God's salvation and especially of his 'social justice.' Both songs announce a new era and thus combine personal and political elements. Finally, they also form an appropriate introduction to the stories that follow.

7. The list above contains two references to the song of Moses in Exodus 15, the first of a series of songs by individuals about God's liberation; other songs in this series in addition to the songs of Moses, Hannah, and Mary are the songs of Deborah and Barak (Judges 5), David (2 Samuel 22), and Hezekiah (Isaiah 38:9–20)

8. Luke reports that Simeon was looking forward to 'the consolation of Israel' (Luke 2:25). The word 'consolation' or comfort' is one of the numerous echoes of the prophecies of Isaiah, in this case of Isaiah 40:1,

'Comfort, comfort my people.' In this way Luke refers to the entire passage in Isaiah that begins with these words. Isaiah had promised comfort to Israel and this promise had so far not been completely fulfilled. God was now going to do so through Jesus.

9. In respect of Anna Luke uses almost the same words as about Simeon: the people around her 'were looking forward to the redemption of Jerusalem' (Luke 2:38), in accordance with the promises in Isaiah 46:13, 52:9 and above all 59:20: 'The Redeemer will come to Zion, to those in Jacob who repent of their sin.' Do also read these words in their context. These promises are now being fulfilled!

Elijah and Elisha

Luke uses not only Hannah and Samuel as models, but also other characters from the Scriptures, especially the prophets Elijah and Elisha, although he never tells you.

In Luke 4:25–26 Jesus himself compares his ministry to that of Elijah. He refers to the story in 1 Kings 17 in which the prophet does well to foreigners, which is a preview of the proclamation of the Gospel in the whole world which Luke will describe in Acts.

Jesus' miracle in Luke 7:11–17 recalls that of Elijah in his contact with the widow in Zarephath (1 Kings 17:7–24). In both stories a woman's only son comes to life again and the witnesses recognise God's work. Both stories contain the comment that the son was returned to his mother. Perhaps even the inhabitants of Nain saw the similarities between Elijah and Jesus, for they say: 'A great prophet has appeared among us' (verse 16). Yet they overlook the fact that Jesus was not dependent on God for this miracle but performed it in his own power: 'I say to you …' (verse 14). So he is more than Elijah.

Luke looked at the narrative of Elijah in Samaria (2 Kings 1:2–15) before writing his story about Samaria in Luke 9:52–56; but whereas Elijah lets fire come from heaven, Jesus refuses to do so. Thus the reaction of Jesus' disciples James and John shows that they do not understand how different Jesus is from Elijah.

The call narrative which follows (Luke 9:57–62) recalls 1 Kings 19:19–21. Both stories are about ploughing and other work on the land; both emphasise God's radical call for disciples to leave their previous life.

The description of Jesus' prayer on the Mount of Olives (Luke 22:39–46) echoes the situation and prayer of Elijah at Mount Horeb (1 Kings 19:1–18): both men are threatened with death, both are frightened despite knowing God, both leave their companion(s) behind, and both receive help from an angel.

According to the Septuagint, King Ahab addresses Elijah as 'he who perverts Israel' and Elijah responds that he is not perverting Israel (1 Kings 18:17–18); when the Jewish leaders blame Jesus at the beginning of the trial before Pilate (Luke 23:2) they use exactly the same words about him. Of course, neither Elijah nor Jesus had done wrong, but both had resisted the evil leaders of the people and were thus seen as a threat to the authorities. In reality, Ahab himself was the bad leader – and the Jewish leaders exposed themselves by using the same words as he. What an irony!

The chapter on Acts below contains even more parallels between Elijah and Jesus. Yet the narrative of the transfiguration (Luke 9:28–36) shows that Jesus is not a reincarnation of Elijah, but a different person.

Jesus is also compared to the prophet Elisha, Elijah's successor. In Luke 4:27 Jesus himself refers to the narrative in which Elisha cures a foreigner (2 Kings 5:1–14), announcing that his ministry will not be limited to Israel either. Both Jesus and Elisha cry over the coming devastation of Israel (2 Kings 8:11–12, Luke 19:44) and Luke must have been aware of this similarity.

There is a further parallel between 2 Kings 6 and the Emmaus story. Elisha's servant is at first unable to see what is there, and at Elisha's request the LORD opens his eyes. Later Elisha opens the eyes of the opposing soldiers (2 Kings 6:17, 20). The two persons on the road to Emmaus at first do not recognise Jesus either, so he opens their eyes (Luke 24:31). These situations are described in the same words. For both the servant and the two disciples, the ability to 'see' makes the difference between despair and hope. Together these parallels form a clear echo.

So far a few examples of Luke's dealings with Scripture. His stories show how God acts in recognisable patterns, without using a 'promise and fulfilment' scheme. This allows him to write a very different book about Jesus than Matthew.

Further Reading

Bauckham, Richard, *Gospel Women* (London/New York: T&T Clark, 2002).

Hays, Richard B., *Echoes of Scripture in the Gospels* (Waco: Baylor University Press, 2016).

Koet, Bart J., 'Holy Place and Hannah's Prayer,' in Koet, *Dreams and Scripture in Luke-Acts* (CBET 42; Leuven: Peeters, 2006) 123–146.

Riet, Peter van't, *Lukas versus Matthew* (Kampen: Kok, 2005)

Chapter 26: John

Pope Gregory the First said about the Scriptures that they are:

> A kind of river … which is both shallow and deep, in which both the lamb may find a footing and the elephant float at large.

These words are surely true of the Gospel of John. This Gospel is easy to understand yet at the same time it has enormous depth. John's use of the Old Testament, which pervades the entire Gospel, surely contributes much to this depth. John does not use the Old Testament in such a striking way as Matthew and Paul, but what he does is even more compelling. In this chapter I once again make a limited selection from the material.

Quotations

I start with what is most visible, the direct quotations from the Old Testament. John does not quote often and the boundary between quotations and allusions is rather thin. Quotations occur in any case in 1:23; 2:17; 6:31, 45; 7:38, 42; 8:17; 10:34; 12:13, 14–15, 38, 40; 13:18; 15:25; 19:24, 36 and 37. In 12:8, Jesus uses words from Deuteronomy 15:11 without John saying anything about it, so this verse is an allusion rather than a quotation. In addition, 17:12 and 19:28 mention fulfilment of the Scriptures without reference to a particular text.

John does not quote as often as Mark, and Matthew and Luke have even more quotations. The literal quotations in John are sometimes words spoken by Jesus himself, sometimes they are statements by another person in the story or commentary by the evangelist. Some quotations also occur in one or more of the other Gospels, but not all.

When you read the above verses, you notice that John does not often use quotations in order to prove that Jesus is the Messiah, as do Matthew and Acts. Such quotations, which mention the word fulfilment, only occur from chapter 12 onwards, in the description of the passion of Jesus.

John quotes only short passages from the Old Testament and sometimes does so fairly freely, as in 7:42 and 8:17. In 7:42 he assumes that a few words suffice for readers to think of Micah 5:2. John uses both the Hebrew text and the Septuagint. He clearly assumes that most of his readers have the Septuagint, but he is not bound by this translation. For example, in 6:45 he prefers the Septuagint but in 19:37 he uses the Hebrew text. I can show this by giving literal translations of the texts. John 6:45 is simple:

Hebrew Isaiah 54:13	Greek Isaiah 54:13	John 6:45
All your children will be taught by the LORD	All your sons are taught by God	They will all be taught by God

The difference is small, but John chooses the word 'God' that appears in the Septuagint, while the Hebrew has LORD. But in John 19:37 it is different:

Hebrew Zechariah 12:10b	Greek Zechariah 12:10b	John 19:37
They will look on me, the one they have pierced, and they will mourn for him	They will look at me because they have danced	They will look on the one they have pierced

The Septuagint has confused the Hebrew word for pierce (*daqar*) with the word for dance (*raqad*), and the result is a nonsensical translation. John therefore rightly follows the Hebrew text.

'Quotations' not Exact

Sometimes John creates problems for those of us who think literally. For example, in 6:31 he uses the introductory words 'as it is written,' so you expect a quotation; yet the words 'He gave them bread from heaven to eat' (6:31) occur nowhere in the Old Testament. Yet the idea that God feeds people with supernatural bread is thoroughly biblical: the Jews who speak these words are combining ideas from Exodus 16:4, 15, Nehemiah 9:15 and Psalm 78:23–25, and they clearly to justice to the *intention* of the Old Testament. Yet they don't see that Jesus is the fulfilment of these texts. Something similar occurs when Jesus declares:

> As the scripture has said, 'Out of the believer's heart shall flow rivers of living water.' (John 7:38, NRSV)

For these words you search in vain in the Hebrew Bible and in the Septuagint – nor do they occur in the apocryphal writings. However, it appears that Jesus freely combines ideas from Psalm 78:16 and 20 with Zechariah 14:8 (and perhaps Exodus 17:3–6 and Ezekiel 47:1–12). You see that John and Jesus treat Scripture with respect and reverence, but not as literally as you might expect.

Out of Context? (John 10:34)

In John 10:34–36, Jesus seems to take the words of Psalm 82:6 completely out of their context:

> Jesus answered them, 'Is it not written in your Law, "I have said you are 'gods'"? If he called them "gods", to whom the word of God came – and Scripture cannot be set aside – what about the one whom the Father set apart as his very own and sent into the world? Why then do you accuse me of blasphemy because I said, "I am God's Son"?'

Yet from a Jewish perspective this is no problem, for Jesus is following the Jewish logic 'if this, then surely that.' This way of reasoning presents something small as a precedent or evidence for something larger. We still do this: 'If a hundred pounds is much money, surely a thousand pounds is more?' or 'If manslaughter is wrong, how much worse is murder?' This argument *a fortiori* occurs throughout in the New Testament, most often in Hebrews, and it was also known in the surrounding Greek culture. Our only problem is that Jesus uses this 'how much more' argument implicitly.

So what do his words mean? Jesus does not argue that God can simply call humans 'gods,' because that would contradict the Old Testament. The key to understanding him is to see that the text does not contain a word like 'people' or 'humans.' In Psalm 82, God is rather addressing the idols or the princes of other nations, giving them an opportunity to prove themselves. Jesus' reasoning is therefore: if even idols get an opportunity, how much more does he, God's representative and deputy on earth, deserve the opportunity to prove that he is God. Whether the evidence is convincing, depends on the audience.

A few more things strike us here, firstly that Jesus is referring to the psalm as 'your Law'; he therefore refers to the entire Scripture as law, while we prefer to reserve that word for the books of Moses. Secondly, Jesus speaks tremendously positively about Scripture: it is always in force and authoritative. And finally, it is clear that it is Jesus who can call on Scripture, not his Jewish opponents, despite their claim that they are faithful to it. Scripture is about him, and as long as they do not recognise this, they are wrong. They do not have the key.

Beginning (John 1:1)

In his Gospel, John does much more with the Old Testament than merely quoting it! I give some examples of the influence of the Old Testament on John 1–4. This begins in the very first verse, for no Jewish reader can have missed that the Gospel begins with the same words as the Hebrew Bible, 'In the beginning....' Although Genesis and John have only two words in common in the Greek, because these are the opening words you cannot miss this loud echo.

The Gospel of Mark also begins with the word 'beginning,' as we saw, and it is possible that John is nodding at the book of his colleague. In that case he means to say: 'Dear readers, Mark has told you about the beginning of Jesus' ministry; I will now tell you about the beginning of the world.'

Whereas in Genesis it is God who acts, in John it is the Word, Jesus, who is emphatically equated to God (1:1). The evangelist also states that the Word acted as creator, suggesting that Jesus *is* not only God but also *acts* like God. This thought will be repeated throughout the book.

The term 'the Word' for Jesus is itself likewise taken from the Old Testament, but also surpasses it. The word of God is strong and creative (for example, Psalm 33:6; Isaiah 40:8; 55:11; Jeremiah 23:29), but under the old covenant it is still impersonal. John has combined it with the wisdom, which is represented in the Old Testament as a person (for example in Proverbs 9:1–6) and who even speaks (Proverbs 8:22–36). This means that Jesus combines traits of God's Word and God's wisdom, but as God-in-person he also surpasses these.

God's Son (John 1:14, 18)

Jesus is referred to as God's only Son in 1:14 and 18; here older translations have 'only begotten' because John does not use the ordinary word for 'only,' but the special word *monogenēs*. In the Septuagint this word often renders the Hebrew word for 'beloved' and is used, among others, for Isaac (Genesis 22:2, 12 and 16). Therefore Hebrews 11:17 calls Isaac *monogenēs*. John's choice of word thus implicitly puts the Lord Jesus next to Isaac. What does this mean? Isaac was the beloved, only son who was willing to be sacrificed by his father!

Occasionally the people of Israel as a whole are also referred to as God's son, for example in Exodus 4:22–23; and in 2 Samuel 7:14 God promises David that his son and successor will be God's son. These things also resound in John 1:14 and 18.[13]

John the Baptist (John 1:19–28)

The conversation between John the Baptist and his Jewish interrogators in 1:19–28 presupposes knowledge of the Old Testament; failing that, we will not understand it fully. The Jews expected a Messiah (verse 20); that is not a name but a title, which means 'anointed one.' Under the old covenant between God and the people leaders such as kings, priests, and prophets were equipped for their task by anointing with oil (see for example 1 Samuel 16:1–13; 1 Kings 1:32–40; 19:16; Leviticus 8:10–12). The saviour whom God would one day send would also be anointed in this way, and he was therefore called Messiah, 'anointed one.' In addition the Jews also hoped for the return of the prophet Elijah, taking Malachi 4:5–6 literally; and according to John 6:14 they expected the great prophet about whom Moses had spoken in Deuteronomy 18:15–18.

---

[13] On John 1:14–18, see also chapter 2.

Jesus' contemporaries often cited Isaiah 11:1–5 with respect to their expectation of the Messiah. The words of John the Baptist on the role of the Holy Spirit in the life of Jesus (1:32–33) fulfil Isaiah 11:2. Isaiah wrote that the Spirit would rest on the great descendant of David and John does not accidentally use the same word, 'rest' (CSB) or 'remain.' Previously, the spirit had 'rested' on Moses and the seventy elders of Israel (Numbers 11:25–26), so Jesus is part of a strong scriptural tradition!

Nathanael (John 1:43–51)

During his meeting with Nathanael, Jesus shows his supernatural knowledge by saying that he had seen Nathanael under a fig tree (1:48). In 1 Kings 4:25, sitting under one's own fig-tree is a description of peace and prosperity; later in the Old Testament it became a description of the messianic time of salvation (Micah 4:4; Zechariah 3:10). Jesus' remark characterises Nathanael, 'a real Israelite' (verse 47), as a type of – and an example for – the people who believe in Jesus and who experience the happiness of the messianic era.

The fact that Nathanael is 'an Israelite in whom there is no deceit' (verse 47) makes him the opposite number of Jacob, the ancestor of Israel, who was a deceiver (Genesis 27:12, 35, 36). God had later given Jacob a new name, Israel (Genesis 35:9–12), and Nathanael bears that name with honour. If this Nathanael says that Jesus is 'the Son of God' and 'the king of Israel' (verse 49), his declaration must be reliable. In 1:51 Jesus clearly alludes to the story of Jacob in Bethel (Genesis 28:12):

> You will see heaven open, and the angels of God ascending and descending on the Son of Man.

It is not immediately clear what he means, but when you read on, the Gospel itself provides more clarity. Several times John writes that Jesus, the Son of Man, will be lifted up on the cross (John 3:14; 8:28; 12:32, 34). He uses the word 'lift up' ambiguously. Literally, the point is that Jesus will hang on the cross, high above the earth; but at the same time it means 'raised,' 'elevated,' 'glorified,' 'receiving honour.' Humanly speaking Jesus' elevation on the cross was of course an insult, because crucifixion was a deep humiliation. But, miraculously, from God's perspective it is rather his exaltation (12:28)! On the cross

Jesus shows who he is and defeats the enemy, death, on its own territory.

So is the cross a kind of stepladder, or are we dealing with similarities between Jacob, the old Israel, and Jesus as the new Israel? No, John means that henceforth heaven is open and that Jesus is now the connection between heaven and earth, a kind of stepladder between the people and God. As Jacob's ladder stretched to heaven, so Jesus' work on earth has effect in heaven.

As you see, the Old Testament sheds light on the story of Nathanael in many ways. It especially shows that in Jesus God's new era has begun on earth. When you read Isaiah 52:13, the beginning of the well-known chapter Isaiah 53, and you connect this verse to the next verse and with the entire chapter that follows, with this new understanding of the meaning of 'lift up' in mind, you see that 'lift up' has the same double meaning here. Because Isaiah 53 contains so many contrasts between glory and suffering, Isaiah's use of 'lift up' probably inspired that of Jesus and John. This is all the more likely because John 12:38 is a quotation of Isaiah 53:1.

Wedding in Cana (John 2:1–11)

Whatever some people may say, the fact that the wedding in Cana takes place 'on the third day' (2:1) has no Old Testament parallel, and later Judaism has no tradition that people married on the third day of the week either. This is simply an event that takes place three days after the previous one; when you read more closely, you see that John is reporting the first complete week of Jesus' public ministry in 1:19 through 2:11. This first week is the counterpart of the last week of Jesus' life, which is described in great detail in John 12–20.

Nonetheless, there are clear allusions to the Old Testament in 2:1–11. First of all, there is the theme of the wedding. In the story the actual groom remains in the background, giving room to the Old Testament idea that the era of the coming of the saviour would be a kind of wedding feast (Isaiah 54:1–8; 62:4–5). The saviour comes to take Israel as his wife and make her happy. That this explanation is correct is confirmed in John 3:29, where John the Baptist calls Jesus the bridegroom; see also Mark 2:19–20, where Jesus refers to himself as the groom.

A second theme from Scripture is the wine that Jesus brings in abundance. In Judaism at the time of Jesus, wine was a symbol of the Torah, God's good instructions for his people. But more importantly, according to the Old Testament the time of God's redemption would be characterised by an abundance of good wine (Isaiah 25:6; Amos 9:13–14; Hosea 14:8). By bringing such good wine, Jesus signals that he is the promised saviour and that the good new era of God's salvation has now begun. God has indeed saved the best until last.

Some find it farfetched, but I think there is also significance in the fact that John tells us that there were *six* water vessels (2:6). They were tools 'for the [Jewish] ceremonial washing' which was made redundant by Jesus' ministry. It helps if you know that six, because it is not seven, was the number of imperfection. So this detail in the narrative shows that Jesus has come to renew the relationship between God and humankind.

Nicodemus (John 3:1–21)

We tend to feel sorry for Nicodemus because Jesus treats him so harshly. 'You are Israel's teacher … and you do not understand these things?' is Jesus's fierce criticism (verse 10). Is Jesus unfair? How could Nicodemus ever know the things Jesus is talking about, such as rebirth and a new heart? Well, as a scholar and scribe he might have thought of Ezekiel 36:25–27, where God says to Israel:

> I will sprinkle clean water on you, and you will be clean; I will cleanse you from all your impurities and from all your idols. I will give you a new heart and put a new spirit in you; I will remove from you your heart of stone and give you a heart of flesh. And I will put my Spirit in you and move you to follow my decrees and be careful to keep my laws.

Jesus is sent by God to do exactly this – and more! Nicodemus must therefore recognise him as the Messiah and receive a new heart himself.

Later the conversation with Nicodemus deals with the snake that saved the people who looked at it in the wilderness (3:14). These words refer directly to Numbers 21:4–9, the narrative about the bronze snake. The point of comparison is of course the necessity of looking up in faith in order to be saved, not anything that Jesus and the serpent would have in common. It says that 'everyone who believes may have eternal life in him' (verse 15).

The Woman in Samaria (John 4:1–42)

Here we see the daring opening of the narrative about the encounter between Jesus and the woman from Samaria. Modern readers probably don't hear how audacious this is, but a Jewish audience was on the tip of their chairs: is this unmarried man, Jesus, sitting at a well in a foreign country? Exciting! 'Comes a man to a well' was a familiar theme, think of the servant of Abraham (Genesis 24:11–20), Jacob (Genesis 29:1–12), and Moses (Exodus 2:15b–20). In each of these situations a nice lady had appeared on scene, water was drawn, and the result was a wedding!

John does not suggest anything untoward and neither do I, but as the opening of a story the theme, 'comes a man to a well' is brilliant. Should the woman have doubted Jesus' intentions, then his request to call her (own) husband (verse 16) would have helped her out of the dream, especially as he also knows that her past record is not great (verses 17–18). We see the beginning of a spiritual relationship between Jesus and the woman as a result of her radical choice for him. Her choice is more radical than that of most males in the Gospel of John, and this links in with John 3:29 again, to which I have already referred.

There are even more parallels between Genesis and John 4. Just as Rachel runs home with good news (Genesis 29:12), so this woman – hastily, but with good news – returns to her town without her jar (4:28, see also 39–43). Other people, who know this woman, also come to the well to meet the man (Genesis 24:28–32; John 4:30, 39–40).

The narrative also shows how Jesus fulfils two Old Testament expectations. As I noticed in 1:19–28, he is the great prophet who was expected. The Samaritans shared this expectation of a coming prophet:

they recognised only the first five books of the Old Testament, but these do contain the promise of the prophet like Moses (Deuteronomy 18:15–18). The woman recognises Jesus as such in verse 19. In the second place, Jesus is the one who gives living water (verses 10–15); he himself says more about this in John 7:37–39, see below. In Jeremiah 2:13, God complains that his people have left him, 'the spring of living water,' and the prophet does the same in Jeremiah 17:13; in Jesus, God comes offering living water again.

At the beginning of the conversation, the woman asks whether Jesus is more important than Jacob (verse 12); the answer in verses 25–26 does not come unexpectedly: yes, he is, for he is the promised Messiah, the Saviour of Jews, Samaritans, and the whole world.

Festivals (John 5–10)

In the middle section of his Gospel, John focuses on Jesus' participation in the Jewish feasts in Jerusalem and his teaching on the temple. It seems as if the evangelist quite systematically follows the Jewish feasts. Every time Jesus and his Jewish opponents discuss the interpretation of the Old Testament in detail; both sides invoke Abraham and Moses, the great heroes of the history of Israel's faith.

In John 5 Jesus probably attends the Feast of Weeks that was also called Pentecost, although John does not mention it. Originally this was a harvest festival, but in Jesus' time the Jews primarily celebrated the legislation by Moses. During this feast, but far from the temple, Jesus heals a paralysed man. Healing of the paralysed was a promise for God's glorious future, which has now come in Jesus; see for example Isaiah 35:6; Jeremiah 31:8; Micah 4:6–7; and Zephaniah 3:19.

The teaching of Jesus at this feast concerns the issue of testimony. These witnesses are God (5:32), John the Baptist (33–35), Jesus' own work (36), and the Scriptures (37–40). And while the Jews think that Moses is on their side in their opposition to Jesus, Moses is precisely their accuser, for he has already written about Jesus – but the Jews do not believe him (45–47, see also 1:45).

John 6 is set at the time of the Passover festival and presents Jesus as the fulfilment of all that was commemorated at this feast: the Exodus from Egypt and God's care for the people of Israel in the wilderness by means of food and drink (see Exodus 17:1–7 and Numbers 20:1–13). Jesus' teaching has the form of a sermon in Jewish style, which takes its point of departure in two texts from different parts of the Hebrew Bible:

> Come, all you who are thirsty, come to the waters; and you who have no money, come, buy and eat! Come, buy wine and milk without money and without cost. Why spend money on what is not bread, and your labour on what does not satisfy? Listen, listen to me, and eat what is good, and you will delight in the richest of fare. (Isaiah 55:1–2)

> Yet he gave a command to the skies above and opened the doors of the heavens; he rained down manna for the people to eat, he gave them the grain of heaven. (Psalm 78:23–24)

Both passages are being fulfilled in the coming of Jesus.

Both John 7 and 8 revolve around the Feast of Tabernacles, of which in Jesus' time water and light were the important symbolic elements. Every morning water was brought to the temple while the people were singing Isaiah 12, with the core words 'With joy you will draw water from the wells of salvation' (Isaiah 12:3). Jesus' words in John 7:37–39 echo the fulfilment of passages such as Psalm 36:8–9; 78:16 and 20; Isaiah 35:6; 41:18; 43:19–20; 44:3; and Zechariah 14:8. In the evening, there was dancing by the light of torches which recalled the pillar of fire and cloud that had protected Israel from the Egyptians (Exodus 14:19–25). Jesus responds to this by calling himself the light for the world (8:12). His arrival is the beginning of the real feast!

Finally, John 10:22–39 is set during Hanukkah, the feast of Temple Renewal. The temple was deconsecrated in 167 BC by the pagan king Antiochus IV, but in 164 reconquered by the Maccabees, cleansed, and re-consecrated; you can read about this in 1 Maccabees 4:36–59. This final feast is, therefore, not strictly an Old Testament festival (although some churches include the Books of the Maccabees in the canon), but it is of course part of the background of Jesus' ministry. Already in 2:13–22 the Lord had hinted that his coming would make the temple redundant. Now he says that he was set apart by the Father and sent to the world (10:36), which again makes him a superior alternative to the existing temple, the place set apart for God.

The Creation

At various places in the Gospel, John refers to the creation of the world, again without quoting any specific texts. He does this to indicate that Jesus was already present at creation and thus pre-existed with the Father (1:3, 10; 17:5, 24). Consequently, Jesus is on the side of God, not of created reality. This of course implies that he was already there before Abraham (8:58) and Moses (5:45–47). In the present, Jesus is doing the same things as God the Creator (9:3–4) and, like God, he has power over creation, which is apparent, for example, from his walking on water (6:16–21). Habakkuk 3:12–15 is about God's ability to do this; and listen to Job 9:8:

> He alone stretches out the heavens and treads on the waves of the sea.

And to Job 38:16, where God asks Job:

> Have you journeyed to the springs of the sea or walked in the recesses of the deep?

Because he is God, the meaning of Jesus' person and work is not limited to the land and people of Israel; note the expression 'all people' in his words in 12:32:

> And I, when I am lifted up from the earth, will draw all people to myself.

Jesus is the one who 'gives light to everyone' (1:9), enabling them to become children of God (1:11–12).

In the narrative of the resurrection John mentions twice – and therefore with emphasis – that it took place on the 'first day of the week' (20:1, 19). Here you hear Genesis 1 again. The old week is over; the old creation is behind us. The resurrection of Jesus is the beginning of a new creation week. Looking back, you might also notice that Jesus had died on Friday, the sixth day of the Jewish week. As God completed the creation on the sixth day (Genesis 1:31–2:2), so on the sixth day Jesus could say that his work was finished (John 19:30). On the seventh day God rested of his work as creator, and Jesus rested in the tomb after his work on the cross. So the resurrection of Jesus is the beginning of the new creation!

Unity

The concept of unity occurs in two ways with John, both of which are connected to the Old Testament. First, there is the unity of God, a very important element of the faith of Israel, for example in the confession of Deuteronomy 6:4:

> Hear, O Israel: the LORD our God, the LORD is one.

The Jews in Jesus' time still found this of great importance, see John 8:41 (NRSV):

> They said to him, 'We are not illegitimate children; we have one father, God himself.'

Contrary to what Jews and Muslims think, this unity of God is not threatened by who Jesus is. Although he is equal to God, he and the Father are *one* – as he emphatically declares in 10:30, 17:11 and 22 – and therefore not two gods. Hence we can recognise Jesus as God without giving up the unity of God.

Second, there is the ideal of the unity of all those who believe in God. The unity of the people of Israel was broken by the formation of two separate kingdoms after King Solomon, and later by the exile and the fact that many Jews had not returned to the promised land but spread over the world. The renewed unity of the people was therefore an important ideal for the prophets, expected for the end times (Ezekiel 34:13; 37:15–24; Hosea 2:3; Micah 2:12; also in Jewish texts outside the Bible). This hope includes the prospect that there will be one leader again. Jesus emphatically prays for this unity in John 17, and he achieves it according to 10:16 and 11:52. In this way he shows that he is the expected Saviour and that the time of God's salvation begins with him. In the words of John's Gospel you hear the echo of the prophets.

Finally

It is clear that the Old Testament has profoundly influenced most of the thoughts, concepts, and speeches in the Gospel to John. All kinds of elements of the Old Testament find their deeper meaning or fulfilment in Jesus. John's book is entirely based on the Christological reinterpretation of the Old Testament. Consequently, we live with the tension that there is continuity in God's plan, but the advent of Jesus changes everything. The message of Jesus Christ is completely in line with the Old Testament yet it radically changes the meaning of the same Old Testament. John shows this without using many proof texts. His many allusions and echoes assume that the readers know who Jacob, Elijah, Isaiah, and the others are, so they can appreciate his allusions.

Further Reading

Bauckham, Richard, *The Testimony of the Beloved Disciple* (Grand Rapids: Baker Academic, 2007).

Crutcher, Rhonda G., *That He Might Be Revealed: Water Imagery and the Identity of Jesus in the Gospel of John* (Eugene: Pickwick, 2015).

Hays, Richard B., *Echoes of Scripture in the Gospels* (Waco: Baylor University Press, 2016).

Menken, Maarten J.J., *Old Testament Quotations in the Fourth Gospel*, CBET 15 (Kampen: Kok Pharos, 1996).

Sosa Siliezar, Carlos R., *Creation Imagery in the Gospel of John*, LNTS 546 (London: Bloomsbury T&T Clark, 2015).

Wright, Tom, *Surprised by Scripture. Engaging with Contemporary Issues* (London: SPCK, 2014).

Chapter 27: Acts

This chapter presents a selection from the material available, because like the other books of the New Testament, Acts frequently uses the Old Testament. It is important to remember that Acts was written by Luke, the person who also wrote the Third Gospel.

The Scriptures as Model

Luke not only uses quotations, allusions, and echoes, but he also takes the Old Testament as a *model* for his own books. Here are some examples.

The transition between Luke and Acts marks the transition from Jesus to the apostles, and resembles the transition between the ministries of Elijah and Elisha in 2 Kings 2. Both times there is an ascension that is indicated by the expression 'take up' (2 Kings 2:1; Luke 24:51; Acts 1:2, 9). The number of eyewitnesses to these ascensions is limited: only Elisha in the case of Elijah, only the eleven disciples in the case of Jesus. These eyewitnesses are the successors of the one who is taken up. And just as Elisha performed the same miracles as Elijah (2 Kings 2–9), so the disciples of Jesus do the same miracles as he (Acts 2:43; 5:12). Finally, the Old Testament narrative emphasizes the spirit of Elijah (2 Kings 2:9, 15), which seems to be a type of the Holy Spirit (see also Luke 1:17).

These parallels between the two stories are a promise and a challenge for the church. Just as the ministry of Elisha was not inferior to that of Elijah, so the ministry of Jesus' disciples and of the whole congregation does not need to be inferior to that of the Lord Jesus.

Later in Acts we encounter another echo of Elijah, because the stories about the evangelist Philip have similarities with the narrative about Elijah, as you see in the following list:

Similarity	Elijah in 1 and 2 Kings	Philip in Acts 8
Active in Samaria	1.18 to 1.21	verses 5–8
Meets courtier	1.18:3–7	verse 27

Angel of the Lord	1.19:5–7	verse 26
A chariot	1.18:44–46; 2.2:11–12	verses 28, 29, 38
'Together,' 'both'	2.2:6–8, 11	verse 38
Suddenly removed	1.18:48; 2.2:3, 5	verse 39
No longer visible	2.2:12	verse 39

We note that Luke used the Elijah narrative as a model for his own text by emphasising the similarities between these two men. Perhaps he did this to give Philip, who was not an apostle but one of the helpers of Acts 6:1–6, more authority. Because the agreements are fairly superficial and the stories are about different subjects, the parallels probably have limited meaning.

The narrative of the call of Paul (Acts 9:1–9, see also 22:4–11 and 26:12–18) has similarities with the stories about the call of Jacob (Genesis 31:11–13), of Moses (Exodus 3:2–10), and of Ezekiel (1:28–2:1). Both Paul and Ezekiel see something supernatural, they hear a voice and fall on the ground, and are finally sent out by God to preach. When you see this, you understand that Luke is introducing Paul as someone with great potential.

An interesting parallel between Acts and the Scriptures is not bound to a particular narrative, but is seen in the so-called we-form of Acts. The bulk of Acts is a narrative in the third person, which is about 'they' and 'he.' However, there are also some so-called we-passages, in which a person who is present in the narrative is the narrator. These we-passages can be found in 16:10–17; 20:5–15; 21:1–18; and 27:1–28:16. Remarkably, the narrator does not mention his name, but he is probably the author of the book, Luke. Because this we-form begins in chapter 16, the narrator probably joined Team Paul in Troas.

The unexpected transitions between the 'he-passages' and the 'we-passages' in Acts are unique in ancient literature. However, the Old Testament contains similar inconsistencies. The book of Ezra begins in the he-form and holds it until 7:28, where for the first time 'I' is used. The I-form can be found in Ezra 8 and 9, after which chapter 10 is once again in the he-form. The book of Nehemiah is largely in the I-form, but in 8:9 and 12:26, 47 it refers to the main character in the he-form. The book of Daniel again resembles Ezra: it begins in the he-form but from chapter 7 uses the I-form. It is therefore quite possible that Luke took these parts of the Old Testament as models for the we-form of Acts. Although this explanation still leaves us with some questions, it is the best explanation we have.

The Speeches

A quarter of Acts consists of spoken word, mainly in the form of long speeches: four speeches by Peter in Acts 2, 3, 4 and 10; one by Stephen in Acts 7; and four by Paul in 13, 17, 22 and 26. In these discourses the speakers proclaim Jesus, doing so by reminding their hearers of what had happened recently in Jerusalem (cross and resurrection) – but also by presenting extensive explanations of the Scriptures. The only speech that hardly uses the Scriptures is the last one: in Acts 17 Paul is addressing the Athenians, gentiles who did not know the Scriptures, so it would not have made sense for Paul to refer to the written Word of God. Thus, the speech in Acts 17 is the exception to the rule. The other speeches were given to Jewish audiences and therefore the speakers were bearing witness to the fact that in Jesus the Scriptures are fulfilled. If you see the use of the Old Testament in the New anywhere, it is here.

As an example, we look at the rather unknown speech in Acts 13:16–41, given in Antioch in Pisidia, which Luke intended as a model of how Paul spoke in synagogues – and he often spoke in that context. This evangelistic speech primarily seems to be a history lesson! Paul reminds his Jewish hearers of many good things from their book of national history, the Old Testament (verses 16–22). Then he tells about John the Baptist and about Jesus, continually referring positively to the same Scriptures (verses 23–31). In verse 32 he arrives at the present of the hearers, but he continues to base himself on the Scriptures. Yet he uses remarkably few real quotations (only in verses 22, 33, 34, 35 and 41, so especially towards the closing of the speech) and these quotes are fairly short as well. (In verse 25, John the Baptist is quoted, with words similar to John 1:20, 27 and Luke 3:16.) So if you only paid attention to these five quotations, you would overlook the fact that Paul's speech is rife with the Old Testament. The first quotation is 13:22:

> After removing Saul, he [God] made David their king. God testified concerning him: 'I have found David son of Jesse, a man after my own heart; he will do everything I want him to do.'

The words in the quotation marks are not an exact quotation, but a combination of words from Psalm 89:20, 1 Samuel 13:14, and Isaiah 44:28. Notice the unique expression that God *found* David. The combination of the words 'David' and 'find' only occurs in Psalm 89:20, so it is fairly obvious that Paul is making a conscious allusion. This is all the more probable, because in the following verse (Acts 13:23) he uses the word 'promise,' which expresses the central thought of Psalm 89. And there is another connection between Paul's proclamation and Psalm 89, for at the climax of this psalm (verse 51) the word 'anointed one' (Messiah) occurs.

Psalm 89 asks the question when God will finally fulfil his promise to David. The answer of Paul and Luke is that God has done this now, in our time, in Jesus! For Paul's hearers in Antioch and for us as readers, this means that we may also relate the following words from Psalm 89 to Jesus:

> My hand will sustain him; surely my arm will strengthen him. The enemy will not get the better of him; the wicked will not oppress him. … He will call out to me, 'You are my Father, my God, the Rock my Saviour.' And I will appoint him to be my firstborn, the most exalted of the kings of the earth. I will maintain my love to him for ever, and my covenant with him will never fail. I will establish his line for ever, his throne as long as the heavens endure. (Psalm 89:21–22, 22–29)

Acts 13:22 not only refers to Psalm 89, because the phrase 'a man after my own heart' comes from 1 Samuel 13:14. And the comment that David will do the will of God is based on Isaiah 44:28, where doing the will of the LORD relates to King Cyrus of Persia, who is then called God's anointed in the next verse, Isaiah 45:1. Paul's uses of Scripture carries the suggestion that Jesus combines qualities of the kings David and Cyrus, and that he fulfils what God had promised about these two leaders in the Scriptures.

In 13:33, the second quotation in Paul's speech comes from Psalm 2. We saw in chapter 3 that Psalm 2:7 is often cited in the New Testament and I will say no more about it here. It is striking that Paul uses the expression 'the second Psalm,' because references to the Old Testament are usually much vaguer as a consequence of the fact that there was no chapter division yet and only the psalms were numbered.

In 13:34, Paul quotes the Septuagint of Isaiah 55:3, which differs from the Hebrew. In Isaiah the phrase 'the blessings promised to David' refers to God's eternal covenant. God had promised David that his covenant with him would be eternal: there would always be a descendant of David on the throne (2 Samuel 7:12–16).

By using the words of Isaiah while speaking about the resurrection of Jesus, Paul says that Jesus' resurrection was already announced in Scripture. How else could God's covenant with David be eternal? Paul also gratefully takes up Isaiah's use of 'you' (plural) in 'I will make an everlasting covenant with *you*' to show that what God once promised to David, now benefits all hearers and readers through Jesus. And finally, the subsequent verses in Isaiah (55:4–5), in which there are even more rich messianic promises, also echo in the ears of people who know the Scriptures.

In Greek, the transition from Acts 13:34 to 13:35 is by association, for the Greek for 'the sure blessings (promised to David)' in verse 34 is *ta hosia* whereas verse 35 uses almost the same words, *ton hosion*. This word *hosion* means 'trustworthy or holy person' and it is translated as 'holy one.' By associating the Greek words (*hosia* and *hosion*) Paul makes the transition from Isaiah 55 to Psalm 16. The final part of this psalm gave many Jews reason to look out for a resurrection of the dead at the end of time. The readers of Acts still remember that Peter had already quoted extensively from Psalm 16 in Acts 2:25–28 and commented on it in Acts 2:29–32. The readers understand that what they read in Acts 2 is still valid here in chapter 13. Nevertheless, in verses 36–38 Luke does add Paul's explanation of the psalm in order to show that Peter and Paul are proclaiming the same gospel.

Unlike what the Jews thought, Psalm 16 is not about the general resurrection at the end of time, but about our time, the 'now' of the church. The words of the psalm say more about Jesus than about David, because they are prophetic words. Now, in the midst of time, the Messiah has been raised from the dead! He has not seen decay.

In 13:41, Paul quotes the Septuagint of Habakkuk 1:5, in which the warning has a sharper tone than in the Hebrew text. He means to say that his hearers cannot ignore God's word, just as it could not be ignored under the old covenant. The last word in the verse, 'told' or 'tell' (NIV, NRSV), is a weak translation of the Greek which means 'unfold,' so the CSB correctly has 'explain' and the NASB 'describe.' The same Greek word occurs not only here in Habakkuk, but also in the Septuagint of the messianic Psalm 118:17: 'I ... shall *recount* the deeds of the Lord.' By using this word, even if it is only one word, Paul and Luke once again allude to the messianic Psalm 118 which plays such a great role in Luke's Gospel. It is remarkable that Paul's sharp warning does not repel his Jewish audience, as evidenced by their reaction in verses 42–43. Discussions between Jews can often be hard and direct, yet without any sign of anger or alienation.

As I said, Paul's speech contains far more allusions to Scripture than quotations. Together they show that Paul bases his representation of history in verses 16–22 firmly on the Scriptures. Here is a list without much comment:

Acts 13	Old Testament	Comment
:17	Deuteronomy 7:6–8; 10:15	chosen
:17	Deuteronomy 4:34, 37	summaries
:17	Exodus 6:1, 6 Septuagint	'uplifted arm' (NRSV)
:18	Exodus 16:35; Numbers 14:33–34	forty years
:19	Deuteronomy 7:1	seven nations
:20	Judges 2:16	judges

:20	1 Samuel 3:20	Samuel as prophet
:21	1 Samuel 8:5, 10	asking for a king
:21	1 Samuel 10:1	Saul
:23	2 Samuel 7:12, 22:51; Isaiah 11:1; Jeremiah 23:5–6	David's descendant

Note also that the verses 23–31 have many parallels with the Gospels.

Isaiah

The prophet Isaiah plays an important role both in Luke's Gospel and in Acts. We already saw how Isaiah appears in Acts 13, and I will now give some other examples of Luke's use of his book.

1. At important moments Luke introduces quotations from Isaiah. In the Gospel this is when the main characters begin their ministry. In Luke 3:4–6 John the Baptist quotes words from Isaiah 40 as his programme and Jesus does the same in Luke 4:18–19 with words from Isaiah 61. In Acts 7:49–50 it is Stephen who cites Isaiah 66:1–2 at the end of his speech. This speech follows the history of Israel, increasingly focusing on the question where God resides. God's criticism of what people think about the temple, as expressed in Isaiah 66, is an appropriate conclusion of this speech.

Philip, the first person to proclaim the Gospel to a gentile (Acts 8:32–33), hears that this man is reading from Isaiah 53 and uses this chapter to explain to him 'the good news about Jesus.'

In his first speech, among other things, Paul makes use of Isaiah 55:3 (in Acts 13:34, see above). Later in this same speech he brings out the significance of his work by quoting Isaiah 49:6 (13:47). Finally, the very last quotation in Acts (28:26–27) also comes from Isaiah (6:9–11).

Three of these passages from Isaiah which are used in Acts, also play a role in Luke's Gospel. Isaiah 6:9 is already used by Jesus long before Paul's ministry (Luke 8:10), the old Simeon already claims that the promise of Isaiah 49:6 finds fulfilment in Jesus (Luke 2:32), and Jesus applies Isaiah 53:12 – and thus of course all of Isaiah 53 – to himself

(Luke 22:37). All these things together show that Luke is an excellent writer: he first uses passages of Isaiah in his Gospel, but he does not 'use them up,' so that there is plenty left for Acts without falling into repetition. I am not saying, of course, that Luke was freely inventing the words of the speakers, but that he is making a conscious and appealing choice from the large quantity of material available to him.

2. In Acts 8:26–40 the quotation from Isaiah 53 is not only theologically the most important part of the story, it is also at its centre because the narrative has a so-called concentric structure, which looks like this:

A 8:26–27a Philip en route.

B 8:27b–29 Meeting of Philip and the Ethiopian.

C 8:30–31 Philip speaks with the Ethiopian.

D 8:32–33 Quote from Isaiah 53:7–8.

C' 8:34–35 Philip speaks with the Ethiopian.

B' 8:36–39 End of meeting of Philip and the Ethiopian.

A' 8:40 Philip en route.

This story confirms that Jesus is the fulfilment of the promises in Isaiah 53, the prophecy of the suffering servant of God who takes away the sin of the world. In the verses which the Ethiopian reads aloud in Philip's presence, the emphasis is on the innocence, the willingness, and the humiliating suffering of the servant. These things were already described in Luke's Gospel; in Acts it is the followers of Jesus who must suffer innocently (as for example in 7:58–60; 9:16; 12:2, 3–5) and who thus walk in the footsteps of their Lord.

In 8:32–33 Luke is following the Septuagint of Isaiah 53:7–8. Critical readers have wondered why he omits the last sentence of verse 8, 'for the transgressions of my people he was punished.' Does this omission show that Luke did not believe that Jesus had suffered vicariously for humanity? This is not a good question. First of all, remember that when a word or phrase is quoted, the entire text around it (the context) resounds. Secondly, this story mainly focuses on *who* the servant of Isaiah 53 is, not on what he *does*. Thirdly, the words 'my people' in the omitted line might have created the misunderstanding that Jesus had died only for the Jewish people, while the story is about how the very first *gentile* joins the believers in Jesus. Luke therefore probably omitted them to avoid this misunderstanding.

Besides the quotation, the narrative about the Ethiopian also contains some echoes of Isaiah. Directly at the beginning there is the combination of 'desert' ('wilderness,' NRSV) and 'road' (verse 26). The Greek word for 'desert' (*erēmos*; 'lonely') is the same word which in Isaiah 40:3 is translated as 'wilderness,' so Luke's introduction echoes Isaiah 40. The expression 'good news' or gospel in verse 35 translates a word which you also find in Isaiah 61:1 and which is also quoted by Jesus in Luke 4:18; the word occurs again in verse 40. This means that Philip follows in the footsteps of Jesus as bringer of good news.

3. Many places in Isaiah 40–55 focus on the servant of the LORD, and the Septuagint normally uses the word *pais* to render 'servant,' for example in Isaiah 42:1, 50:10 and 52:13. This everyday word has a deep meaning to the prophet. As a title, in the Old Testament sometimes uses it to refer to the entire people of Israel (for example in Ezekiel 37:25; Isaiah 42:1; 48:20) but sometimes to an individual, the expected saviour. These two usages of the word are not always neatly distinguished, for example in Isaiah 42. The most important passage about the servant is Isaiah 53, which clearly has an individual in view. In the New Testament, Jesus is five times called the servant (*pais*), four of which are in Acts: Matthew 12:18 (in a quotation from Isaiah 42:1) and Acts 3:13, 26, and 4:27, 30. Moreover, Jesus introduces himself as the servant (Luke 4:16–21) and he quotes Isaiah 53:12 as fulfilled in him (Luke 22:37). Thus, the message of the New Testament is that Jesus is the one who fulfils the prophecies of Isaiah about the servant of the LORD. The ambiguity between people and individual is solved because Jesus takes the role of the people of Israel, suffering innocently in place of the people. He brings God's light to the ends of the earth, with the help of his apostles. Because Luke focuses so heavily on Isaiah 53, it is probable that the title 'The Righteous One' for Jesus in Acts 3:14, 7:52, and 22:14 (and in 1 John 2:1) is based on Isaiah 53:11, which mentions 'my righteous servant' (NIV, CSB; 'the righteous one, my servant,' NRSV, ESV).

4. Even after Paul's speech in Acts 13, Isaiah comes to word. In the unpleasant discussion that follows a week later (verses 42–52), Paul and his colleague Barnabas address the jealous Jewish leaders:

> Then Paul and Barnabas answered them boldly: 'We had to speak the word of God to you first. Since you reject it and do not consider yourselves worthy of eternal life, we now turn to the Gentiles. For this is what the Lord has commanded us: '"I have made you a light for the Gentiles, that you may bring salvation to the ends of the earth."'

The first part of this response (verse 46) is unremarkable, for Paul unfortunately had to say something like that to unbelieving Jews more often (Acts 18:6 and 28:28, see also 19:8–9). But in verse 47, Paul and Barnabas quote words from Isaiah (49:6) which you would think are about Jesus. Was not Jesus destined to be 'a light for the Gentiles, that [God's] salvation may reach to the ends of the earth?' Yes, in Luke 2:32 these very words were applied to Jesus, and the parallel place Isaiah 42:1–6 is also about him (see Matthew 12:18).

But of course Paul and Barnabas do not err when they apply these words to themselves, and so we learn that not only the Lord Jesus, but also his apostles Paul and Barnabas are 'a light for the Gentiles,' called to go 'to the ends of the earth.' This conclusion follows on from the beginning of Acts, where Luke reports that Jesus applies the expression 'the ends of the earth' to the work of his apostles when he sends them into the world (Acts 1:8).

All this borrowing from Isaiah has the result that things are not simple and one-dimensional. Israel is God's servant – Jesus is too. Jesus is a light for the nations – Paul and Barnabas are as well. The prophetic words of Isaiah have multiple layers. You can read all of Isaiah 49:1–13 as a promise that first pertains to the people of Israel (verse 3), but then also to Jesus, and finally to his apostles. These are all called to proclaim God's salvation to the whole world.

However, I would like to make a distinction within the collection of prophecies about 'the servant of the LORD' as you find them in Isaiah 42:1–9; 49:1–11; 50:4–9; 53; and 61. For while many of these texts are fulfilled in Israel *and* in Jesus *and* in his apostles, others are only fulfilled in Jesus. He is the only one who takes away the sin of the world (53:4–6).

5. The conviction that God's good news is destined for both Israel and the nations helps us to understand the end of Acts. At the end of the book Paul arrives in Rome; after his long journey he wastes no time before inviting the city's Jewish leaders for conversations about Jesus (Acts 28:17, 23). Verse 23 suggests that he speaks to them in the same way as, according to Acts 13, he had spoken in most synagogues, see above. Not unexpectedly, the Jews of Rome become just as divided about Jesus as the Jews everywhere else. Some accept him as their Messiah, others do not (28:23–25a). At the farewell, Paul gives them the words from Isaiah 6:9–10 which he attributes to the Holy Spirit (28:25). In this way Paul declares that he is now free to proclaim the gospel to the gentiles in Rome and elsewhere (28:28), but this does not mean the end of the proclamation to those Jews who are open to it. By telling us at the end of his book that Paul uses Isaiah 6, Luke suggests that the unbelief of the Jews has opened the way for the proclamation of the gospel among the gentiles without replacing the Jews. Paul agrees with this view and explains this in great detail in Romans 11, especially in verses 11–12. Isaiah 49:6, which mentions Israel and the nations together, is fulfilled!

6. In Acts the words 'witness' and 'witnesses' are important descriptions of the task of the apostles, which is missional speaking about Jesus. You can find these words in 1:8, 22; 2:32; 3:15; 5:32; 10:39, 41; 13:31; 22:15, 20; 26:16, and previously in Luke 24:48. In the Old Testament these words often occur in connection with legal affairs; in the missional sense, 'witness' is an expression from Isaiah 40–55, where God first appoints the people of Israel as witnesses of his great deeds (43:10, 12; 44:8) and then his messianic servant (55:4). Again, you see how Isaiah has influenced Luke.

7. Of course Acts is the book in which Luke tells about the coming and the work of the Holy Spirit. Is it a coincidence that of all Old Testament books it is Isaiah which contains the most about the Spirit of God? For this reason, some overlap was to be expected anyway, but Luke consciously makes connections with Isaiah. On the one hand, Stephen alludes to Isaiah 63:10 when saying that the Jews often opposed the

Holy Spirit (Acts 7:51). On the other hand, in the synagogue in Nazareth Jesus uses words from Isaiah 61 to claim that he is filled with the Spirit (Luke 4:18). Luke also tells how Peter refers to these words of Jesus (Acts 10:38), so that a further connection with the book of Isaiah arises. The third connection between the two books is Acts 1:8, the important verse that states the programme for Jesus' followers. It is no coincidence that the words 'when the Holy Spirit comes on you' echo Isaiah 32:15.

Amos

The book of Amos is almost never cited in the New Testament and there are very few quotes from it. However, in Acts 7:42–43 Stephen quotes from Amos 5:25–27, and James quotes from Amos 9:11–12 in Acts 15:16–17. It is remarkable that both times Luke does not mention the name Amos, instead referring to 'the prophets,' so that Amos is not mentioned by name in the New Testament. (What Luke does is understandable because in the time of the New Testament – and still today – the Jews treated the books of the twelve minor prophets as one book.)

The two quotes from Amos are in strategic places in Acts. Acts 7 is the last part of the description of the community of believers in Jerusalem, just before Luke reports the start of the gospel proclamation outside the city; Acts 15 is the moment when this 'foreign mission' and the inclusion of the gentiles into the Christian church are being accepted by all followers of Jesus. In between Acts 7 and 15 Luke describes the struggles surrounding this great change: Peter learns how to make contact with gentiles, Philip tells the first non-Jews about Jesus, and Paul – the apostle who will be used by God as apostle to the gentiles – begins his ministry.

In Acts 7, Stephen points to all kinds of wrong developments in the history of Israel; their idolatry resulted in judgement and exile. The critical words of Amos, as cited by Stephen, nicely summarise all of this. In the other hand, however, at the Jerusalem meeting in Acts 15 words of promise from Amos are quoted: for the end times, God promises recovery, rebuilding, and the participation of the gentiles! The emphasis in Amos 9:12 is on the nations (Hebrew *gojim*). You see that the way in which Amos is used in Acts draws attention to the big picture of Luke's narrative and shows that the inclusion of the nations in the church was planned by God long ago.

We still have to look at some details. In both quotations Luke uses the Septuagint quite literally, but in Acts 7:43 he writes that the exile will bring the people 'beyond Babylon' instead of Amos' 'beyond Damascus.' The message of Amos was about the exile of Israel in Assyria, but the text is now adapted to the exile in Babylon, which took place later. It is possible that Luke made this change to the text of Amos, but it is more likely that it was Stephen who updated the Scriptures in this way, or that it had been done before Stephen.

Another interesting detail is that a little earlier in his speech (Acts 7:40) Stephen quotes from Exodus 32:1, where the people of Israel ask Aaron for gods who can go with them. The ironic answer to their question comes in verse 43 in the words of Amos: they may take their preferred gods, Molek and Rephan, to Babel in exile.

In both quotations from Amos the word 'tent' or 'tabernacle' occurs. In Acts 7:43 the people are criticised for carrying the tent of the idol Molek or Moloch (NRSV), while Acts 15:16 is God's promise that he will rebuild the fallen, dilapidated tent of David. Stephen also uses the theme of the tent in his references to Scripture in Acts 7:44–45, creating a contrast with the idea of a permanent house for God in verses 46–50.

In Acts 15 James and Luke make good use of some minor differences between the Hebrew text and the Septuagint of Amos 9:12:

Amos 9:12 Hebrew	Amos 9:12 Septuagint
'So that they may possess the remnant of Edom and all the nations that bear my name,' declares the LORD, who will do these things.	In order that those remaining of humans and all the nations upon whom my name has been called, says the LORD God who does these things.

The Hebrew text has *'edom*, but the Septuagint has interpreted this as *'adam,'* people. That was possible because originally there were no vowels between the consonants *'dm*. As a result, the Septuagint declares that God will search for the remaining *people* and this word made it into Acts 15:17. It fits in well with what is at issue in Acts 7–15, the mission to all people. In addition, the Hebrew text has 'possess' but the Septuagint has 'seek.' The Septuagint is based on a difference of only one letter in Hebrew: *yarash* was read as *darash*. As is the case more often, the Septuagint prepared the way for God's continuing revelation.

Further Reading

Doble, Peter, 'The Psalms in Luke-Acts' in Steve Moyise and Maarten J.J. Menken (eds), *The Psalms in the New Testament* (London and New York: T&T Clark, 2004) 83–117.

Genz, Rouven, *Jesaja 53 als theologische Mitte der Apostelgeschichte: Studien zu ihrer Christologie und Ekklesiologie im Anschluss an Apg 8,26–40.* WUNT 2,398 (Tübingen: Mohr Siebeck, 2015).

Koet, Bart J., 'Isaiah in Luke-Acts' in Koet, *Dreams and Scripture in Luke-Acts* (Leuven: Peeters, 2006) 51–79.

White, Aaron W., 'Revisiting the "Creative" Use of Amos in Acts and What It tells Us About Luke,' *Biblical Theology Bulletin* 46.2 (2016) 79–90.

Chapter 28: Paul

Paul wrote a large part of the New Testament and used the Old Testament so extensively that he has already been mentioned in many places in this book. The index at the back of the book will guide you. For the present chapter I have chosen a few new subjects which give you some insight into the person and ministry of Paul, without repeating what has been said before.

General Comments

1. Paul has such a high respect for the Scriptures that you can definitely read Romans 15:4 as his declaration of principle:

> Everything that was written in the past was written to teach us, so that through the endurance taught in the Scriptures and the encouragement they provide we might have hope.

When you read Paul's letters, you notice that he is serious about what this statement expresses. His attitude was a source of inspiration for my own writing and I hope that as readers you will think of Scripture in the same way. In chapter 2 I showed how Paul illustrates the enduring importance of the Old Testament in his comments on Exodus 34 in 2 Corinthians 3. You heard that he believed that 'the letter kills' (2 Corinthians 3:6), but that the Scriptures have lasting value when they are read with the help and guidance of the Holy Spirit.

2. For this reason Paul does not read the Scriptures as timeless texts, but as books which suddenly look very different as a result of the coming of the Messiah, Jesus. Many things that were still mysteries under the old covenant (Romans 16:25–26; 1 Corinthians 2:7; Ephesians 3:3–12; Colossians 1:25–27) have now become public and clear. Paul's conviction regarding the central place of Jesus is audible, for example, in his use of Isaiah 49:8 in 2 Corinthians 6:2 where he writes: 'Now it has happened, Scripture is fulfilled.' And in Galatians 3:8 he introduces the Scriptures as a speaking person who proclaims the gospel; this is the gospel as Paul came to understand it when Jesus revealed himself to him as the risen Lord (Acts 9:1–9; Galatians 1:16).

3. The apostle primarily uses Genesis, Deuteronomy, Isaiah and the Psalms, so books from all three parts of the Hebrew Bible, the books of Moses, the Prophets and the Writings.[14] Like the other writers of the New Testament – and like Jesus himself – Paul draws far more examples from the stories in Genesis and Exodus than from the stories in Joshua through Kings.

The quotations and allusions are rather unevenly distributed over the letters. Paul often quotes in Romans (but barely in Romans 5–8), in Galatians and in both letters to the Corinthians, and he does not quote in Philemon at all. Someone has found more than a hundred quotes and allusions in Romans 9–11 alone. How much Paul decides to use the Scriptures is clearly dependent on his subject and his readers.

4. Contrary to popular opinion, Paul does not quote Scripture without attention to the context in which the words stand. I have already shown this in many places in this book. Yet his handling of the Word is often not easy to understand, and sometimes only later interpreters discover his true intentions. His colleague Peter was surely right when he claimed that many of Paul's readers found him a difficult writer (2 Peter 3:15–16).

5. In his handling of Scripture Paul does not follow any particular system or fixed method. Some texts he takes literally, other texts he interprets in a more figurative way. Sometimes he quotes accurately, sometimes he adapts the wording. He applies some texts to Jesus, others to the church, others to himself or to the future. Note that he often makes connections between the Old Testament and the Christian church, so not merely between the Old Testament and Jesus. For example, he sees Abraham as a forerunner of the believers of the new covenant, but not as a forerunner of the Lord.

Here are some examples of the great diversity in Paul's approach:

- An example of literal explanation is his application of the prohibition to covet; simply compare Romans 7:7 with Exodus 20:17 and Deuteronomy 5:21. Paul also takes Habakkuk 2:4 literally in Romans 1:17, although in the former text NIV has

---

[14] On these three parts see for example my *Enduring Treasure*, chapter 9.

'faithfulness' rather than 'faith' which you find in NKJV, NRSV, NASB, ESV and CSB.

- In Galatians 4:21–31, on the other hand, Paul gives an allegorical explanation of the persons Hagar and Sarah in Genesis 16. This means that he does not pay attention to the events in Genesis but regards the two women as symbols of two covenants (Galatians 4:24–25). Yet Paul knows very well what he is doing, as he writes in verse 24. This verse has interestingly different translations, which all show the point:

> These things are being taken figuratively. (NIV)
>
> Now this is an allegory. (NRSV)
>
> This is allegorically speaking. (NASB)
>
> Now this may be interpreted allegorically. (ESV)
>
> These things are being taken figuratively. (CSB)
>
> Which things are symbolic. (NKJV)

The Greek text indeed has a form of the word 'allegory' here. Although in this passage Paul allegorises the two women, he would never deny that Hagar and Sarah, like Abraham, were also historical persons. In this case, however, he brings out the deeper meaning of what happened to them.

- Paul usually respects the (historic) value of Old Testament events, taking many of them as foreshadowings of Jesus or the church. What he does in such cases is called typology. A good example of typology is 1 Corinthians 10:1–13, where Paul argues that the experiences of Israel in the wilderness are 'examples' for us (verses 6 and 11; the Greek here has forms of the word *typos*, type). In a typological reading, therefore, the original event is not seen as a prophecy but as something whose deeper meaning becomes apparent in the light of Jesus.

- Sometimes Paul seizes a detail in the text to build an argument. When he does this, he is closest to the approach of many contemporary Jews. For example, he writes in Galatians 3:16:

> The promises were spoken to Abraham and to his seed. Scripture does not say 'and to seeds,' meaning many people, but 'and to your seed,' meaning one person, who is Christ.

In Genesis the word 'seed' is indeed in the singular, and therefore refers to one person. Paul has Genesis 13:15 and 17:8 in mind, but 2 Samuel 7:12–16 and Psalm 89:3–4 probably resound as well. Paul knows very well that precisely while he using this Jewish approach, he is now reading the Scriptures in a radically different way from the other Jews and from how he himself used to read them as a Pharisee, not yet recognising Jesus as the Messiah. Yet for a follower of Jesus this is the best interpretation of Genesis.

- Paul can use the same passage in different ways, depending on what suits him. Thus he uses Habakkuk 2:4 in Galatians 3:11 to say that no one is made righteous by the law, but in Romans 1:17 to summarise the gospel.

- Sometimes he strings quotations from all over the Scriptures into a long chain, as in Romans 3:10–18; 9:25–29; 10:15–21; 11:8–10; 15:9–12; and in Galatians 3:10–13. This gives his words additional authority, of course, because the Scriptures have authority.

- In four places Paul even cites a pagan author in order to make a point. In 1 Corinthians 15:33 it is the saying 'Bad company corrupts good character,' a general truth found in a Greek author (see NIV footnote). Likewise, Paul quotes in Titus 1:12, and Luke includes quotations used by Paul in his speeches in Acts 17:28 and 26:14. By means of these quotes he builds a bridge to his audiences and their cultural background.[15] Yet he never quotes from the apocryphal books.

Paul and Jeremiah

In a number of places, Paul uses the book of Jeremiah as he speaks about himself and his work as an apostle.

---

[15] An accessible book in English is Steve Moyise, *Paul and Scripture* (London: SPCK, 2010). My friend Harm-Jan Inkelaar is the author of the scholarly study *Conflict over Wisdom: The Theme of 1 Corinthians 1–4 Rooted in Scripture* (Leuven: Peeters, 2011).

Uprooting and Tearing Down

At his call, Jeremiah receives authority from the LORD 'over nations and kingdoms to uproot and tear down, to destroy and overthrow, to build and to plant' (Jeremiah 1:10). Here God uses four negative words and two positive ones for the work he instructs the prophet to do. Later in the book of Jeremiah, the same words are repeated, so they form a refrain in the book (18:7–10; 24:6; 31:28; 42:10). In 2 Corinthians 10–13 Paul uses the same metaphoric language to describe his work – at the beginning and at the end of this passage, to be exact. At the beginning he appeals to 'the authority the LORD gave us for building you up rather than tearing you down' (2 Corinthians 10:8); and this is mirrored by his words at the end of the passage: 'the authority the Lord gave me for building you up, not for tearing you down' (2 Corinthians 13:10). The imagery from Jeremiah thus encloses chapters 10 to 13, which form a close-knit unit.

Of course, Paul knows full well what he is doing; his choice of words leaves no doubt that he understands his ministry in the light of Jeremiah's. As the prophet had to denounce the sins and injustices of his contemporaries, so Paul firmly tackles the Corinthians. Perhaps he uses the words of Jeremiah because his situation is similar to that of the prophet. Jeremiah had many problems with *false* prophets (see in particular Jeremiah 23 and 27) and Paul calls his opponents *false* apostles (2 Corinthians 11:13; cf. 11:5; 12:11). Just as the false prophets approved of everything the people did (for example, Jeremiah 6:13–15), these false apostles were much too tolerant of sin (2 Corinthians 11:4; 12:20–21). Only by first 'tearing down and uprooting,' Paul would be able to 'plant and build' again in Corinth later.

Boasting Competitors

A well-known passage in the book of Jeremiah states:

> This is what the LORD says: 'Let not the wise boast of their wisdom or the strong boast of their strength or the rich boast of their riches but let the one who boasts boast about this: that they have the understanding to know me, that I am the Lord, who exercises kindness, justice and righteousness on earth, for in these I delight,' declares the Lord. (Jeremiah 9:23–24)

Paul also uses the word boasting and in 2 Corinthians 10–13 it is even a central theme (10:8, 12–17; 11:10–12, 16–18, 21, 30; 12:1, 5–9). Both in 1 Corinthians 1:31 and in 2 Corinthians 10:17 Paul cites Jeremiah's words about boasting. Both Jeremiah and Paul know that they themselves are not strong, but that their strength lies in God (see also 1 Corinthians 1:23–25). By means of his conscious allusions to Jeremiah, Paul shows that this prophet was not only a precursor of Jesus – in the way he suffered from his opponents and responded to them – but also of Paul.

Call

At his call, the LORD says to Jeremiah:

> Before I formed you in the womb I knew [NIV footnote: chose] you, before you were born I set you apart; I appointed you as a prophet to the nations. (Jeremiah 1:5)

Likewise the servant of the LORD says about himself in Isaiah:

> Before I was born the LORD called me; from my mother's womb he has spoken my name. I will also make you a light for the Gentiles, that my salvation may reach to the ends of the earth. (Isaiah 49:1b, 6b)

The apostle Paul clearly alludes to these words when he writes about himself that 'God set me apart from my mother's womb and called me by his grace' (Galatians 1:15). What unites these three people – Jeremiah, 'the servant,' and Paul – is that their calling is not a human idea but originated in God. All three also know that they have been sent by God to the pagan peoples (for Paul see Galatians 1:16).

There are two more similarities between Isaiah 49:1–13 and what Paul writes about himself in Galatians. The words of Galatians 1:24, 'And they praised God because of me,' resemble Isaiah 49:3 in the Septuagint; and Galatians 2:2b echoes the thought of Isaiah 49:4 about labouring in vain.

So Paul alludes to the words of both Jeremiah and the servant of the LORD to clarify his situation and to defend his work against his opponents. Undoubtedly this insight gives him both comfort and cause for concern.

Experiences

There are two more similarities between Jeremiah and Paul, one of which is merely implied, namely that both are unmarried. Although about Jeremiah we read this in 16:2, for Paul we merely suppose it to be the case. Explicitly, the agreement is that both declare that they are incompetent speakers (Jeremiah 1:6 and 2 Corinthians 11:6), although in both cases it is probably false modesty. After all, they have a vocation which makes them speak much in public.

At the end of this section we note once more that for Paul the Scriptures not only illuminate Jesus and the church, but also his own person and ministry.

The Psalms in Romans

In Romans Paul quotes from the psalms fifteen times, six of which are in Romans 3. The following list comes from the recent edition of the Greek New Testament:

Romans	Psalm
2:6	62:12
3:4b	51:5
3:10–12	14:1–3 (= 53:1–3)
3:13a	5:9
3:13b	140:3
3:14	10:7
3:18	36:1b
4:7–8	32:1–2

8:36	44:22
10:18	19:4
11:2a	94:14
11:9–10	69:22–23
15:3b	69:9
15:9b	18:49
15:11	117:1

These quotations are very diverse and are therefore representative of Paul's varied use of Scripture. Among other things, you can note the following:

Choice of Psalms

Paul uses some well-known psalms like 32 and 51, but also unknown ones such as 5 and 44. Only three of these psalms are also used elsewhere in the New Testament, namely 62, 69, and 94. Paul's choices are thus quite original, which underlines that he was an independent thinker with an enormous knowledge of Scripture. He uses different types of psalms, such as laments and songs of praises, but in Romans 3 he only uses laments. That will be a conscious choice because the passage is about sin.

Introductions

Paul normally uses some introductory words to indicate that he is about to quote, for example, 'As it is written' (Romans 15:9b) and 'Again, it says' (15:10). In Romans 11:9 his introduction is: 'And David says.' But some quotations appear without an introduction, as in Romans 11:2 where it says: 'God did not reject his people' without any indication that these words form a quotation. Consequently, the CSB has not printed these words in bold. Nonetheless, the use of the rare word 'reject' leads readers who know their Bible or who use a search engine to Psalm 94:14.

For the sake of clarity Paul has replaced the word 'LORD' from Psalm 94:14 with 'God'; instead of the future tense he uses the past, because he is writing at a later moment in salvation history than when the psalm was written.

Romans 10:18 also lacks an introduction to the quote, although some modern translations like the Good News Translation have added clarifications like, 'as the Scripture says.'

In any case, Paul mainly cites psalms whose inscription refers to David. About half of all psalms have such an inscription, so Paul seems to have a clear preference for this group. Yet Paul does not apply Davidic psalms like 32 and 51 to Christ but to the church.

Textual Differences

Most translations enable you to see rather clearly that the quoted psalm and Romans use the same words, but sometimes you don't see this so readily. This may be in cases when Paul used the Septuagint, the translation the Romans knew, as and when it differs from the Hebrew text. For example, the use of Psalm 5:9 in Romans 3:13a is obvious because there are only minor differences between the Hebrew text and the Greek translation of the psalm. However, the use of Psalm 10:7 in Romans 3:14 is more difficult to spot. The psalm states:

> Him whose mouth is full of cursing and bitterness and deceit; under his tongue are grief and hardship.

Yet Romans 3:14 has: 'Their mouths are full of cursing and bitterness.' The word 'bitterness' is not in the Hebrew text, but comes from the pen of the translators of the Septuagint. Paul has also put the text in the plural, so that it fits his argument better.

On one occasion Paul has adapted the text to the subject of Romans, which is about justice and righteousness. In Psalm 14 the word 'righteous' does not occur, but Paul still uses it in his quotation in Romans 3:10: 'There is no one righteous, not even one.' In this way he sticks to what the psalm means to say, and he applies this to his subject. You can see this as an example of the freedom which the Spirit gave Paul.

Subject

Paul sometimes uses words from the Old Testament which are about people in general, but also words about Israel or the church. After declaring that all people are sinners (Romans 3:10–18), he uses as 'proof texts' verses which originally describe 'bad people,' applying them to all people. In this way he strengthens the meaning of what these psalms are saying. Thus in the New Testament it turns out that the harsh words of David in Psalm 14 about the fool are applicable to all people! In another twist, in Romans 8:36 he puts the complaint of the people of Israel from Psalm 44 about persecution because of their faith into the mouth of the church of Christ.

The quotations in Romans 3:4b and in chapters 9–11 are about Israel. And in fact only one of Paul's psalm quotations is about Jesus Christ, namely that in Romans 15:3b. This is a striking observation, showing again that according to Paul and the other apostles the Old Testament is much more than a set of predictions of the coming of Jesus. The Old Testament also speaks of God's plan to form a world-wide community of believers, and so it speaks about us and to us.

It is clear that Paul is not only a careful reader of the Scriptures but that he also reflected deeply on his readers whilst writing.

Philippians 2

The Letter to the Philippians has a very different character from Romans, Galatians, and the two letters to the Corinthians, because Paul does not seem to be using the Old Testament here. Yet although he does not quote from it, it is not absent! Earlier, I showed how you gain a deeper understanding of Philippians 2:5–11 when you read it against the background of the Hebrew Bible. I will now show that the next passage, Philippians 2:12–18, has many connections with the end of Deuteronomy.

Deuteronomy 32 is the song that Moses sings at his farewell to Israel, reflecting on his mission to bring the people into the promised land. Paul knows this chapter well for he also uses it in Romans 10:19; 12:19; 15:10, and in 1 Corinthians 10:20–22 he refers to Deuteronomy 32:17,

21. In Philippians his approach is different, though; he does not quote but alludes to the whole chapter.

Philippians is a late letter of Paul, in which he refers several times to his impending death (1:20–26; 2:17; 3:10), looking back like Moses did in his song. Whether consciously or unconsciously, Paul finds himself in the same situation as Moses. Almost automatically he alludes to Deuteronomy 32 and to Moses' experiences in general.

In 2:12 he raises his absence from the congregation in such a way that he seems to be saying goodbye to them, asking his readers to remain obedient to God even after his time. Yet he is optimistic about this, for while Israel was disobedient (Deuteronomy 31:27), so far the Philippians have been very obedient. Paul's use of words for presence and absence remind us of Deuteronomy 31:27.

His next appeal, 'Do everything without grumbling or arguing' (2:14), contains a general reference to the behaviour of Israel in the wilderness, not to a specific passage. The reference is in the choice of the word 'grumbling,' which was also used for Israel's behaviour in the wilderness (for example in Exodus 15:24; 16:2; 17:3). Older translations used 'murmuring.'

In 2:15 several words remind of the Septuagint of Deuteronomy 32:5; this version is considerably different from the original Hebrew and can be translated into English as follows:

> Blemished children, not his, have sinned; a generation crooked and perverse.

Paul uses these words to contrast sinful Israel to the impeccable readers in Philippi. He has added the word 'God' to the text, but otherwise stays close to the Greek of Deuteronomy. The words 'warped and crooked generation' now refer to people outside the Philippian church, or perhaps also to the opponents he mentions unexpectedly in 3:2 without identifying them. (It seems that with the last words of verse 15, about shining like stars in the sky, Paul is also alluding to Daniel 12:3.)

In 2:16 Paul writes:

It is by your holding fast to the word of life that I can boast on the day of Christ that I did not run in vain or labour in vain. (NRSV)

These words echo several elements of Deuteronomy 32:46–47a:

Take to heart all the words I have solemnly declared to you this day, so that you may command your children to obey carefully all the words of this law. They are not just idle words for you – they are your life.

Both texts state that the word of God is vital, life-giving. Moreover, the words 'idle' in Deuteronomy and 'in vain' in Philippians translate the same Greek word (*kenos*, 'empty').

In conclusion, Paul's farewell in Philippians 2:12–18 places him beside Moses and compares the obedient Philippians to the disobedient Israelites in the wilderness. He achieves this without quoting, merely by using allusions and echoes. Perhaps Paul also saw similarities between Timothy, whom he more or less introduces as his successor (2:19), and Moses' successor Joshua. In any case, both men needed much encouragement (Deuteronomy 31:7; Joshua 1:1–9; 1 Timothy 4:12–16). Yet I wonder how much of this Paul's readers were able to appreciate.

Further Reading

Allen, David, 'Paul Donning Mosaic Garb? The Use of Deuteronomy 32 in Philippians 2:12–18,' *European Journal of Theology* 26.2 (2017) 135–143.

Lalleman, Hetty, 'Paul's Self-Understanding in the Light of Jeremiah. A case study into the use of the Old Testament in the New Testament' in Jamie A. Grant et al (eds), *A God of Faithfulness. Festschrift J.G. McConville* (New York and London: T&T Clark, 2011) 96–111.

Norden, Christopher G., 'Paul's Use of the Psalms in Romans. A Critical Analysis,' *Evangelical Quarterly* 88.1 (2016) 71–88.

Chapter 29: Hebrews

The author of the Letter to the Hebrews is unknown to us, but this chapter will continually show us that he or she uses Scripture differently from Paul, implying that he or she was not Paul.[16] When we read through Hebrews, it strikes us how the writer quotes long passages of the Old Testament. He seems to think that his readers do not have a copy of the text at hand. That could indeed be the case, because the readers were being persecuted for their faith, as we see in 10:32–34; 12:1–4; and 13:3, 13. Among their plundered possessions (10:34) may have been the biblical manuscripts of the congregation. Another striking characteristic of Hebrews is that the writer rarely gives the title of the biblical book from which he quotes, or its author. (The exceptions are 4:7 and 9:19–20, where he mentions David and Moses.) Is this reticence also connected to the fact that the readers are unable to look up the quotations anyway?

Speakers

Theologically more important is a third striking observation: only in 10:7 the writer uses a phrase such as 'It is written' or 'As was foretold by.' Everywhere else he uses the word 'say' about the Old Testament: the Scriptures, God, Jesus the Son or the Holy Spirit *are saying* something. Always in the present tense. This makes clear that for the writer in Scripture God speaks directly to the readers, and it connects well with the statement in 1:1 that in the past God *spoke* to our ancestors. The Scriptures do not just contain the words of David, Isaiah or anyone else from the past! And the writer would undoubtedly state that the same still applies, for in the Bible God speaks directly to us, even today!

It may strike us as rather artificial that the writer puts many quotations into God's mouth instead of the mouth of the human author, although he sometimes ascribes statements to Jesus or the Holy Spirit, and also mentions David and Moses a few times as speaker. There is in fact a strikingly beautiful pattern in the distribution of the speakers.

---

[16] I am emphatically writing 'she' because Priscilla (Acts 18) might well be the author of Hebrews. From here I will revert to the convention 'he.'

Hebrews 1 always says that God speaks, but subsequently Jesus (2:11–12 and 13) and the Holy Spirit (3:7) are mentioned as speakers. Then it is God again who speaks a number of times (for example, in 5:5), but later the writer once again mentions Jesus Christ (10:5) and the Holy Spirit (10:16) in succession. In the final section of the letter, the speaker is again God or someone who is not mentioned. Is this pattern a coincidence, or is it an inconspicuous reference to the Trinity?

Both times when Jesus is introduced as speaking, he speaks *to* God as his Father, declaring that he is obedient to God's will. Jesus is a person with his own task and responsibility, but he carries out God's plan. Both times when the Spirit is introduced, he addresses the people. These things fit well with what we believe about the Son and the Spirit.

The last quotation in the letter is not spoken by God, but by people. The 'we' quote Psalm 118:6 in response to a wonderful promise of God in the preceding verse 5:

> Keep your lives free from the love of money and be content with what you have, because God has said, 'Never will I leave you; never will I forsake you.' So we say with confidence, 'The Lord is my helper; I will not be afraid. What can mere mortals do to me?' (Hebrews 13:5–6)

In contrast to all the exact indications of who spoke in Scripture, there is one funny, vague wording, namely in 2:6, where you read, 'someone has testified somewhere' (NRSV). The words that follow are taken from Psalm 8, a psalm by David, as the learned author of Hebrews knows very well, but he does not want to draw attention to it. Yet overall the approach of the author of Hebrews does not differ much from the way in which Jesus applied the Scriptures to himself, which we studied in the chapters on the Gospels. The readers of Hebrews will also have handled the Scriptures in the same way as the writer, or he would have chosen a different approach in this vitally important letter. For Jesus and for the author and readers of Hebrews, Scripture is not a collection of second-hand books, but the voice of the living God; and this word of God is 'alive and active' ('effective,' CSB) and 'sharper than any double-edged sword' (4:12).

Quotations and Allusions

In light of what you see elsewhere in the New Testament, it was only to be expected that many quotations in Hebrews would come from the Psalms. The Psalms provide the majority of the quotes used in Hebrews! Yet the author is original, citing many passages that are not used anywhere else in the New Testament, such as the Psalms 40, 45, 95, 102, and 104.

Yet Scripture is not only heard as and when the writer quotes it literally. His language is saturated with Old Testament words and ideas, so that the whole letter evokes the world of ancient Israel. Scripture is not something that is brought in from outside, but it is central to the world of the writer and his readers. For example, in Hebrews 9 you find yourself in the heart of the Old Testament, even though the chapter only contains one single quotation, namely from Exodus 24:8 (in verse 20)! This chapter is awash with references to Exodus, Leviticus, and Numbers, which I will omit. The well-known chapter 11 on the heroes of faith works in much the same way: although it is entirely based on the Scriptures, it barely contains any quotations but about sixty allusions to Genesis, Exodus, Joshua, Samuel, Kings, and other books.

Between the lines Hebrews offers you as a reader a complete biblical worldview: God is the creator of everything (11:3) who rested from that work on the seventh day (4:4). He created angels as his servants (1:7, 14). He spoke to all the important persons of the time before Christ (for example 11:4, 8, 18). He made a covenant with Israel (9:15) and guided them by the prophets (1:1; 11:32). But now, 'in these last days' (1:2), Christ has come to bring a 'great salvation' (2:3) and the Holy Spirit is now working in the church (2:4).

Theme

The subject of Hebrews is the Lord Jesus as the one who makes the difference between the old and the new covenant. According to 1:1–4, Jesus is God's final and best revelation. This makes him the key to all revelations in the Old Testament so, like the writer and his readers, we now can and should read that book with him in mind.

The readers are in grave danger of giving up their faith in Jesus and returning to a form of Judaism without Jesus. They are about to give up the conviction that he has inaugurated the new covenant. In response the writer uses all possible means to show them that the new covenant is better because *Jesus* is better than the angels, Moses, Joshua, the sacrificial system, and anything else. Look at Jesus, he appeals to them. And for that reason he shows from the Scriptures who Jesus is.

The following two tables will help your understanding of this beautiful but difficult letter. The first shows that the writer hangs his entire argument on six passages from the Old Testament, most of which he supports with one or more other passages:

Hebrews	Key text	Supporting text	Comparison
2:5–18	Psalm 8:3–6	Isaiah 8:17–18	Jesus – humanity
3:7–4:11	Psalm 95:7b–11	Numbers 14; Genesis 2:2	Jesus – Joshua
5:5–7:28	Psalm 110:1–4	Genesis 14:18–20	Jesus – high priest
8:1–10:18	Jeremiah 31:31–34	Psalm 40:6–8; Exodus 24–26; Leviticus 16–17	Jesus – Sinai covenant and the sacrifices
10:32–12:3	Habakkuk 2:3–4	Isaiah 26:20	readers – OT persons
12:4–13	Proverbs 3:11–12	–	readers – OT persons

I suggest that you read through Hebrews once as a commentary on the six key texts above.

Moreover, in other places in the letter, mainly at the beginning and the end, the writer also draws comparisons, or rather contrasts, between the old and the new covenant:

Hebrews	Key text	Supporting text	Comparison
1:1–4	–	–	Jesus – the prophets
1:5–14	A series of seven quotes (see below)	–	Jesus – the angels
3:1–6	Numbers 12:7	–	Jesus – Moses
12:14–17	Genesis 26–27	–	the readers – Esau
12:18–29	Exodus 19	Haggai 2:6	Sion – Sinai

In the remainder of this chapter I give examples of how the writer uses the Scriptures, but I cannot discuss the complete letter. Moreover, Psalms 2, 8, and 110 have already been discussed in this book.

Hebrews 1:5–14

Jesus is the Son of God, God's image, seated next to God on the heavenly throne and 'superior to the angels' (1:4). To underline this superiority of Jesus, in 1:5–14 the writer presents a series of seven quotations from the Old Testament. He detaches them from their contexts and puts them all into the mouth of God, although in the Old Testament many of these statements are words of humans. In other words, in 1:1–4, the writer claims that God spoke and speaks, and in 1:5–14 he illustrates this assertion directly. Five of the seven quotations come from the Psalms; most of them come from recognisably 'messianic' texts:

Number	Hebrews 1	Source	Comments
1	:5a	Psalm 2:7	'Son'; rhetorical question[17]
2	:5b	2 Samuel 7:14	'Son'

---

[17] A rhetorical question is a question to which you do not expect an answer because everyone knows it; in this case, the answer is, 'Not to any angel, but to Jesus.'

3	:6	Deuteronomy 32:43	'Angels'
4	:7	Psalm 104:4	'Angels'
5	:8–9	Psalm 45:6–7	'You' (son)
6	:10–12	Psalm 102:25–27	'You' (son)
7	:13	Psalm 110:1	Rhetorical question

When you look at this passage in detail, you see that the author of Hebrews is a real style artist. The first six quotations form three pairs. The numbers 5 and 6 are much longer than the other five. For the sake of variation, the third and fourth quotations are not about Jesus but about the angels, who are snubbed as no more than servants.

Very cleverly, the final quotation comes from Psalm 110, as an early signal that this psalm will play a leading role in the letter. (The psalm was already audible at the end of 1:3 in the words 'sat down at the right hand of the Majesty in heaven.')

It is also striking to observe what the writer does *not* do. In Judaism many angels had been given names and there was speculation about various classes of angels, about fallen angels and demons. No such speculation occurs here!

If the quotations from Deuteronomy 32:43 and Psalm 104:4 do not seem to be quite correct, this is because the writer in quoting from the Septuagint, the only version of the Bible which his readers knew.

The series of seven quotations underlines the author's claim that the Lord Jesus is divine, that he is the Son of God. You could make a list of all the points on which he surpasses the angels.

In the rest of the letter there are no more chains of quotations; from now on, the writer is using longer quotations and often making longer comments. In addition, there will be all kinds of allusions.

Hebrews 2:1–4 and Similar Passages

In the short section 2:1–4 the writer is not using any particular verse or passage from the Old Testament, but the whole of it, as in 1:1–4. The 'message spoken through angels' (2:2) is the entirety of God's revelation to Israel, especially as contained in the book of Exodus, which according to Jewish traditions had been mediated by angels. The writer argues that if this divine revelation was valid, and if any violation of the commandments received due punishment, *how much more* will that apply to ignoring the new covenant? This covenant was given by the Lord Jesus, God the Father himself is testifying to it, and it is visible in the presence of the gifts of the Holy Spirit. (Do you hear how he is referring to God as three divine persons?) This is a sharp warning for readers then and now: it would be catastrophic to ignore Jesus, because the salvation he gives is so much greater (verse 3) than what Exodus could ever offer us!

The writer thus uses the argument 'how much more' – if that, how much more this? If that is true, surely this too? The argument compares a less important fact to an important one, making the latter look even stronger or better. We have come across such arguments *a fortiori* twice before in this book.

The author of Hebrews goes on to use the argument *a fortiori* several more times, of which I give two examples:

1. In 9:13–14, he once again compares the entire old covenant – but above all the sacrifices that people had to bring – to the forgiveness of sins thanks to Jesus. He then argues: if the blood of animals is already effective, 'how much more' the blood of the Lord? As background information you could read the old rules in Numbers 19:9–17. Jesus is so much better than those observances! And the effect of our cleansing by him is not outward, but inward, in 'our consciences.' Who would then want to return to the old?

2. The subject of 10:28–29 is the price for apostasy, a sin which was severely punished under the old covenant. 'To reject' is a strong expression that is also used in the Septuagint with regard to repelling a partner (Deuteronomy 21:14) and the breaking of a pledge (Judges 9:23). The writer's question is: if transgression of the law of Moses incurred capital punishment, how much graver will the punishment be for despising Jesus?

The writer thus highlights all kinds of contrasts between the old and the new covenant, yet one contrast is not mentioned because it only exists in the minds of some contemporary believers. Nonetheless, this alleged disparity is very popular in our time: all kinds of people inside and outside the church argue that the Old Testament is hard, strict, and loveless, whereas the New Testament is sweet, nice, and cuddly. Well, that is surely not the impression Hebrews is trying to create! Just read 10:26–31 and chapter 12. Hence the author's urgent warning: do not abandon Jesus!

Hebrews 3:1–6

Our unknown author is the champion of typology: he sees countless similarities between people, affairs, and events from the Old Testament on the one hand and Jesus on the other. The author is not unnecessarily negative about the old covenant and does not deny at all that everything really happened – but Jesus puts all these things in the shadow.

Repeatedly, Moses and Jesus Christ are likened to each other. Earlier in this book you saw that Matthew and John also make this comparison, but each writer does it in his own way. Without naming Moses, the author alludes to him in 1:1, and God's revelation to him is the subject of 2:2 (see above). Later in Hebrews, chapters 4–10 offer a long comparison of the covenant which God gave through Moses and the new covenant in Jesus. As Moses was the mediator of the old covenant, so Jesus is the mediator of the new (see also 9:15). In addition, Moses gets a beautiful, spacious place in the gallery of heroes of the faith (11:23–28).

An ancient Jewish tradition claims that Moses was more important than the angels. This may be the reason why the writer first compares the angels with Jesus (Hebrews 1–2) and then Moses, so that 3:1–6 forms a climax after the chapters 1–2.

The explicit comparison of Moses and Jesus in 3:1–6 is seamlessly connected to the preceding, for in 2:17 the writer calls Jesus 'faithful' or 'trustworthy.' This praise would ring a bell in the ears of the audience, for wasn't Moses also a faithful servant? That is what God himself declares in Numbers 12:7: 'But ... my servant Moses ... is faithful in all my house.' Without saying so, in Hebrews 3:2 and 5 the author quotes these words. And he does not detract from them, he does not weaken Moses' faithfulness and his other qualities. He is probably also thinking of God's appreciative words about Moses at the beginning of Numbers 12 and in Exodus 40:16 and Deuteronomy 34:10. Yet under the new covenant everything is greater and better: the 'house' is better and Jesus is the Son, not merely the servant, of God.

In verse 3, the NIV translates that Jesus was deemed worthy of greater 'honour' than Moses, whereas other translations use the word 'glory.' The latter is preferable because it enables you to see that the writer actually uses the word 'glory' (Hebrew *kabood*; Greek *doxa*). This word comes from Exodus 33–34 and is central to John 1:14–18, as we saw earlier. Hebrews has already used it twice before: in 1:3, the author calls Jesus 'the radiance of God's glory' and in 2:9 states that he was crowned 'with glory and honour.' The connection with Exodus 33–34 tells you that Moses saw something of God's glory, but that Jesus is worthy of much more than he. Jesus is God's glory in person, to borrow John's thought.

The writer could have finished the letter here. Jesus is much better than Moses and the old covenant, so why on earth would the readers want to go back to Judaism? And in our time, why are some Christians embracing a form of legalism which includes all sorts of Jewish laws and customs?

Hebrews 3:7–4:11

The words of God which the author used in 3:1–6 (from Numbers 12) were spoken during the time Israel was in the wilderness. In this new passage he holds on to the thought of the wilderness and draws a comparison between the readers and the unfaithful people of Israel in the wilderness. He begins by quoting the second half of Psalm 95, which remains central in the entire passage and is quoted again in 3:15, 4:3, 5 and 7. In the psalm God is the speaker and the author of Hebrews boldly states that God now speaks to the recipients of the letter in the same way as he appealed to Israel at the time. Please note that the Old Testament is not applied to Jesus, but to the local church.

The original hearers of God's words – the generation of Israelites in the wilderness – did not come through alive, the writer states (3:16–19). As a result of their unbelief, Israel missed the goal – but the readers of Hebrews should do better. This direct appeal to the readers is especially strong because of the way the quotation starts and ends. God's words in the psalm *begin* with, 'Today, if you hear his voice.' The writer takes the word 'today' literally, saying that it also applies to this day and every day (3:13). That is why God's promise exists 'still' (4:1) or 'again' (4:7).

At the *end* of the quotation the author picks up the word which becomes the pivot of the argument, 'rest.' What is this rest? It is both a place and a period of time. It is the destiny of people who believe (4:3). In the psalm it was the promised earthly country, Canaan, where Joshua brought the people of Israel (4:8). Now it is something better, the 'Sabbath-rest' that God has in store for his people (4:9). The writer derives this thought from Genesis 2:2, where the word 'rest' is also used. He does not explain what he means, but the remainder of the letter shows that he is thinking of eternal happiness.

What the writer does not emphasise, but what does resound, is that the leader of the people at the end of the wilderness period was called Joshua (4:8). In Greek this name (*Jēsous*) is exactly the same as the name Jesus. The first Joshua brought the people of God into Canaan, the second Joshua brings them everlasting peace.

Hebrews 5:1–4

The passage 5:1–4 is remarkable for the fact that, for a change, it mainly mentions agreements between the old and the new dispensation. The writer describes the situation under the old covenant without referring to a particular chapter; for the election of Aaron and his descendants see Exodus 28:1–2 and Numbers 3:10; 25:10–13. Hebrews emphasizes God's choice of Jesus also in 5:5 and 10. The fact that priests had to make sacrifices first and foremost for their own sins is evident in Leviticus 4:3; 9:7; and 16:6, 17, and is also emphasised in Hebrews 7:27 and 9:7.

Yet this passage also contains a contrast, namely that Jesus did not need to offer sacrifices for his own sins (verse 3). He had not committed any sin because he did not give in to temptations (4:15). The expectation that a high priest can sympathise with ordinary people (verse 2; 4:15) is not mentioned in the Old Testament. In this respect, too, Jesus is just much better than the high priests!

It is striking that the writer does not say anything about the corrupt priests and the temple service in his own time; he clearly doesn't want to score cheap points, which is to his credit. He is arguing from Scripture, not from bad practice.

Hebrews 5:5–6

In Hebrews 5:5–6 the writer quotes two psalms in quick succession. I discussed both of these earlier in this book. Psalms 2 and 110 are both prophecies about the messianic king. The author uses the fact that God directly addresses this messianic king in both psalms as 'you' in order to show that Jesus is both Son and priest.

But the author does more. Up to this point, the letter was mainly about Jesus as the Son of God, as he is called in Psalm 2. From here, it will mainly be about Jesus as the high priest, as he is called in Psalm 110. Psalm 2 was the most important text in the first part of the letter – now follows the second part, in which Psalm 110 is the most important text. Here the author brings both psalms together to make the transition: from Psalm 2 and the Son to Psalm 110 and the high priest.

Hebrews 8:7–13

The second half of Hebrews 8 contains a lengthy quote from Jeremiah 31:31–34; this is the longest quotation from the Old Testament anywhere in the New Testament. Although Jeremiah 31 is an important text, it is not quoted anywhere else in the New Testament. (Not even by Paul, who alludes to it in 2 Corinthians 3:3.) The reason for this lack of attention might be that orthodox Jews at that time hardly spoke about the new covenant. They did expect the Messiah, but did not combine his coming with the making of a new covenant. Yet that is what God did: he made a new, big, final step in the history of salvation and ratified it with a new, better covenant.

From here the word covenant receives more attention in Hebrews. In 8:8 and 13, the writer emphasizes the word 'new,' but this word plays no further role, unlike what you might have expected. In chapter 10:16–17 the author quotes another part of Jeremiah 31, without the word 'new,' and he derives different ideas from it: the certainty and the completeness of the forgiveness that Jesus gives, and also the promise that God will put his laws in our minds and in our hearts. In this respect, too, the new covenant is superior to the old, and therefore the words of Jeremiah constitute a beautiful conclusion to the whole discussion in Hebrews 9 and 10. In other words, the heart of the letter, 9:1–10:14, is enclosed by words of Jeremiah.

Hebrews 10:37–38

In 10:19–39, the readers are again called to remain faithful to Jesus. Hebrews 10:37 contains a combined quotation of words from the Old Testament, as you also encounter for example in Mark 1:2–3. In Hebrews 10 it is a combination of Isaiah 26:20 and Habakkuk 2:3. The words 'just a little while …' derive from Isaiah, but 'he who is coming will come and will not delay' is from Habakkuk 2:3. The prophet Habakkuk is discussing a vision, to which he refers by using 'it' several times. But the Septuagint had taken the content of the vision as referring to a future person, and so used 'he' rather than 'it':

> Although he might linger, wait for him; he will certainly come, and will not delay.

The use of 'he' in Hebrews is thus based on the Septuagint, and according to Hebrews the person who will come is Jesus Christ.

Staying with Habakkuk 2, the writer again quotes the prophet in 10:38. This time he has swapped the two parts of 2:4. Part of the quotation is hard to recognise in our translations because the Septuagint of 2:4a differs much from the Hebrew text. This is not important, however, because the focus is on the two fundamental attitudes of belief and disbelief.

The warning to not 'shrink back' fits well in the long series of warnings against unbelief in this letter. If you shrink back from God, if you do not really believe, then God is no longer pleased with you, is what the words of Habakkuk add to the argument.

The prophet also promises that righteous people will live by their faith. This promise is also cited by Paul in Romans 1:17. These words of Habakkuk help the writer to move to the next part of his letter (chapter 11), which is about the heroes of faith. You see that that chapter is not detached from the rest of the letter but fits in very well.

Hebrews 12:15–29

Towards the end of the letter the writer uses the Old Testament differently than hitherto, in a more 'conventional' way. Twice he refers to situations of the past without clearly citing the Scriptures. The first reference is to Esau (12:15–17) who had sold his birth right in a whim (Genesis 27). The writer tells the story very briefly, mentioning the tears of Esau for dramatic effect; Genesis 27:38 also states that Esau cried. Hebrews further states that Esau committed adultery; that is not said in Genesis, but it may be a circumlocution for serving other gods (as in Deuteronomy 31:16) or it may refer to Esau's marriage with unbelieving women (Genesis 26:34–35).

The second reference (Hebrews 12:18–21) is to God's revelation at Mount Sinai. The writer gives a short, vivid impression of Exodus 19–20, with a quotation from Exodus 19:12–13 in verse 20b. He also quotes words of Moses, 'I am trembling with fear,' which come from Deuteronomy 9:19. In Deuteronomy 9:8–29, Moses is describing how impressive and terrifying his encounter with God at Sinai was. In that situation it was no shame to be afraid. The call of the writer to the readers is the same as ever: take this awesome God seriously please!

A little further on (12:26–29), he takes up the thought of the earthquakes at Sinai (Exodus 19:18 and Psalm 68:8) and connects it to Haggai 2:6 and 21, which say that God will cause earth and heaven to tremble once more. He applies these words to the last judgement, contrasting it to the 'kingdom which cannot be shaken.'

In the intervening verses (12:22–25), the writer contrasts the warning example of Israel's experience at Sinai with the perspective of another mountain, Mount Zion, on which the heavenly city of Jerusalem is situated. In the Old Testament, Mount Zion is linked to the royal house of David (for example, Psalm 2:6; 132:10–18). Perhaps the idea for the comparison between the two mountains arose because Zion is mentioned in Psalm 110:2, the psalm that is central to the letter. Paul (Galatians 4:26) and John (Revelation 3:12; 21) also use Jerusalem as an image for God's glorious future. Once again the writer makes a comparison *a fortiori* here: if God revealed himself in a special way at Sinai, how much better will be his revelation of the coming eternal glory?! In their minds, in faith, the readers are already standing at the gates of this new city, the symbol of God's goodness. But everything will have been in vain if they now 'refuse him who speaks' (verse 25).

God is called 'the living God' in 12:22 (as in 3:12; 9:14; and 10:31), a title which is also derived from the Old Testament (for example Deuteronomy 5:26 and Joshua 3:10). It strikes me that at this moment in the letter there is even a positive reference to angels (12:22), who had been snubbed so emphatically in Hebrews 1–2.

Conclusion

The Letter to the Hebrews is an artful sermon on Psalm 110 in which many other psalms also play a role. It is unique that the whole structure of the letter is determined by the Old Testament. The prophet Isaiah, who is so important in the rest of the New Testament, has disappeared into the background here. Hebrews brings out the fact that under the new covenant God is at least as strict as under the old covenant.

Further Reading

Fitzmyer, Joseph A., *Essays on the Semitic Background of the New Testament* (London: Geoffrey Chapman, 1971).

France, R.T., 'The Writer of Hebrews as a Biblical Expositor,' *Tyndale Bulletin* 47.2 (1996) 245–276.

Johnson, Luke Timothy, 'The Scriptural World of Hebrews,' *Interpretation* 57.3 (2003) 237–250.

Lane, William L., *Hebrews 1–8*, Word Biblical Commentary (Dallas: Word, 1991).

Malcolm, Matthew, 'God Has spoken: The Renegotiation of Scripture in Hebrews' in Matthew Malcolm (ed.), *All That The Prophets Have Declared* (Milton Keynes: Paternoster, 2015) 172–181.

Rascher, Angela, *Schriftauslegung und Christologie im Hebräerbrief* (Berlin: De Gruyter, 2007).

Smith, Ian K., 'The Letter to the Hebrews' in Mark Harding and Alanna Nobbs (eds), *Into all the World. Emergent Christianity in its Jewish and Greco-Roman Context* (Grand Rapids: Eerdmans, 2017) 184–207.

Chapter 30: First Peter

The First Letter of Peter is the only book of the New Testament that discusses the position of the believers as foreigners in the world. This letter in characterised by its intensive use of the Old Testament. There is no other book in the New Testament with so many quotations and so many allusions relative to the number of words in the text. Romans and Revelation contain more quotations and allusions, but they are much longer. Peter especially uses Isaiah, Zechariah, and the Psalms. His letter is full of elements of the Old Testament that are now applied to the church of Christ. In 1:10–12 he also has important things to say about the nature of prophecy, but I will not treat these verses here as they are not directly based on specific verses in the Hebrew Bible.

Theme

Two key words in 2:11 point to the theme of the letter: the first is 'aliens' (NRSV, NASB), 'foreigners' (NIV), 'strangers' (CSB) or 'sojourners' (NKJV, ESV); the second 'strangers' (NASB), 'exiles' (NIV, NRSV, CSB, ESV) or 'pilgrims' (NKJV). Peter uses these words to characterise his readers, helping them to adopt a fitting attitude in a world in which they are not welcome. This combination of words is unusual, but the same Greek words occur together in Psalm 39:12 (Septuagint), in the same order in which Peter uses them. So Peter has even taken the key words of his letter from Scripture! In the psalm, both words are in the singular, but in view of his readers Peter has put them in the plural.

Peter also uses one of these two words in his heading (1:1), where the English translations again offers various possibilities: 'exiles' (NIV, NRSV, ESV), 'those who reside as aliens' (NASB, cf. CSB) and 'pilgrims' (NKJV). The other key word occurs in 1:17, where it is variously translated as 'foreigners' (NIV), 'exile' (NRSV, cf. ESV) and 'strangers' (CSB). This reveals that in 2:11 Peter brings together the two concepts which he had first used separately in 1:1 and 1:17 respectively, and only so you discover that he has Psalm 39 in mind.

Abraham (Genesis 23:4) and the other patriarchs in the promised land (Psalm 105:12) are also called aliens in the Old Testament. The expression also occurs in Psalm 34:4, where the Greek does not have 'fears' but 'alienation.'

In New Testament time the words 'foreigners' and 'aliens' were generally used to denote the Jews in the diaspora. Peter himself writes that he is writing from Babylon (5:13), by which he means Rome, and this also indicates that he feels like a stranger. Because of the Old Testament background of these words, we should not too soon spiritualise any feelings of alienation by saying that Christians are citizens of heaven. We are rather dealing with a contrast between cultures. Because of their conversion, the readers have become outsiders in their own culture.

Jesus Christ

1. Peter specifically writes about Jesus in 2:21–25 and 3:18–22, but of course in other places as well. Twice he says that Jesus' blood brings atonement (1:2, 19), a thought that is not based on a single Bible verse but on the entire sacrificial practice of the old covenant. In 1:19, he also calls Jesus the sacrificial lamb, which is a reference to Isaiah 53:7, 'he was led like a lamb to the slaughter.'

In 1:11 Peter mentions the suffering *and glorification* of Christ in general, although once again Isaiah 53 is probably on his mind, because in 52:13 and 53:10–12 Isaiah also mentions the glorification after the suffering.

2. In 1 Peter 2:21–25 the author makes more use of the well-known passage Isaiah 53 than any other writer anywhere in the New Testament. In fact, this passage is a kind of poem, based on the words of Isaiah. Peter does not adhere to the order of his source, but he does quote the words of the prophet literally. Thus, according to the Septuagint of Isaiah 53:4, the servant of the LORD 'bore our sins,' while the Hebrew has 'diseases'; from the fact that Peter has 'sins' in 2:24, you see that he is following the Septuagint.

Here are the parallels between Isaiah 53 and 1 Peter 2, in Peter's order:

Isaiah 53	1 Peter 2
9b he had done no violence, nor was any deceit in his mouth	22 he committed no sin, and no deceit was found in his mouth
7 he did not open his mouth	23 he did not retaliate … he made no threats
4a he took up our pain and bore our suffering … 12c he bore the sins of many	24a he himself bore our sins in his body on the cross
5b by his wounds we are healed	24b by his wounds you have been healed
6 we all, like sheep, have gone astray	25 you were like sheep going astray

In his introductory words Peter comments on the meaning of Isaiah's words about the servant of the LORD for the readers (verse 21): Jesus Christ fulfilled this prophecy by showing us what innocent suffering is and, in doing so, he gave us an example.

In 3:9 Peter also offers a direct application of Isaiah 53, in particular of 53:7, in his own words:

> Do not repay evil with evil or insult with insult. On the contrary, repay evil with blessing, because to this you were called so that you may inherit a blessing.

3. Jesus not only suffered innocently, bearing our sins: according to Peter, he is also the cornerstone of the church (2:4–8). This beautiful image of the cornerstone comes from Psalm 118. Peter then involves the readers by asking them to be available as 'living stones' (2:5). This allegorical use of the expression stretches the Old Testament image considerably.

4. In 2:25 and 5:4, Peter calls Jesus the shepherd. He does not seem to have a particular passage in mind, but rather the teaching of Jesus himself, as you find it in John 10:1–18.

Imagery Relating to the Readers

1. Peter discusses the identity of his readers in Christ especially in 1:3–2:10, using various images from the Hebrew Bible. The first metaphor is in fact a contrast: the believers are born again of imperishable seed (1:23) and therefore *not* fleeting like grass and flowers. Here, Peter seems to have the parable of the sower in mind, but to underline that the believers are imperishable, in 1:24–25 he quotes – without any introduction – from Isaiah 40:6–8. He does this more or less verbatim from the Septuagint, but in verse 8 he replaces 'God' with 'Lord.' And he adds that the word of the LORD, which is mentioned by Isaiah, is the gospel. In this way he claims the authority of God's word to the prophets also for the apostolic proclamation of the Lord Jesus.

Peter probably chose Isaiah 40 on purpose, because this passage is the beginning of words of consolation and hope from the prophet for the people who are in exile. The inspiration of Isaiah 40 is also evident when Peter calls the inheritance of the believers one that 'can never perish, spoil or fade' (1:4) and a crown 'that will never fade away' (5:4), because these words again echo Isaiah 40.

2. In his extended metaphor of the spiritual stones (2:4–8), which I mentioned above, Peter also says that the believers form a spiritual house or temple, that they are 'a holy priesthood, offering spiritual sacrifices' (verse 5). Again, the terms temple, priest, and sacrifice take their meaning from the Old Testament, although not from any particular verse.

3. In 2:9, Peter continues by calling the congregation 'a chosen people, a royal priesthood, a holy nation, God's special possession.' That gives you four Old Testament terms in a row, each communicating that the believers are different from the other people, as Israel was different from the gentiles, because their values and norms are determined by God's culture. This thought is particularly strong in Deuteronomy 7:6 and the broad context of that verse:

> For you are a people holy to the LORD your God. The LORD your God has chosen you out of all the peoples on the face of the earth to be his people, his treasured possession.

Yet each of the four terms also comes literally from the Septuagint, the outer two from Isaiah 43 and the inner two from Exodus 19:

- The expression 'chosen people' occurs at the end of Isaiah 43:20; Peter also calls Deuteronomy 7:6–8 and Isaiah 41:8–9 into the minds of his readers.

- 'A royal priesthood' or 'a kingdom of priests' is an expression from Exodus 19:6, where God says that the whole nation of Israel is special and comes under special rules.

- Likewise the words 'a holy nation' come literally from Exodus 19:6.

- Finally, with 'God's special possession, that you may declare the praises of him …' we are back with Isaiah 43:21 (Septuagint). Here Malachi 3:17 also resounds, which contains the promise that the Israelites will be God's treasured possession.

Together these short quotations and the context from which Peter takes them show that the church of the Lord Jesus is joint heir to the role of Israel.

4. Finally, 1 Peter 2:10 contains the notion that a group that once was *not* God's people is now his people. These words, based on Hosea 1:10–2:1 and 23, illustrate that God makes unexpected choices.

You see that Peter has consciously combined expressions from different parts of Scripture to express the continuity between the old and the new covenant. If you listen carefully, you may hear also the echo of Isaiah 42:6; 43:1; and 48:12 in the repeated use of the word 'call' in 1 Peter 1:15; 2:9; 3:9; and 5:10. In this case, it is not certain whether Peter himself intended the echo or whether later hearers just have such sharp ears. But when you hear this echo, you know with even more certainty that Peter sees the church as the co-heir of God's people, Israel.

Psalm 34[18]

Psalm 34 plays a major role in this letter. Above you already saw that one of the key words of the letter, 'aliens,' appears in verse 4 of this psalm (Septuagint). Furthermore, in 3:10–12 Peter quotes Psalm 34:12–15, the longest quotation in the letter. He has adapted the text to the situation of his readers and in the assignments he has replaced the second person ('you') with the third person ('he').

In the New Testament, Psalm 34 is also quoted in John 19. It consists of a combination of thanksgiving to God and wise words such as you find in Proverbs. Peter will have chosen to quote this psalm precisely because it contains advice on how a righteous person should behave during persecution and when in a minority. That is exactly the situation of Peter's readers. The long quotation from the psalm nicely summarises what Peter wrote to his letter so far, before he proceeds to do yet more with it:

1. Psalm 34:13 says:

> Keep your tongue from evil and your lips from telling lies (deceit, NRSV).

In 1 Peter 2:1, Peter asks the same of his readers, partly in the same words:

> Rid yourselves of all malice and all deceit, hypocrisy, envy, and slander of every kind.

It seems that the psalm already resounds here.

2. It says in 1 Peter 2:3, 'now that you have tasted that the Lord is good.' Turning back to the psalm, you see that Peter is quoting verse 8a, 'Taste and see that the Lord is good.' The words are exactly quoted from the Septuagint. When you look at the context, you see that Peter deliberately uses the name of the God of Israel, LORD (Yahweh), for Jesus. And if you listen even longer, you hear how the second part of Psalm 34:8 also echoes in Peter's words: 'blessed is the one who takes refuge in him.'

---

[18] Peter consistently uses the Septuagint of the psalm. In the Septuagint the psalm has the number 33 (because in the Septuagint Psalms 9 and 10 are one song) and so I actually need to refer to 'Psalm 33 Septuagint,' but that would be confusing.

3. Immediately following, 1 Peter 2:4a has the unobtrusive words 'as you come to him.' This very much sounds like an echo of Psalm 34:5 in the Septuagint, which differs so much from the Hebrew text that you do not see the agreement in the translations.

Psalm 34:6 Hebrew (34:5 English)	Psalm 34:6 Greek
Those who look to him are radiant; their faces are never covered with shame.	Come to him, and be enlightened; and your faces shall never be put to shame.

4. Peter and the psalmist also share three terms for the believers:

- 'obedient children' in 1 Peter 1:14 reminds of 'my children' in Psalm 34:11;

- 'servants' from Psalm 34:22 is taken over in 1 Peter 2:16 (NRSV; NIV has 'slaves');

- 'blessed' (Greek *makarios*) migrated from Psalm 34:8 to 1 Peter 3:14 and 4:14.

In these cases Peter probably echoes the words of the psalm automatically, because he knows it so well.

5. Finally, it is remarkable that Psalm 34 and 1 Peter discuss the same theological themes:

Theme	Psalm 34	1 Peter
Praise at the beginning	verses 1–2	1:3
Believers are 'holy people'	verse 9	1:15–16; 2:5, 9; 3:5
Believers are 'aliens'	verse 4 (Septuagint)	1:17; 2:11
The righteous have trouble	verses 6, 17, 19	1:6; 2:19–21; 3:13–14; 4:12–19; 5:10
Fear of God	verses 7, 9	1:17; 2:17–18; 3:2
Salvation	verses 4–7, 17–22	1:5, 9–10; 2:2; 3:21

Because of the many similarities, it could be argued that 1 Peter is a written sermon with Psalm 34 as text. That suggestion cannot be proven, but Psalm 34 certainly plays a large role in the letter. You notice that Peter's use of it is probably both conscious and unconscious. Just reflect on how your own choice of words is unconsciously influenced by movies, series, songs or books which are important to you.

Proverbial Wisdom

Towards the end of the letter, Peter twice more quotes from Scripture without announcing it, so we may overlook it. This happens first in 4:18, when he declares that the suffering of the believers is not unexpected. This verse is a verbatim quote of Proverbs 11:31 according to the Septuagint. Then in 5:5 the words 'God opposes the proud but shows favour to the humble' are a quotation from the Septuagint of Proverbs 3:34, which again differs from the Hebrew text and thus from the English translations.

Once you know that Peter knows his Proverbs, it is not surprising that in 3:6 he hints at Proverbs 3:25, again in the Greek translation, with the words 'do not give way to fear.' And 1 Peter 4:8 echoes the wise words from Proverbs 10:12 that love covers many sins.

Conclusion

I will conclude with a few comments. First of all, it is important to understand that it is not obvious that Peter should be using the Old Testament. He is writing to readers with a pagan background (4:3–4), yet he is simply assuming that the Scriptures are now authoritative for them. The readers must have understood this when they came to faith and joined a congregation of believers.

Second, Peter reads the Old Testament not only with a view to Jesus, but also (and even more) with a view to the church. He brings out the similarities between both the identity (as the people of God) and the circumstances (as foreigners) of Israel and of the church: both are holy people and both are innocently persecuted. It is not hard to see how relevant these things are to us.

Third, he takes many texts typologically, using scriptural materials that you would not regard as prophecy.

Fourth, although Peter uses some texts that are also used by other writers of the New Testament, he uses many which are not quoted anywhere else. His use of the Bible resembles that of Paul, but he does not imitate him.

And finally, like everywhere in the New Testament, 1 Peter contains direct quotations (with or without introductory words) as well as allusions and echoes.

Further Reading

Dubis, Mark, *1 Peter: A Handbook on the Greek Text* (Waco: Baylor University Press, 2010).

Green, Gene, 'The Use of the Old Testament for Christian Ethics in 1 Peter,' *Tyndale Bulletin* 41.2 (1990) 276–289.

Woan, Sue, 'The Psalms in 1 Peter' in Steve Moyise and Maarten J.J. Menken (eds), *The Psalms in the New Testament* (London: T&T Clark, 2004) 213–229.

Chapter 31: Revelation

One of the keys to understanding the difficult book of Revelation is to see how much John is using the Old Testament. Elsewhere I wrote the following:

> It is characteristic of Revelation that John makes much use of the Scriptures of Israel, our Old Testament. However, he never quotes them literally and he does not refer to them either; it is up to us as readers to find out where and how he works with the Old Testament. The Old Testament sources of Revelation are found especially in the prophets Isaiah, Ezekiel and Daniel; in second place we have Genesis 1–2, Exodus 7–15, the Psalms and the other prophetic books. In [chapter 1] John describes his call in a way that recalls the call narrative of Ezekiel, and this book also plays a role in the structure of Revelation.[19]

I must add immediately that John handles the Old Testament very freely and that he often gives a new meaning to the elements he uses. Many of the symbols in Revelation are familiar to us from the Old Testament but, like acquaintances whom you have not met for a long time, they now look pretty different.[20] Let me give a few examples of such changes.

- Revelation 1:14 describes the Lord Jesus as he appears to John:

  > His head and his hair were white as white wool, white as snow. (NRSV)

  John has borrowed this description from Daniel 7:9:

  > His clothing was white as snow, and the hair of his head like pure wool. (NRSV)

  The difference is, however, that in Daniel 7 these words describe God, while John uses them to describe Jesus. John thus intentionally represents Jesus as God, yet without saying this in so many words, and the message is clear: Jesus is God.

---

[19] See my *The Lion and the Lamb*, 11–12.
[20] The expression is in McComiskey, 310.

- Revelation 1:7 says that 'every eye will see him,' the coming Jesus, 'even those who pierced him,' and that 'all peoples on earth will mourn because of him.' There is another passage that mentions seeing someone who has been pierced and mourning over him, which is Zechariah 12:10. In this case, too, it is clear that John has taken his words from the Hebrew Bible. But Zechariah writes that it is the people of Israel, 'the house of David and the inhabitants of Jerusalem,' will see 'the one they have pierced,' and the effect of this is thus limited to the land of Israel, as is also clear in the subsequent verses. Once again the message of Revelation is clear – unlike what Zechariah thought, faith in God's murdered messenger will not be confined to the people of Israel, but members of 'all peoples on earth' (Revelation 1:7) will believe in him.

- The greatest change from the Old Testament is probably that John, although he is familiar with the book of Ezekiel including the chapters 40–48, denies that there will be a new physical temple. This suggests that the promises to Ezekiel will find their fulfilment in God himself.

It is not always clear what John means, and I am puzzled by the following change. Ezekiel 1:5–14 describes four identical creatures who each have traits of a lion, a bull, an eagle, and a human. Yet in Revelation 4:6–7 John sees four different creatures: a lion, a bull, an eagle, and a human. The symbolism is the same: these four creatures represent the entire creation; but the significance of the change is not clear to me. Yet another change I do understand: the creatures in Ezekiel each have four wings, but those John sees have six wings (Revelation 4:8). This is because the vision of John is influenced here by another piece of Scripture, Isaiah 6:3 to be exact, which states that God is praised by seraphs with six wings saying 'holy, holy, holy.' In his own vision John hears these very same words of praise.

Earlier in this book I have already discussed the temple, the river, and Babylon (Babel), which are important themes in Revelation; we also saw how often Psalm 2 resounds in Revelation. Here we first look at some important single texts and then at issues and themes from the

Hebrew Bible. After discussing the larger structures of Revelation, I will conclude with John's use of Isaiah.

I am referring to the writer of Revelation as 'John.' That is only one side of the matter, though, because according to Revelation 1 it is Jesus who appears to John in person and who shows him the visions he writes down. This makes Jesus the original author of what is described; it is therefore he who shows John things that have their origins in the Jewish Bible. Instead of 'John' it is therefore often possible to read 'Jesus' in this chapter. But John is the actual writer, and it is quite possible that he explains the visions he was shown as coming from Scripture without Jesus explicitly saying so.

If you wonder why I regularly use the word 'symbols' and why I interpret much of Revelation symbolically, then read Psalm 18 and pay attention to the unnumbered introduction before verse 1, which is an integral part of the text. This psalm is just such a kind of text as Revelation, describing historical events in pictorial, symbolic language.

Important Texts

We will first look at some important ideas which stem from the Hebrew Bible.

1. The announcement at the beginning that Revelation is about 'what must soon take place' (1:1) strongly reminds of Daniel 2:28–29, where these words appear twice in the Septuagint in roughly the same form; NIV 'what will happen in days to come' and NRSV 'what will happen at the end of days.' The opening words of Revelation thus deliberately evoke the book of Daniel, a book that resembles Revelation because both are about world history. But contrary to Daniel's book, which had to be sealed (closed, made unreadable) 'until the time of the end' (12:4), Revelation (22:10) is not sealed. There is even a promise of blessing for all who read and hear the book (1:3, see also 22:7).

2. In the introductory chapters John three times refers to God as the one 'who is, and who was, and who is to come' (1:4, 8 and 4:8). This title plays with the verb 'to be' and it derives from the name of God which he revealed to Moses: 'I AM WHO I AM' (Exodus 3:14). Once you

see this connection, you understand better that God is the Eternal One, who comes to us from the future.

3. John's description of the great vision of the risen Jesus (Revelation 1:13–16) combines several scriptural elements:

- The main source is Daniel 7:9, 13–14: The Lord looks like a human being but he is much more than that as well. The Lord comes with the clouds (1:7), he is dressed in white clothes and his hair is white. Both texts also contain flaming fires. Both Daniel 7:13 and Revelation 1:13 use the title 'son of man.'

- Daniel 10:4–10 resounds in the flaming eyes, the bronze of the feet, and the loud voice described in Revelation 1. The recipient of the vision falls face to the ground and is touched for comfort. The announcement of a vision about the future also connects Daniel 10:14 with Revelation 1:1.

- Ezekiel 43:2 supplies the thought that God's voice sounds like rushing water (Revelation 1:15).

The effect of this combination of texts is that the risen Jesus (verse 18) resembles the God of the Old Testament in all respects, without John having to say this explicitly. At the same time he also seems to be the human person of Daniel 7:13, who is the model for the 'son of man' in the New Testament. In other words, this 'son of man' is himself God.

4. Revelation 21:3 contains a great promise about the end of time:

> God's dwelling-place is now among the people, and he will dwell with them. They will be his people, and God himself will be with them and be their God.

This is an ancient promise, for God already made it to the people of Israel in Leviticus 26:11–12, repeating it in Ezekiel 37:27. But the way in which God is with the people is becoming more and more delightful in the transition from the Old Testament to Jesus and the Holy Spirit, to the future new earth, and this promise now applies to all of humanity.

There are also less significant texts that become clearer when you see that John is using the Hebrew Bible. Here are a few examples:

1. The notion that an enemy has ten horns occurs in Daniel 7:7 and in Revelation 12:3; 13:1; 17:3, 7, 12, 16. A horn is a symbol of strength and power, as you can see, for example, in Zechariah 2:1–4 and Psalm 92:10. Ten is a large number so ten horns indicate much power. The Lamb on the other hand does not have ten horns but seven (Revelation 5:6), which means that his power is perfect.

2. If God gives you a new name, that is a great blessing. In this respect, Revelation 2:17 makes use of a thought from Isaiah 62:2 and 65:15.

3. If God blesses you, your (former) enemies will come to you, throw themselves at your feet, and acknowledge God as Lord. Revelation derives this expectation from Isaiah 45:14; 49:23; and 60:14.

Biblical Objects and Themes

Revelation mentions many terms, phrases, events, and names from the Hebrew Bible in a way which assumes that they would be known by the readers. For example, the author assumes that the reader knows who Jezebel is (2:20), and that symbols such as the lion and the lamb come from the Hebrew Bible (from Genesis 49:8–10 and Isaiah 53 respectively) and that they are messianic titles. The author writes about known divine institutions such as the temple, the priesthood, and the twelve tribes of Israel, but he also mentions lesser known things such as the Song of Moses (15:3), the Day of the LORD (1:10), and the majesty or glory of God (Greek *doxa*, 15:8 and 21:11, 23).

John uses geographical terms such as Mount Zion (14:1), Sodom and Egypt (11:8), Babylon, and the Euphrates. These things are not taken from one specific text of Scripture, but from the world of the Jewish people which is reflected in the Hebrew Bible.

I will explain the background to some things in some more detail.

1. Twice John uses the difficult expression 'the seven spirits of God' (1:4 and 5:6). The interpreters agree that he means the Holy Spirit and the fullness of his work. Yet it helps to know that the prophet Zechariah had written that impossible things are made possible by the help of God's Spirit (4:6), and that this verse is in a chapter in which the number seven plays a major role. Thus in 4:10, the 'eyes of the

LORD that range throughout the earth' are symbolised by (not two but) seven lamps.

2. The cloud(s) mentioned in Revelation 1:7; 10:1; 11:12; and 14:14–16 can be found earlier in the Bible, for example in Exodus 13:21–22; 19:16; 1 Kings 8:10–12; Isaiah 19:1; Ezekiel 10:3–4; Mark 13:26; 14:62. Clouds are not part of the weather forecast or even divine means of transport, but they symbolise the coming and the presence of God and his Son. John's choice of words was especially inspired by Daniel 7:13.

3. The book of life (3:5; 13:8; 17:8; 20:12, 15; and 21:27) was previously mentioned in Exodus 32:32–33, Psalm 69:28, and Daniel 7:10; 12:1; in all these places it is a register of persons who belong to the people of God.

4. One of the most beautiful images that John uses for the future is that of the meal, the wedding supper of the Lamb (Revelation 19:7, 9). He derives this image from Isaiah 25:6–12 and it is also used in Matthew 22:1–14. It has aspects such as 'tasty' and 'abundance' as well as 'together,' 'home at last,' and deep intimacy.

One name, however, is a riddle to us: Armageddon (16:16; Harmagedon NRSV). This name does not occur in the Old Testament or in any other text. Our best guess is that it is a deformation of the Hebrew *Har Megiddo*, 'Mountain of [the city of] Megiddo.' This city was the location of the death of the promising king, Josiah (2 Kings 23:29–30), but other famous battles had taken place there as well, such as the victory of Deborah and Barak over the Canaanites (Judges 5:19) and the violent death of Ahaziah as a result of the actions of Jehu (2 Kings 9:27).

But Megiddo lies in a valley; Mount Carmel is miles away and that mountain was never called Mountain of Megiddo anyway. It is therefore unclear what John means by Armageddon. Does he think of Megiddo as the place where great kings died or of the weeping in the *plain* of Megiddo in the last days, which is mentioned in Zechariah 12:11?

Agreements Between Larger Passages

John not only uses loose items and texts from Scripture, he has also modelled sections of his book into longer sections of Scripture. I mention the most important of these in the order of our Old Testament.

- The descriptions of the creation, the paradise situation, and the invasion of sin in Genesis 1–3 have influenced John's description of the new world and of the disappearance of evil in Revelation 21–22. The end will look like the wonderful beginning: there will be no more evil, God and humanity will have direct contact, there will be a tree of life again, God's river will flow and nature will radiate God's peace.

- The ten plagues of Egypt in Exodus 7–11 are the model for the misery caused by the trumpets and the bowls according to Revelation 8–9 and 16. John handles the material from Exodus quite freely, but the similarity tells us that just as the plagues of Egypt were meant to allow the pharaoh to listen and to set free God's people, so God's judgements in Revelation are meant to force the disobedient people to listen. But they do not listen.

- The vision of God on his throne in heaven (Isaiah 6) resounds in Revelation 1 as well as Revelation 4–5. The apocalyptic passage of Isaiah 24–27 has had influence on Revelation 19–20.

- Jeremiah 50–51 play a major role in the description of Babylon in Revelation 17–18.

- Ezekiel chapters 1–3 and 10 resonate especially at the beginning of Revelation (chapters 1, 4–5, 10). We meet Ezekiel 38–39 (including the names Gog and Magog) and Ezekiel 47:1–12 at the end of Revelation (chapters 17–22). See for example how the vision in Revelation 4 makes use of the precious stones, the rainbow, the crystal sea, and the four creatures from the vision in Ezekiel 1.

- Daniel 7–8 echoes in Revelation 12–13, 17 and 19; this means that John's description of the anti-Christian powers does not contain much that is new in comparison to what we already know from the Scriptures.

- The locusts of Joel 1–2 were the obvious model for the locusts in Revelation 9:1–11, although the latter are much worse than the former.

- Amos 1–2 consists of seven short prophecies addressed to as many nations and was possibly the model for the seven short letters to the churches in Revelation 2–3.

- Various elements of Zechariah 4, such as the two anointed persons, the olive trees, and the lamp stands, have found a place in the description of the two witnesses in Revelation 11:1–13, where they are combined with traits of Moses (the ability to cause plagues) and Elijah (the ability to withhold rain). But in their death, resurrection, and ascension, the witnesses of course follow Jesus.

- Zechariah 1:8 and 6:2–3 provide the inspiration for the four coloured horses that ride across the earth according to Revelation 6:1–8.

All these links put John and his book on a par with the prophets and books of the old covenant.

Verses from Isaiah

Interpreters of Revelation agree that John often uses the books of Ezekiel and Daniel; but they disagree as to which of these two books is more important. I will not take sides in this discussion but would instead draw attention to John's use of Isaiah. Only in Revelation 21 Isaiah echoes more than any other book of the Hebrew Bible, yet the prophet's words occur everywhere in Revelation. Here are some thought-provoking examples.

1. At the beginning of the present chapter I already showed that Revelation 4:8 is based on Isaiah 6:3.

2. In Isaiah 22:22 (and only there in the Hebrew Bible) you find the expression 'the key to the house of David.' Because John uses almost the same expression in Revelation 3:7, you could conclude that he knows Isaiah well. This key is probably the same as 'the key(s) of the kingdom of heaven' which Jesus mentions in Matthew 16:19. In his time, Isaiah promised this key to one Eliakim, who could not live up

to the high expectations. Jesus the Messiah is the one who has authority over God's kingdom, although he delegates this authority to Peter and the church.

3. The LORD God calls himself 'the first and the last' in Isaiah 44:6 and 48:12; this title is taken over in Revelation 1:17 and 22:13 but applied to the Lord Jesus. The expression 'the Alpha and the Omega' (the first and the last letter of the Greek alphabet; Revelation 1:8; 21:6; 22:13) is also based on these words of Isaiah. You can see that the expression is used both for the God and for his Son Jesus. God is at the beginning and the end of the world; he took the initiative and he will complete his work.

4. The description of the fighting Jesus in Revelation 19:13 and 15 is unusually fierce:

> He is dressed in a robe dipped in blood, and his name is the Word of God. … Coming out of his mouth is a sharp sword with which to strike down the nations. He will rule them with an iron sceptre. He treads the winepress of the fury of the wrath of God Almighty.

This picture is partly taken from the equally fierce and unexpected eruption of God in Isaiah 63:1–6, which also echoes at other places in Revelation. It is Isaiah who uses terms such as 'tread the winepress' and images of blood-stained clothing. John combines them with the sharp sword from Isaiah 49:2 (see also Revelation 1:16) and the iron staff (rod, sceptre) from Psalm 2:9.

5. And as we are at chilling imagery, the image of the smoke that rises for ever after the destruction of Edom (Isaiah 34:10) is used by John in Revelation 14:11 and 19:3, who applies this punishment to the immoral city of Babylon.

6. Conversely, beautiful images of blessing also originate from Isaiah, such as the abundance of water in a normally dry country (Isaiah 49:10 in Revelation 7:16) and wiping the tears from all eyes (Isaiah 25:8 in Revelation 7:17 and 21:4). Isaiah 40:10 gave John the image of the Lord who brings wages (reward) with him when he comes to save his people (Revelation 22:12).

7. Isaiah often writes about future blessings for the city of Jerusalem, which he usually calls Zion (after the mountain on which it is built). Much of this has been taken over by John in his description of the celestial city of Jerusalem which will descend to earth and which is therefore an image of the eternal happiness of God's children. Thus you read about a bride who dresses beautifully and eagerly anticipates the bridegroom (Isaiah 52:1; 54:5; 61:10; 62:4–5 in Revelation 21:2, 9); about ornaments with gemstones (Isaiah 54:11–12 in Revelation 21:19–20); about keeping all evil outside the city (Isaiah 52:1 in Revelation 21:27); but also about gates which are always open (Isaiah 60:11 in Revelation 21:25) and how God himself will be the light of the world (Isaiah 60:1–3, 19–20 in Revelation 22:5). When you read through Isaiah 54 and 60, you may discover even more things that re-appear in Revelation.

8. Even the familiar expression 'a new heaven and a new earth' (Revelation 21:1) was not conceived by John himself, but found in Isaiah (Isaiah 65:17 and 66:22; see also 2 Peter 3:13). But as always, John does not say, 'as is written by the prophet Isaiah' or a similar phrase – he simply expects the reader to see and evaluate the connection. In this particular case, it pays off if you read Isaiah 65:17–20 as a whole.

Finally

You wonder if there is anything in Revelation that John has *not* taken from the Old Testament! His use of it permeates everything: two out of every three verses of Revelation contain an element from the Old Testament. This show us that Jesus' appearance to John brings together many – if not all – threads of the Bible. It makes Revelation a very fitting conclusion of the collection of sacred books of the Christian faith. Their unity is barely hidden!

Further Reading

Lalleman, Pieter J., *The Lion and the Lamb. Studies on the Book of Revelation* (London: Faithbuilders, 2016).

McComiskey, Thomas E., 'Alteration of OT Imagery in the Book of Revelation. Its hermeneutical and theological significance,' *Journal of the Evangelical Theological Society* 36 (1993) 307–316.

Ryken, Leland, James C., Wilhoit and Tremper Longman III (eds). *Dictionary of Biblical Imagery* (Leicester: IVP, 1998).

Tõniste, Külli, *The Ending of the Canon: A Canonical and Intertextual Reading of Revelation 21–22* (LNTS 526; London: Bloomsbury T&T Clark, 2016).

Chapter 32: Epilogue

My way of reading the Bible is strongly influenced by Richard Hays, who calls his approach 'a hermeneutics of trust.' He also uses the term 'figural interpretation.' David Aune and Mark Stibbe speak of charismatic exegesis in this regard; that is, interpretation led by the Holy Spirit. In my view, especially Hays has helped us to understand how the New Testament authors were reading the Old Testament, and how later believers can do it. This way of reading is increasingly gaining ground in the twenty-first century.[21]

With the above authors and others, I believe that the meaning that the New Testament gives to the Old Testament is the meaning that God intends, even though its human writers may not have been aware of the meaning of everything they wrote. For Christians, the New Testament is therefore the best commentary on the Old Testament. Conversely, the Old Testament is indispensable when reading the New. Many things in both parts of the Bible rise above themselves when they are read in the context of the entire canon. Much in the relationship between Old and New Testaments is about the fulfilment of prophecies, but also about the unexpected 'fulfilment' of things which originally did not seem to be predictive prophecy at all. God's continuing revelation in Jesus and in the church sheds new light on ancient words and phrases. Conversely, the older text, the Hebrew Bible, explains the younger, for the writers of the New Testament assume familiarity with the older text.

Fulfilment

Speaking about fulfilment, the fulfilment of Scripture is something other than its abolition or making it redundant. As I wrote elsewhere:

> We believe that the Scriptures were fulfilled in Jesus Christ. In him God has revealed himself deeper than ever before. Predictions of the coming of the Messiah have come true and now the Scripture is fulfilled. This means that the status of this ancient book has changed. The idea of fulfilment occurs in texts

---

[21] David Allen, *According to the Scriptures* (2018) appeared too late to be considered.

such as Luke 4:21; 24:26–27, 44–48; John 5:39; Acts 3:18 and James 2:23. But many people misunderstand this notion of fulfilment: they think that the words which are fulfilled have been crossed out, made inoperative, set aside. This is a painful misunderstanding. When a promise has been fulfilled in everyday life, it means that we have received what was promised. Our expectation has been fulfilled, we have the promised thing in our hands and we can go on to enjoy it. Likewise, the biblical meaning of fulfilment is not elimination or abolition, but rather: becoming full-grown, becoming fully effective, mature. In Jesus the Old Testament has reached its goal. Therefore, it is of great value to us, next to the New Testament.

The misunderstanding of the concept of fulfilment was bolstered by a mistranslation of Romans 10:4, where the King James Version reads:

> Christ is the end of the law for righteousness to everyone that believeth.

And even the NRSV (cf. ESV, CSB) has:

> Christ is the end of the law so that there may be righteousness for everyone who believes.

What Paul writes is that Christ is the *telos* of the law; and the Greek word *telos* can mean much more than just 'end.' It often means 'goal' or purpose'; hence the 2011 version of the NIV correctly has 'culmination':

> Christ is the culmination of the law so that there may be righteousness for everyone who believes.

And the New Living Translation helpfully says:

> Christ has already accomplished the purpose for which the law was given. As a result, all who believe in him are made right with God.[22]

---

[22] Slightly edited from my *Enduring Treasure*, 14–15.

Against the Enlightenment

Most of today's theological books offer a different way of reading the Old Testament than this book, because many theologians are strongly influenced by the scholarly model of our time. Yet this is actually the model of the past, of the era of the Enlightenment. The Enlightenment model has the pretension to offer an exact form of scholarship, in which exact references to sources and 'scientific' evidence are central elements. Through Enlightenment spectacles scholars study the Bible critically to see if everything is correct, with a 'hermeneutics of distrust.' This model only allows the scholars to accept quotations and allusions if they have objective evidence for the thought processes of the biblical writers. The result is that the Bible becomes a fragmented collection of books, with some scholars denying that the Old Testament knows anything about Jesus Christ.

This Enlightenment model does not suit the study of the Bible and can even be deadly for faithful Bible reading. As believers, we can only approach the Bible on the basis of trust, in the same way as Jesus and his first followers approached the Scriptures. Jesus claimed that the Scriptures bear testimony to him (Matthew 21:42; 26:54; Luke 4:21; 24:27; John 5:39, 46). His followers had surprising experiences with him, after which they went back to the Scriptures – and their eyes were opened! The first Christian communities and the writers of the New Testament discovered countless connections between earlier and later persons and events, between the Scriptures they had and the events in their own time. For them and for us, the Lord Jesus is the key to the Old Testament.

What we do as Christian readers of the Bible and as Christian scholars cannot be followed or imitated by non-believing theologians. Our reading and understanding is based on our faith in the triune God: the Father who reveals himself, Jesus Christ who fulfils the Old Testament, and the Holy Spirit who *first* inspired the Bible writers and *now* illuminates the minds of the readers. Jews and Muslims also read the Hebrew Bible differently from us, because they have different starting points. They do not recognise Jesus as the key.

Going Further

The present book contains some examples of texts in which contemporary interpreters see a link between Old and New Testament which is not mentioned in the New Testament itself. Is that not a bridge too far? Should we not limit ourselves to what the New Testament says? I do not think so, because I believe that Christians who are led by the Holy Spirit in their reading of the Bible are not limited to the conscious intentions of the original writer or to a literal interpretation. It is a matter of discovering God's intention with his word, regardless of whether the human author was aware of it.

Therefore, in the reading of the Bible much depends on the person of the reader. A good reader is a Christian surrounded, encouraged, inspired, and corrected by the Christian church (the congregation), a person who has sufficient knowledge of the Bible, the history of the church and the important ancient confessions such as the Apostolic Creed and the Creed of Nicaea, and who affirms these confessions. These notions of agreement and participation are important for someone who merely reads the Bible, even someone calling themselves a theologian, but who is not spiritually connected to the cause of Jesus Christ and his church, cannot acknowledge certain links in the Bible which believers see and believe. A believing reader, on the other hand, sets out to follow Jesus Christ, who was the first to apply the Scriptures to himself, thus setting his followers an example.

I am of course aware of the lurking danger of individualism. An individual Christian discovers something new in their Bible, in this case a link between the two Testaments, and thinks that this is *the* correct interpretation of the text. Our readings must therefore always be tested by others. If we let ourselves be guided by the wisdom of the church of the ages, we can contain the risks of individualism. Individual readers must therefore have knowledge of, and be involved in, the church and its history, so that new insights can be properly assessed.

The First Readers

Did the first hearers and readers of, for example, Mark's Gospel, Romans, and Revelation hear all the quotations, allusions and echoes which we hear? Maybe not. We have seen that many quotations are marked by the writers, so they could not be missed. But unmarked quotations, and some allusions and echoes, will not always have been picked up. Much of course depended on whether the readers were Jews and thus familiar with the Scriptures (as the first readers of Matthew and Hebrews likely were) or whether they had a pagan background (as with Mark and Philippians). It is striking that – of all books – Matthew and Hebrews mark their quotations so clearly! Perhaps Jewish readers expected this more than readers with a pagan background?

Other factors that played a role in recognising allusions and echoes were the availability of manuscripts of the constituent parts of the Old Testament, the length of time that readers were already following Jesus, and – in the case of letters – the explanation given by the person who transmitted the letter, such as Phoebe (Romans 16:1–2) and Epaphroditus (Philippians 2:25–30).

Many of the first readers will have missed some quotations and allusions, and this also applies to many later readers. I do not think that this is a big problem, however. Connections between the two Testaments are still being discovered, enriching and deepening our understanding, but they do not basically change the meaning of the message of salvation in Jesus.

Prophecy

One of the things which connect the Old and the New Testament is prophecy, and I must make a few comments on this subject. The prophets of Israel predicted persons and events, such as the Messiah and his coming, and the New Testament shows how their expectations were fulfilled. But we cannot always put a simple equal sign between prophecy and fulfilment; you have seen many examples of that on the preceding pages. The idea that there is always one prediction in a prophetic word, and one fulfilment, is much too simple. A prophetic word may have multiple fulfilments; its meaning may not be 'used up' by one event or person. I give two simple examples of what I mean. Isaiah's expectation of a child to be born (7:14) was first fulfilled in the time of the prophet himself, but later also in Jesus. The expectations of

Jesus' coming were partially fulfilled in the first century AD, but they will be further and definitively fulfilled at some moment in the future.

A second remark is that the prophets are not so much predictors of the future, fore-tellers, as people who primarily comment on their own time, forth-tellers. Certainly, they also mention things that will happen in the future, but these things are often especially as a result of human behaviour in the present.[23] In some cases it is not yet (not even now) clear what a prophet exactly meant. That is what the apostle Peter realised, as he wrote about the prophets:

> They inquired into what time or what circumstances the Spirit of Christ within them was indicating when he testified in advance to the sufferings of Christ and the glories that would follow. (1 Peter 1:11 CSB)

My third remark is that this book has shown that many things which do not appear to be prophetic within the Old Testament, which do not present as prophecy, yet appear to have an element of prediction in them. Even if the older text is not strictly speaking an announcement or prediction, it often turns out to be a foreshadowing of a later person or event exactly in the light of the coming of that later person or event. We have seen this phenomenon especially in the psalms. This means that our definition of prophecy must be much broader than 'texts that explicitly predict or discuss the future.' You can compare the situation with reading a detective or watching a movie: only at the end you begin to understand why certain things were said or shown earlier in the story. When you view the movie again or reread the book, you will probably notice more hints to 'whodunit' which you had missed the first-time round.

The Septuagint

It is a remarkable fact that the early church did not preserve the words of Jesus in their original language, Aramaic, but rather in Greek. All four evangelists chose to use Greek for recording the story of Jesus, not Aramaic or Hebrew, even when they are quoting his very words. (For exceptions to this practice, see Mark 5:41; 7:34; 14:36; and 15:34.) This

---

[23] See for example my *Enduring Treasure*, 77–78.

is true even for Matthew, who probably wrote for a Jewish audience. Greek was the most widely used language in the first Christian communities. As a consequence of these choices, it is not surprising that the New Testament authors normally use the Septuagint when they quote from the Old Testament: it was the Bible of most followers of Jesus, and it was convenient to use a ready Greek text in their own writing of Greek.

I am discussing this issue because the Septuagint is more than just an ordinary, literal translation. Hence its use is not neutral. Firstly, we saw above that the translators had sometimes made mistakes or introduced deliberate but immaterial changes. Secondly, the text was sometimes adapted, or depended on another version of the Hebrew text, as in Amos 9:12. Thirdly and most importantly, at other moments you can see this translation as a continuation of God's revelation, because it sheds new light on things. This development is, for example, visible in the choice for the Greek word *parthenos* to refer to the young woman in Isaiah 7.[24] Here the Septuagint makes something visible which was still hidden in the Hebrew Bible, namely the virginity of the mother of the promised child.

The exact relationship between the Hebrew text and the Septuagint is far too complicated to be discussed here. My basic assumption is that the Holy Spirit was guiding the writers of the New Testament in dealing with these two text forms of God's word, the Hebrew and the Greek texts. They handled the differences in such a way that they made the best choice in their own recording of God's word.

Judaism

This book contains hardly anything about Jewish customs and ideas in the period after the Old Testament. This omission is not because these things are unimportant or because they do not help our understanding of the New Testament, but because this is a book about the Bible and its (hidden) internal unity, not about human traditions and their influence. The Jewish way of thinking in the post-Old

---

[24] See chapters 9 and 23.

Testament period and the Jewish practices in Jesus' time are the material for another book.

Combined Quotations

In various places, especially in the chapter on Mark, I have pointed to the use of combined quotations. They are not uncommon in the New Testament, but almost impossible and inconceivable in our time, because we 'modern people' are much stricter in our handling of sources than the people in antiquity. Interestingly, the topic of combined quotations is currently being studied by scholars who are bringing out how Greek and Roman authors, including the church fathers, as well as the writers of the New Testament, sometimes combined words from two or more sources into one quotation. The use of such quotations is therefore not a matter of carelessness or bad memory, but a conscious choice of such famous writers as Cicero, Seneca, and Plutarch, and also of some authors of the Dead Sea Scrolls and other Jewish texts.[25] However, at the moment it appears that combined quotations are more common in the New Testament than elsewhere.

And What Should We Do?

The year 2018 saw the publication of a book in which the author states that the way in which the writers of the New Testament treat the Old is normative for us. In other words, we *must* read the Bible just as they did. I think that things are not quite so simple. The writer of that book, Abner Chou, uses the argument that the writers of the New Testament always did justice to the *conscious* intentions of the Old Testament writers. And he is convinced that there is not a glimmer of light between God's intentions and the conscious intentions of the human writers. I find both these claims unbelievable because my book has shown that the New Testament often discovers meanings in the Old of which 'Moses and the prophets' were clearly unaware themselves. In a sense, in my opinion the conservative Chou is as strongly influenced by the Enlightenment as many 'modern' theologians. He does not

---

[25] Sean A. Adams and Seth M. Ehorn (eds). *Composite Citations in Antiquity. Two Volumes* (London: Bloomsbury T&T Clark, 2016, 2018).

leave any room for the work of the Spirit in the writers and in us as readers. Because we are dealing with charismatic exegesis, in other words, with a hermeneutics of trust, modern scholarly methods of interpretation are inadequate and we need to leave room for God's work in the unconscious area. We also cannot turn what is happening in the New Testament into a prescriptive method for us.

Conversely, Richard Longenecker answered his own question, 'Can we reproduce the exegesis of the New Testament?' in the negative.[26] Without further interacting with Longenecker here, it will be clear that I reject this position as well. A strange gap would open up between the Bible writers and us if we were to believe that they were correct in their time and that the Bible is authoritative for us, but that we have to use the Bible very differently from them. In fact, we can readily agree with a large part of their dealings with the Hebrew Bible. I have been suggesting that, at some points, we might go even further than they, as we sometimes hear more gospel in the old book than the authors of the New Testament. But I would be unhappy to use the word 'normative' in this context. If we do that, we are in danger of trying to control the work of the Holy Spirit.

Further Reading

Allen, David, *According to the Scriptures: The Death of Christ in the Old Testament and the New* (London: SCM, 2018).

Aune, David E., 'Charismatic Exegesis in Early Judaism and Early Christianity' in James H. Charlesworth and Craig A. Evans (eds), *The Pseudepigrapha and Early Biblical Interpretation* (Sheffield: Sheffield Academic Press, 1993), 126–150.

Chou, Abner, *The Hermeneutics of the Biblical Writers: Learning to Interpret Scripture from the Prophets and Apostles* (Grand Rapids: Kregel, 2018).

---

[26] 'Can we reproduce the exegesis of the New Testament?' is the title of his article in *Tyndale Bulletin* 21 (1970) 3–38; see more extensive R.N. Longenecker, *Biblical Exegesis in the Apostolic Period* (Grand Rapids: Eerdmans, 1975; reprint Carlisle: Paternoster, 1995). See also David Allen, *According to the Scriptures: The Death of Christ in the Old Testament and the New* (London: SCM, 2018)

Hays, Richard B., *Echoes of Scripture in the Gospels* (Waco: Baylor University Press, 2016) especially 347–366.

Malcolm, Matthew (ed.), *All That the Prophets Have Declared* (Milton Keynes: Paternoster, 2015).

Stibbe, Mark, 'This is That: Some thoughts concerning charismatic hermeneutics', *Anvil* 15.3 (1998) 181–193.

Index of Bible Passages

INDEX